ON THE CUSP

King Labour: The British Working Class, 1850–1914
The Secretary of State
The Chancellor of the Exchequer
Bobby Abel, Professional Batsman
Archie's Last Stand: MCC in New Zealand, 1922–23
The Financial Times: A Centenary History
WG's Birthday Party
Cazenove & Co.: A History
The City of London, Volume 1: A World of Its Own, 1815–90
The City of London, Volume 2: Golden Years, 1890–1914
LIFFE: A Market and Its Makers
Phillips & Drew: Professionals in the City (with W. J. Reader)
The City of London, Volume 3: Illusions of Gold, 1914–45
The City of London, Volume 4: A Club No More, 1945–2000
City State: How the Markets Came to Rule Our World (with Richard Roberts)
Siegmund Warburg: A Centenary Appreciation
Austerity Britain, 1945–51
Family Britain, 1951–57
Modernity Britain, 1957–62
The Lion Wakes: A Modern History of HSBC (with Richard Roberts)
Till Time's Last Sand: A History of the Bank of England, 1694–2013
Arlott, Swanton and the Soul of English Cricket (with Stephen Fay)
Engines of Privilege: Britain's Private School Problem (with Francis Green)
Shots in the Dark: A Diary of Saturday Dreams and Strange Times

ON THE CUSP

DAYS OF '62

David Kynaston

BLOOMSBURY PUBLISHING
LONDON · OXFORD · NEW YORK · NEW DELHI · SYDNEY

BLOOMSBURY PUBLISHING
Bloomsbury Publishing Plc
50 Bedford Square, London, WC1B 3DP, UK
29 Earlsfort Terrace, Dublin 2, Ireland

BLOOMSBURY, BLOOMSBURY PUBLISHING and the Diana logo are trademarks
of Bloomsbury Publishing Plc

First published in Great Britain 2021

A catalogue record for this book is available from the British Library

ISBN: HB: 978-1-5266-3201-2; EBOOK: 978-1-5266-3202-9

2 4 6 8 10 9 7 5 3

Typeset by Newgen KnowledgeWorks Pvt. Ltd., Chennai, India
Printed and bound in Great Britain by CPI Group (UK) Ltd, Croydon CR0 4YY

To find out more about our authors and books visit www.bloomsbury.com
and sign up for our newsletters

This book is dedicated to the memory of Micky Sheringham
(1948–2016)

Contents

Author's Note

On the Cusp continues *Tales of a New Jerusalem*, a projected sequence about Britain between 1945 and 1979. The most recent volume, *Modernity Britain*, ended in June 1962; the next intended volume, *Opportunity Britain*, is likely to run from October 1962 to May 1967. This book is about Britain in 1962 in those months between June and October, with Britain on the cusp of the 'real' 1960s – a moment marked by the release of the first Beatles single and the premiere of the first James Bond film on the very same day. It is not intended as a comprehensive portrait of Britain at this time; but it is a snapshot, and it does include thematic treatment of some significant aspects (including the rural experience, the Welsh experience and the immigrant experience) given less detailed coverage so far in the sequence. A book largely written during the lockdown of spring and summer 2020, *On the Cusp* is about a country where doors and windows were about to be pushed open a little wider.

I

Nothing to Offend

'Dad & I went to church,' noted Veronica Lee on the second Sunday of June 1962. She was seventeen, her father was a farm manager on a landed estate, and they lived near Crediton in Devon. 'New parson, who looked like a sparrow & whistled. He started the service as if we were wound up, at about seventy miles an hour, but gradually good old Shobrooke [the village] slowed him down, till at last we were at snail's pace. How can one believe in God in an atmosphere like that?' Fewer doubts this Whit Sunday in Lancashire, where the Rev. W. A. Wood attended his first scramble by invitation of the Accrington and District Motor Cycle Club. 'I don't blame any of you for coming to Green Haworth and spending the afternoon in this way, the air is fresh, and I like coming up here myself to enjoy it,' he told a crowd of nearly 2,000. And he went on in his five-minute address to compare motor-cycle scrambling to the 'scramble of life', which got everybody 'out of breath' from time to time; and just as the riders had to clean their machines, so people had to clean up their lives through reading the Bible and prayer. A few hours later, at 6.30, England's footballers began their World Cup quarter-final against Brazil, played in the pinetree-ringed Sauzal stadium at Viña del Mar, Chile. Not an easy one to follow: no coverage on the BBC's only television channel (instead, hymn singing from the Tabernacle Welsh Presbyterian Church in Bangor as the match kicked off; *Wagon Train* in the middle; Trolle Rhodin's Swedish Circus at the end); nor on ITV (77 *Sunset Strip* taking the honours); but at least radio's Light Programme offered, though not until 9.45, a recording of the second half. Still, perhaps no great loss, as England were knocked out 3–1, with compensatory

plaudits going to Jimmy Greaves, as he went down on all fours to
snare a spirited dog which had wandered on to the pitch. 'Once more,'
reflected *The Times*'s Geoffrey Green, 'we were finding that courage
and determination were insufficient against the superior ball skill,
easy rhythm, and smooth movements of the Brazilians.' The match
was over by the time the BBC gave its screen to *The Sunday Night
Play*, this week *Worm's Eye View*, with Ronald Shiner recreating
his original role as the lead-swinging Private Sam Porter in the R. F.
Delderfield wartime comedy about aircraftmen billeted in a Lancashire
seaside boarding house. 'There were occasional complaints that the
play was dated, trivial and unamusing,' recorded Audience Research.
'Usually, however, viewers appear to have been highly diverted by this
"happy go lucky" and "typically English" comedy, with its delightful
characters and heart-warming humour, bringing back memories of
the lighter side of the war.' Or as one approving viewer put it, 'sincere
and innocent, with nothing to offend any susceptibilities'. Unlike on
the beach in Brighton that night, a scene of several thousand sleeping
in cars, several hundred dancing, and leather-jacketed motor-cyclists
lighting bonfires. 'We have been jiving all night in bare feet,' Miss June
Verrall (a shop assistant from Burgess Hill) and Miss Miriam Geal (a
bank clerk from Haywards Heath) told a local reporter soon after 6
on the Monday morning. 'Why? Well, it's just something different
to do.' Damage to boats, whether through being used as lavatories
or being ripped apart to provide wood for midnight bonfires, was
considerable. 'They're no good to anyone,' was one boat-owner's
unforgiving verdict on the beachniks. 'They are just like a pack of
animals, only not so clean.'[1]

Whit Monday, 11 June, was a bank holiday. Moderately dismal
weather failed to dampen the spirits of Diana Griffith, a 13-year-
old living in West Worthing. 'Went by 'box to smashing show at
Leatherhead. (Vale Lodge Stables). I rode Angela Proud's Friday 13th
in Trotting & came 3rd! 5/-, 2/6 to Angela (she led me). Nowhere in
musical hats [a kind of equestrian musical chairs].' In Manchester the
unusual absence of sunshine saw crowds somewhat down (never more
than four deep) to watch the famous annual Whit Monday Walks, their
161st iteration; but some 20,000 people from more than forty churches
in the area still turned out to do the actual marching, as they processed
from Albert Square through the city's streets. 'The organisers of 1801',

reflected one observer, 'would have been perplexed by the "Kiss me Quick" and "I'm in charge" on hats worn by spectators as banners declaring "Jesus said I am the light of the world" were carried past. Children in white dresses walked by carrying a flower-decked sign saying "Purity" under the large Guinness sign on Piccadilly.' Further north, not a happy day for Nella Last, veteran diarist of Barrow-in-Furness. 'So chilly & wild this morning. I washed when it wasn't fit to go out, & after our lunch of soup, salad, ham & the last bit of chicken we rested.' Worse was to come. 'The T.V. *was* so bad – both channels,' she lamented. 'We accept the fact that B.B.C. is bad if there's bad weather about – but *no* picture was possible – just when "Sailor Beware" & "The Judy Garland Show" was on. We could not "hold" I.T.V., it kept fading in both sight & sound. I'll ring Kelly's in the morning.' All of which meant that Nella and her far more self-pitying husband Will were unable to get their usual *Coronation Street* fix – this particular evening, a memorable episode in which the jilted and depressed Christine Hardman has gone on to the roof of Elliston's Raincoat Factory where she works, and threatens to jump. Eventually, after a policeman fails, it is Ken Barlow who manages gently to talk her down, though not without Christine saying she will blame him if things don't change for the better in her life. 'Girls like me are stupid,' she remarks. 'An' we don't get anythin' – the only way we can get owt different is by gettin' married.'[2]

No TV, as was still the case in many middle-class homes, for the Haines family in Chingford. 'John back to the grind,' recorded Judy on Tuesday about her husband returning to his office job. 'I to the dentist's grind! The filling didn't hurt at all!! I *was* relieved.' Nella Last, after ringing Kelly's, finished her ironing, tidied the bedrooms, dusted round generally and had just made lunch when the man arrived to look at their rented set. 'Not our "usual", but a very nice person. After a general examination & test, he said he would have to take it down to the workshop. I caught sight of the positively stricken expression on my husband's face & asked if it was at all possible to return it tonight & he said he would, adding "*no* one wants to be without their TV set now".' Another diarist, Kenneth Johnson of Letchworth, was being sent that day a letter from Rutland County Council's Alan Bond, thanking him for his letter 'in support of our "Fight" to retain our independence'. 'We believe', declared Bond, 'that the "battle" we are waging is not merely for the preservation of Rutland but for the maintenance of democracy as a whole.' If that was one struggle, another and much bigger one lying ahead would be for racial equality. The results were declared this day of a secret ballot among members of the National Union of General and Municipal Workers employed at the Alcan aluminium works in Banbury. 'Should coloured workers be admitted to the factory?' was the question – to which 205 answered 'yes' and 591 answered 'no'. But for the 14-year-old Gyles Brandreth, at the progressive co-educational private school Bedales (near Petersfield in Hampshire), it was a day in 'the San' while down with German measles. 'I have seen the school doctor who I have to say is no Dr Kildare! He is more Dr Gillespie (Ma's favourite), old and grumpy. Nobody likes him very much. The girls say that he takes his time putting his stethoscope across their chests and is quite creepy!'³

'Complacency is Labour's Danger' warned a *Scotsman* headline on Wednesday, and indeed the political event of the week was the West Lothian by-election on Thursday. That day, a supremely unconcerned Kenneth Williams went to Hyde Park. 'Full of girls who sit up, bending over their male companions who are lying down, receiving their kissings & caressings. It is disgusting to watch. No wonder Billy Graham thought our parks so foul. But I'm sure Hyde is the worst. There is so much riff-raff living near.' In the new issue of *Country Life*, 'The Urgency of Urban Renewal' was the editorial's title, in the context of a newly published report by the Ministry of Housing and Local Government. Gratified that in the past two years some sixty schemes for 'the redevelopment of central areas of towns and cities' had been submitted for the approval of the Housing Minister (Dr Charles Hill, the one-time 'radio doctor'), the magazine proclaimed that 'undoubtedly this phase of urban renewal is capable of yielding not only relief to the intense pressure for more housing, but a most impressive improvement in the appearance and convenience of towns and cities throughout the country'. Not much urban renewal to be seen yet at the premises of Steptoe and Son, rag 'n' bone merchants of Oil Drum Lane, Shepherd's Bush. 'A large number felt that this was not only most lively and piquant comedy writing, but also a combination of humour and pathos in which a peculiarly crabbed but also whimsical relationship between a working-class father and his son had been subtly and sympathetically observed,' was BBC Audience Research's summary of viewer reaction (including a notably high 'Reaction Index' of 83) to the showing this Thursday evening of 'The Bird', second episode in the first series of the new tragicomedy by Ray Galton and Alan Simpson. 'There was marked feeling in the sample at large that, at this rate, the series was going to be "a winner" for entertainment value and a "must" for future viewing.'⁴ They called it right; and something about the thwarted aspirations of Harold – revealed in this episode as thirty-seven years old, still living with his father a quarter of a century after he had been forced by Albert to leave school at twelve and go into the antediluvian family business – clearly struck a chord.

As for Dr Hill, real-life Steptoe-type housing was the focus of his three-day tour this week of Lancashire. On Wednesday, after a look at some of Manchester's slums (out of a total in the city, he reckoned, of at least 60,000 'slum and unfit houses'), he went on to Oldham (an estimated 15,000 slum houses), where he 'picked his way over the rubble of demolition sites and ducked under lines of torn nappies strung across the back courts'. 'Why', he asked local officials when he stopped in the middle of a gravel patch in the St Mary's district full of small Victorian terraced houses with peeling walls and inadequate sanitation, 'are you waiting for the clearance of the whole area before making a start with the building?' On Thursday it was the turn of Rochdale (nearly 5,000 slum houses). 'We have seen almost without exception', he declared after nearly three hours going into back-alley cottages, 'the way the housewives keep the inside of the houses superbly clean. Perhaps in human terms that is one of the liveliest impressions gained – this contrast between the outside and inside of houses where there is a house-proud housewife.' And on Friday he finished in Liverpool (more than 80,000 unfit homes), where in Windsor Street he was met by some seventy angry tenants, including women with prams, who formed a human barricade to halt the official coach party. 'Get out of the bus, Dr Hill, and talk to the people,' blared a loudspeaker. Later, behind closed doors but confidently reported, he told council leaders that he had 'never seen squalor to equal that in parts of Liverpool'; that 'nowhere else on his tour had he seen so much dangerous litter lying about'; and that 'the corporation's housing programme was totally inadequate'.⁵

By this time the West Lothian result was known. Traditionally a safe Labour seat, it had, in the eloquent words of the historian Christopher Harvie, 'a landscape which anthologised the condition of Scotland: old royal burghs, anonymous colliery villages, run-down factories and docks, looming over them the surreal dereliction of vast red tips of burnt shale'. In a field of five, two candidates stood out: for Labour, 29-year-old Old Etonian and local laird Tam Dalyell, who had conducted his campaign on what he called 'a high, intellectual level' and was described by a reporter as 'intense'; for the largely moribund Scottish Nationalists (hitherto known as 'the Tartan Tories'), 38-year-old William (Billy) Wolfe, joint managing director of his family's Bathgate-based spade and shovel firm and described by Harvie as 'no tactician, no theorist, not even an organiser', but who during the 1960s and 1970s would 'symbolise' his party 'through an Orwellian "decency"'. The declaration at Linlithgow, around lunchtime on Friday, revealed that both men, after energetic campaigns, had triumphed: Dalyell by winning comfortably, Wolfe by coming second, with more than double the votes of the deposit-losing Conservative. Speaking from the steps of the county buildings to a crowd of about 350, the victor insisted that the people of West Lothian were determined in the future to have a government – a Labour government, not the present Tory one – which understood technological change, adding that 'if old industries are to close down they must be replaced by new ones'. Wolfe for his part interpreted the result more in terms of raw emotion: 'The people of Scotland are fed up and are protesting but this is not a protest vote. But if they are in the gutter and being kicked they will protest.' As for the SNP specifically, he declared, entirely justifiably, that 'this is tremendous for us' – the start, as it turned out, of the modern political history of Scottish nationalism. Yet, for the moment, the last word perhaps went to a 60-year-old miner, thrown out of work by the recent closure of the West Lothian shale-oil industry. 'Me? I'd vote for anyone who'd give me a job,' he told a young reporter from London. 'But what hope is there when you're our age? No one will take you on. We're on the bru for good now. You don't know what the bru is? The dole, lad, the dole.'[6]

Different problems in Salop. 'Already we have visiting practically every day of the week,' was how the *Shrewsbury Chronicle* on Friday quoted the cross response of a senior local matron, Miss D. M.

Montague, to the recent request from the Health Minister, Enoch Powell, that hospitals wherever possible allow daily visiting. 'If only', she continued, 'people would visit intelligently, say for 10-minute periods, everyone would be happy. Gone are the days when patients sit in hospital convalescing. People in hospital nowadays are ill and too long a visit can often tend to exhaust them.' Powell in his letter to hospitals had also wanted mothers in maternity wards to be allowed whatever visitors they liked, not just their husbands; but on that the article was silent. The day's crop of magazines included in the *TLS* a dismissive single-paragraph review of Joseph Heller's *Catch-22* ('this unedifying tale ... spread very thinly over a great many pages') and Colin MacInnes having a go in the *New Statesman* at its jazz and pop critic Francis Newton (aka Eric Hobsbawm). 'When he writes of jazz, he praises the artists while castigating the promoters; when he writes of pop, the promoters take a beating, but his artists get no kindly word. If this is so – if Mr Newton esteems all pop is really rubbish – I do wish he'd say so, and frankly declare he finds the taste of millions of his fellow creatures corrupted and deplorable.' Probably neither man tuned in late that afternoon to the pre-recorded (at the Playhouse Theatre in Manchester) *Teenager's Turn – Here We Go* on the Light Programme, featuring a trio of numbers by the Beatles (including a Lennon and McCartney original, 'Ask Me Why') in their second radio outing. 'The surviving recording', notes Mark Lewisohn, 'reveals much clapping along, some between-songs screams and, just before "A Picture of You" [a cover of the current Joe Brown hit], a plainly audible flutter as one of the Beatles did something he shouldn't on BBC radio. There's also laughter during the song's instrumental middle-eight, as if John, Paul and George had gone into a little jig.' An hour and a half later, it was time for Associated Rediffusion's debut edition of *Needle Match*. It all looked good on paper: new British records pitted against new American records (or 'invaders', as *TV Times* called them); eleven members (all from overseas) of the studio audience giving their verdict by waving flags; an unknown David Frost in charge of the flags and responsible for collating votes; Keith Fordyce as referee; Oliver Reed introducing the British records and David Gell (Canadian) the American ones; a guest artist (Kenny Lynch this week) offering an opinion on these new releases; and a team of 'dazzling' dancers providing viewers with something to look at while the records were played. What could go wrong? Plenty in the event, and the *Stage*'s merciless verdict was that 'the disc programme was not only ragged and under-rehearsed, but involved so many people that it was almost impossible to keep track of who-did-what-and-why'.[7]

Elvis's 'Good Luck Charm' in the middle of a four-week run at No. 1, Cliff's 'I'm Lookin' Out the Window'/'Do You Want to Dance?' at No. 2, Mike Sarne's 'Come Outside' perched at No. 3 and heading for the top – the conventional retrospective wisdom that by 1962 it was time for a shake-up is hardly wrong. On Saturday the 16th, *Juke Box Jury*, overseen as ever by David Jacobs, comprised Nelson Riddle, Carole Carr, Anne Heywood and Pete Murray (average age thirty-five); over on ITV, *Thank Your Lucky Stars*, hosted by Brian Matthew (a mere thirty-three, but seemingly much older), included the Kenny Ball Jazzmen ('Green Leaves of Summer', currently No. 10), Craig Douglas ('When My Little Girl Is Smiling', recently departed the charts) and the Polka Dots, as well as a clip of Bobby Vee from the recent Billy Fury movie *Play It Cool*. Away from the box and out in the suburbs, it was a day of Janus-faced Bromley, pointing simultaneously to the past and the future. That afternoon, the local MP and increasingly beleaguered Prime Minister, Harold Macmillan, and his wife put in an appearance (including gamely driving the engine of a miniature train) at a Conservative fete; afterwards, he recorded, 'we had some trouble in getting away, owing to the Anti-Bomb brigade, who lay on the ground in front of our car. Dorothy (who was driving) was very calm and nobody was hurt.' The other fete that day was put on by Bromley Technical School's PTA and was attended by nearly 4,000 people. 'In a continental-style café,' reported the *Kentish Times*, 'one could sip soft drinks while a group of young instrumentalists played music on guitars, saxophone and drums.' The six-piece group played on the entrance steps of the main school building; their name was the Konrads, mainly playing familiar numbers by the Shadows; on sax was the 15-year-old David Jones (later Bowie) – his first formal public appearance; and according to a Bowie chronicler, the performance ran well over time and prompted 'such a commotion among the gathered schoolboys' that it ended only when the music teacher abruptly turned off the power.[8]

Spanning this sun-blessed weekend was the well-attended Festival of Labour at Battersea Park, organised by the party's Merlyn Rees, not yet an MP.[9] 'The first party to risk good money for a purely cultural purpose,' declared Anthony Wedgwood Benn on the eve of the event, but his leader, Hugh Gaitskell, was more circumspect: 'Don't think we want to dictate to people how to spend their leisure, oh my goodness, no!' Attractions included two jazz bands, Arthur Rubinstein playing with the Philharmonia Orchestra, an athletics meeting starring shot-put champion Arthur Rowe (the Labour-supporting blacksmith from Yorkshire), country dancing by the Woodcraft Folk, the Flying Cobinas on a high wire, the Cresswell Colliery Band, the inevitable handicrafts tent ('home-made jam and shapeless cardigans', according to one observer) and on the Sunday a parade of forty-seven floats (representing 'Labour in the Sixties'), followed by speeches, with a crowd of several thousand listening to an unusually personal attack by Gaitskell on Macmillan and his 'pathetic waffling', as well as sarcastically congratulating Hill on having discovered that there were slums in Liverpool. How well overall did the festival work? The young writer Nell Dunn, living nearby, was not quite convinced. 'Why was there no good art on the spot?' she asked. 'It would also have been nice to have had a bit more socialism about the place – not the platform kind – as well as floats and circuses. The trouble with the festival was a certain easygoing dowdiness, as of mass amusements, bank holidays and the telly.' Still, 'easygoing': that was surely a step in the right direction for the people's party.

Gaitskell, accompanied by his colleague Denis Healey and the Liberal leader Jo Grimond, had the day before met a bearded freedom-fighter on the run.[10] 'In London I resumed my old underground ways, not wanting word to leak back to South Africa that I was there,' recalled Nelson Mandela about his ten-day visit, now nearing its end. On the Sunday, he went sightseeing: a famous photograph shows him in Parliament Square outside Westminster Abbey, very deliberately taking the measure of the moment. 'The education I received was a British education, in which British ideas, British culture and British institutions were automatically assumed to be superior – there was no such thing as African culture,' reflected Mandela many years later. 'Despite Britain being the home of parliamentary democracy, it was that democracy that had helped to inflict a pernicious system of iniquity on my people.' Next day, he and Oliver Tambo flew to Khartoum, on the trusted carrier BOAC.

Our Friend Telstar

'It is understood that Councillor Smith would introduce proposed town centre developments for our subsequent examination and acceptance or first refusal,' stated on Monday, 18 June a confirmatory letter by Harry Vincent of the giant contracting company Bovis about a recently reached secret agreement. 'It is understood that Councillor Smith would then have done the great majority of his work and he would then be entitled to a payment of 1 per cent on the estimated building costs of the scheme. If, after that, approval is obtained from the local authority, with ourselves as developers, then he would be entitled to another half per cent for his remaining work.' Councillor Smith was T. Dan Smith, leader of Labour-controlled Newcastle City Council, chair of the housing committee and probably the most powerful single figure in the north-east – a man for whom idealism and self-interest were increasingly indistinguishable.

The rest of the week saw the wheels of the redevelopment juggernaut turning fast: from Glasgow, news that the Murrayfield Real Estate Co. had been 'given the contract to develop the main commercial centre of the new eight-acre redevelopment area that was once the Gorbals', with the £1 million project to be designed by the most prestigious architect of the day, Sir Basil Spence; from London, news not only that the old Peter Robinson building just off Leicester Square was to be redeveloped into a 'Swiss Centre', complete with tower block and 'a sectionally rotating advertisement mast', but also that the green light had been given for the London County Council's highest block of flats yet – a twenty-five-storey tower block near the Elephant and Castle roundabout intended to be 'a "twin" to 25-storey offices

planned on the corner of London Road and Newington Causeway',
and below the coming attraction of 'the huge new shopping centre
soon to arise'. Not quite everyone was signed up to the future. Angry,
'keep off' villagers at Lymm in Cheshire were continuing their long-
standing fight against Manchester planners who wanted to build large
'overspill' council estates there for thousands of the city's inadequately
housed families. 'Those people who live out there have no idea how it
feels for 250 to live in one acre,' Alderman Sir Richard Harper, leader
of the city's Conservative group, bitterly complained on the Monday.
'Many of the private houses have an acre to themselves. We are tired of
trying to secure consideration from so-called Christian people. We are
ignored and objected to everywhere.' Next day, Oxford University
met in congregation to vote on the proposed building in the Parks of
a 260-foot tower to house the new zoology department. The classicist
Sir Maurice Bowra advocated pragmatic acceptance ('we have got to
make up our minds whether we are going to have this tall, thin tower
or something like a battleship lying across our path'); the historian
Robert Blake strongly disagreed ('it would be an act of reckless folly
to ruin prosperity, the skyline of Oxford, and to destroy the whole
atmosphere of the Parks for the sake of this ingenious and perverse
monstrosity'); and by 275 votes to 122 the dons sided with Blake.
'Once this area has gone it has gone for ever,' reflected Balliol's Marcus
Dick (philosopher father of Cressida): words too seldom heard in
those many cities and towns far from dreaming spires.[1]

Not least in Salford, where a day earlier the demolition men had
moved into the Windsor Theatre, a heap of rubble by the end of the
week. That same Monday, the local government officer Anthony
Heap, most assiduous of first nighters, went to the Aldwych to
see a double bill of one-act plays, comprising Strindberg's *Playing
with Fire* and Harold Pinter's *The Collection* (which Associated
Rediffusion had bravely broadcast a year earlier). He did not enjoy
either, not helped by the playwright in the latter 'laboriously seeking
to create a portentous atmosphere of mystery to conceal its essential
hollowness and pointlessness'. Paid critics largely agreed: 'gratuitous
mystification ... desultory episode ... adding up to what might be
called "La Semaine Dernière à Leeds"' (Philip Hope-Wallace, with a
nod to the recent *L'Année dernière à Marienbad*); 'very trivial Pinter
with all the tricks showing like a frayed collar' (Carl Foreman); 'one

stops bothering about formal balance and interplay of motifs, and starts to long for content' (Irving Wardle). Even so, Pinter's critical stock remained high, unlike Noël Coward's or Terence Rattigan's half a decade after the great theatrical revolution. Three nights later, Heap was at the Savoy for Coward's *Sail Away*, his first musical for eight years. 'Never entertaining and yet never exactly boring', in short a 'non vintage effort', and again the professionals mainly concurred, with Wardle calling it 'smooth' and 'well-drilled' (Elaine Stritch the star), but ultimately 'as musicals go nowadays a lightweight affair'.[2]

Increasingly, he might have added, the most rewarding drama lay elsewhere. 'A born television writer', conveying 'dynamic urgency', was how the *Listener*'s Derek Hill praised David Mercer after his second TV play, *A Climate of Fear*, had been shown on Friday the 22nd – albeit it left 'a considerable minority' of BBC viewers dissatisfied ('Just a lot of words and no action'). Its central character was a nuclear scientist, and many predictably saw bias at work ('C.N.D.-ites are given enough publicity daily without the aid of television entertainment'). Two days later, the BBC's *Sunday Night Play* was Michael Voysey's *A Member of the Family*, especially written for its co-star, Eartha Kitt. The story of a mixed marriage (her husband played by Richard Todd), it carefully avoided the word 'colour' as it showed the corrosive effects of racial prejudice on the part of his family. 'It tackles a vital and major problem of our time and presents both sides sympathetically and fairly,' Todd told the press ahead of transmission. And Kitt observed about being married herself to a white man: 'As long as two people are sensible, handle themselves with dignity and, yes, perhaps bravery at times, there is nothing to fear.'

The box in the corner – still showing just the two channels – was becoming an ever more central part of most people's daily life, but during these June days not alas for the unmarried, middle-aged Jennie Hill, living in a village near Winchester with her tyrannical nonagenarian mother. 'M. not interested in T.V. any more,' she noted on the 18th. 'Cannot help feeling very depressed at no T.V. now,' she added on the 19th. So she probably missed, two evenings later, the fiftieth episode of the latest soap, set in the offices of a women's magazine. Fading out considerably at the point where Maggie's labour pains began, it went down well with the viewers:

Compact gets better and better – full of interest – one is never bored. I only wish it were longer!

We all enjoy watching *Compact* – such a refreshing change from hospital and North country serials.

It's light, pleasant fun, whatever some miserable professional critics say.

Moreover, noted the report, 'several commented appreciatively on the attractive costumes and hair-styles – "always in the latest fashion"'. Less than an hour later came 'The Piano', the third episode of *Steptoe and Son*. 'What goes up can bleeding well stay there!' says Harold at one point, reputedly the first time that anyone had – however mildly – sworn on television. If *Steptoe* was TV's groundbreaking comedy of 1962, then *Z Cars* (five months old by June) was just as much the groundbreaking drama series. 'I like it for its realism,' commented one viewer (a personnel officer) after the episode 'Contraband' aired on the 26th. 'Because everybody behaves and reacts so naturally in situations which in themselves are credible, with nice touches of humour, plenty of human interest, and plenty of thrills.' 'This seems', noted the report, 'to be a very widespread opinion'; the episode earned the high RI of 75; and when it came to ranking Newtown's finest, 'Lynch and Steele are slightly more popular than Fancy and Jock, while quite a number seem to have a rather soft spot for Sgt Twentyman.'[3]

Madge Martin, married to an Oxford clergyman, was in London on Monday the 25th. After lunch – a 'lovely small steak' at 'the excellent Grill and Cheese Room, of the Tottenham Court Road Lyons Corner House' – she went to the National Gallery 'to see the famous Leonardo da Vinci's Cartoon [of the Virgin and the Child, attracting large crowds since going on display at the end of March] which they are trying to save for England by huge appeals'. 'It is beautiful,' she added, 'but is it worth £800,000?' The same day, the editor of the *Fife News* received a letter from Miss Helen Fisher; a 65-year-old New Zealander living in London, she was a member of the Keep Britain Out campaign and had set out six weeks earlier from Land's End, planning to reach John o'Groats in three weeks' time. 'During this walk I talk to various people I encounter, ask their opinion of Britain's possible entry into Europe and hand out leaflets. The conclusion come to is that, while the majority know little of what is involved and are anxious to know more, they are definitely against the idea of joining, and more so against any idea of the break-up of the Commonwealth.' W. Norman (no first name given) completely disagreed. 'As a teenager I realise that we will lose some sovereignty, but if Europe is to unite in the accented sense of the word, so will others,' argued his letter appearing next day in the *Bath and Wilts Evening Chronicle*. 'It seems to me loss of some national pride, always a dangerous thing, is a little enough price to pay for peace, prosperity and unity.' In sum: 'Entry into Europe is a challenge. May Britain be equal to it.' Vere Hodgson, one of the very best of London's wartime diarists but now living in Church Stretton in Shropshire, had other public matters on her mind. 'This country goes on its way committing suicide with extreme wage claims etc,' she complained that Tuesday. Moreover, 'Dr Beeching [still formulating his overall Plan but already on the march] is annoying me considerably by cutting down all the railways.' For, as she pointed out with irresistible logic: 'In the event of an evacuation [because of nuclear attack?] how will the people be moved if all have to come by road? Why should we be driven on to the roads to be killed when we could go safely by train?'[4]

Stephen Spender spent Wednesday in Oxford, where All Souls hosted Dean Rusk, Charlie Chaplin, Graham Sutherland, Yehudi Menuhin and others after the conferring of honorary degrees. Over drinks and then lunch, he chatted with Sutherland ('has a very Kenneth Clark manner'), was told by the *Observer*'s Nora Beloff how 'marvellous' the much feted Russian Yevgeny Yevtushenko was and found Robert Graves, sitting opposite, 'a bit remote'. But the day's main action was in London. At the National Gallery, a 56-year-old artist called Franz Weng threw a bottle of ink at the Leonardo cartoon, shouting soon afterwards to the policeman who arrested him, 'Yes, I did it. Would you be prepared to die to protect it? I do not think you would. I am sorry the bottle did not break.' And some 4,000 cotton workers from Lancashire – winders, beamers, reelers, doublers, grinders, ring jobbers and blowing-room men, accompanied by five pipe and brass bands – marched along Oxford Street demanding that the government take action to reverse the steep decline (two-thirds of cotton mills closed down since the war) in the textile industry. 'Cut slave-rate imports', 'Lancashire before China!', 'Get weaving Mac – stop the imports', 'Support us now – soon it may be your turn': the banners made their message clear. 'The feeling which emerged in the march was one of jaunty resilience,' noted an observer. 'There was no heart-tugging hopelessness.' But would it be possible to defy crude economics? 'I went to buy pyjamas for my husband last week,' a woman from a Chorley mill told the reporter. 'There were some from Hong Kong at 17s 6d – but I bought Lancashire ones for 27s 11d in the end. It was a wrench, I don't mind telling you.'[5] Economic nationalism had largely ruled during the middle decades of the century, and it still played a central part in the economic thinking of both main political parties, especially Labour; but the world was starting to re-internationalise, Britain was applying to join the Common Market, and the scrapheap ultimately beckoned – whatever the social cost – for those industries unable or unwilling to keep pace.

'The public wants what the public gets,' the Jam would sing eighteen years later. These summer months of 1962 included two surveys focusing on what people apparently did want and one report which, for better or worse, was markedly less attentive and more prescriptive.

The first survey, conducted during May and June, was under the auspices of Mark Abrams, inventor a few years earlier of the phrase 'the teenage consumer' and still drilling down into youthful habits, in this case a sample comprising 3,500 respondents aged between fifteen and twenty-four.[6] The results were in the form of shillings (20 to the £) spent per four weeks, as shown in the table.

Consumer spending by the young

	Middle-class boys	Working-class boys	Middle-class girls	Working-class girls
Vehicles	44	32	6	2
Clothes	31	30	57	58
Cigarettes	24	33	9	14
Holidays	16	12	13	9
Radios etc	5	7	2	3
Records	6	5	4	3
Books	5	2	3	1
Toiletries and shaving equipment	2	2	–	–
Cosmetics	–	–	7	6

In total, middle-class boys spent 1s 6d more per week than working-class boys; middle-class girls spent 1s 3d more per week than working-class girls; and boys generally spent almost 15s more per week than girls generally. Or put another way, gender seems (at this stage of life anyway) to have trumped class. Abrams also found that whereas just under half of his sample regularly watched BBC television, almost two-thirds regularly watched ITV; 40 per cent visited the cinema at least once a week; nearly 30 per cent went dancing at least once a week; almost half listened to Radio Luxembourg at least three times a week (causing the widespread use of 'the small transistor radio set'); and, once they'd left school, 'the great majority' of these young people did not actively participate in sports and outdoor games.

The other survey, conducted between mid-May and early July by R. Wilkinson (an economics lecturer at Leeds University), focused on attitudes to moving house on the part of those living in eight different slum-clearance areas in Leeds.[7] 'Moving', explained Wilkinson in his subsequent analysis of the results, essentially meant moving not just to different living accommodation, but also out of the very immediate area; and strikingly, from his sample of almost a thousand slum-dwellers, over four-fifths were in favour of such a move, principally on the grounds of the opportunity for a better standard of housing in a more pleasant environment. Predictably enough, the minority who wanted to stay put in their particular immediate area tended to be older (over three-quarters of them being aged fifty or more), had fewer children and enjoyed a lower general level of income, including spending less on hire purchase and being less likely to rent a television set. The most surprising – and arguably revealing – finding was that for would-be remainers, and not just would-be leavers, the factor of being near to friends and relatives was relatively unimportant; whereas those who wanted to stay put were appreciably more concerned about economic reasons such as increased rent or cost of travel. They certainly did prioritise proximity to friends and relatives appreciably more than leavers did – but that proximity was *not* their dominant concern. What price, then, 'community'? Perhaps not very high in the decaying inner-city areas of what was still in some sense recognisably industrial Victorian Britain – whatever the feel-good impression to the contrary given by all those feature films, documentaries and soaps about precisely such areas.

One of the survey's eight slum-clearance districts was Hunslet: 'a highly industrialised area near the river and canal and cut by the mainline railway', in Wilkinson's words, but already immortalised, through powerfully evocative autobiographical and descriptive passages, in Richard Hoggart's *The Uses of Literacy* (1957). Hoggart himself gave much of his time in the early 1960s to the Pilkington Committee on Broadcasting, set up by the government in 1960 and publishing its eventual report on the day the Lancashire textile workers marched. Pilkington was Sir Harry Pilkington, chairman of his family's glassmaking company in St Helens and described by Hoggart's biographer Fred Inglis as 'toweringly tall, formidably authoritative, honestly public-spirited'; Joyce Grenfell embodied the vital qualities of humour and shrewdness; and the recently retired footballer Billy Wright represented sporting celebrity. No one doubted, though, that the Committee's most influential member was Hoggart, with his (Inglis again) 'unshakeable resolution that democracy be served at the same time as its moral standards, without which democracy is mob rule, be given strength and youthfulness' – a broad-brush but timeless concept of public service broadcasting. Director-general of the seemingly under-threat BBC (given commercial TV's generally much higher ratings) was Hugh Greene, younger brother of Graham. He played a blinder. 'At endless dinners and lunches, over drinks at parties, he subtly manoeuvred the conversation,' notes a biographer, Michael Tracey. 'Greene set out to create a climate in which the virtues of the BBC, as opposed to the vices of the commercial opposition, would become received truth in the minds of not just the members of the Pilkington Committee, but anyone at all who might possibly have influence.' To establish exactly what those virtues were, Tracey refers to the D-G's 'democratised and humanised version of the missionary role of the BBC to bring "sweetness and light" to people not because they needed it, but because without quite having realised it they in effect wanted it'. His man in charge of music on the Third Programme perhaps played less of a blinder. What, the Committee asked the incorrigibly anti-mainstream William Glock, did he want to offer the BBC's listeners? His impromptu reply was unyielding: 'What they will like tomorrow.'[8]

The report itself, signed unanimously, made a series of recommendations, including that it should be the BBC which provided a new third channel for viewers to watch; that colour TV should be introduced as soon as possible; that local radio services should be provided solely by the BBC, not financed by advertising; and that the idea of substituting for the licence fee a subscription, pay-as-you-view television service should be rejected because that was 'necessarily much the dearest way of providing a service'. One recommendation, however, stood out above all others: that ITA (the Independent Television Authority), and not the television companies themselves such as Granada or Associated Rediffusion or Tyne Tees, should be directly responsible for planning programmes and selling advertising time – on the grounds that the current independent (non-BBC) television service 'does not successfully realise the purposes of broadcasting'.

But if that recommendation was striking, so too was the very feel of the report, significant parts of it drafted by Hoggart. 'No one can say he is giving the public what it wants, unless the public knows the whole range of possibilities which television can offer and, from this range, choose what it wants to see,' it insisted. 'For a choice is only free if the field of choice is not unnecessarily restricted. The subject matter of television is to be found in the whole scope and variety of human awareness and experience ... What the public wants and what it has the right to get is the freedom to choose from the widest possible range of programme matter. Anything less than that is deprivation.' The language could hardly have been loftier or more high-minded. And in its section on triviality, the final sentence was a quotation from the great ethical and moral socialist R. H. Tawney: 'Triviality is more dangerous to the soul than wickedness.'

Had the puritans, the anti-trivialisers, overplayed their hand? Harold Macmillan certainly thought so when, some weeks ahead of publication, he got an advance sight of the report. 'Happily for us,' he privately reflected, 'the tone and temper is deplorable. Such spleen and bias are shewn in every sentence, that the recommendations (wh might be *very* troublesome) are weakened in force and persuasiveness.' More generally, he predicted, 'there will be a splendid political row over this – for, unlike economics, here is something on which everyone can have an opinion – highbrow and low-brow, rich and poor.'⁹

A day before publication, the BBC's chairman, Sir William Haley, reckoned it was job done. 'I do hope you enjoy the Pilkington report,' he wrote to none other than Lord Reith, forty years after the birth of the Corporation. 'I have only skimmed it so far but it seems to me to be the most forthright vindication of all you said broadcasting should be.' And after noting that he could 'well believe that ministers are taken aback', Haley went on: 'It is the most root-and-branch condemnation of *their* creature [that is, commercial television] that there has been. It is heartening to find someone restoring purpose into broadcasting. The Tories never accepted that.' By contrast, the men in charge of the independent TV companies were appalled – none more so than Westward Television's Peter Cadbury, who marked the moment by holding a garden party at which a large copy of the report (or, according to other accounts, an effigy of Pilkington himself) was ceremoniously burnt on a bonfire.

What about the press? Francis Williams's analysis at the time was revealing. The *Mail*, the *Mirror*, the *Sketch* and the *Herald*, all members of newspaper groups with substantial commercial television interests, were unequivocally hostile, typified by the *Mirror*'s memorable headline, 'TV PILKINGTON TELLS THE PUBLIC TO GO TO HELL'; whereas those without such interests, including *The Times*, the *Guardian* and the Beaverbrook papers, were much more positive, typified by the *Evening Standard* calling it 'a document to warm the hearts of those who feared that standards of taste, intelligence and morality might be slowly worn away by the grey relentless tides of commercialism'. The major exception to the pattern was the *Telegraph*: no commercial interest, but calling the report 'arrogant' and 'grossly insulting to popular taste', through its 'haughty conviction that whatever is popular must be bad'. Standing back from it all was the typically perceptive Mollie Panter-Downes, still writing her 'Letter from London' for the *New Yorker*. 'Most people feel that the Pilkington Report sees the old firm at Broadcasting House through too rosy glasses, and the commercial newcomers – whose standards, as in some of their excellent current-affairs documentaries, can be as high as anything put out by the B.B.C. – through too dark ones,' she reckoned a week after publication. 'Lots of serious people who would agree, by and large, with the committee's findings but instinctively dislike its Miss Prism-like accents think that Sir Harry's committee may have antagonized a lot of support, in Parliament and out, by pitching its praise and blame so steeply.'

'Who', asked Macmillan during the Cabinet's largely hostile discussion of the report, 'is responsible for this?' To which Lord Kilmuir – the notoriously reactionary Lord Chancellor – reputedly responded, 'Some lecturer in a provincial university'. The more complicated response was Labour's. In theory it backed Pilkington, but in practice there were limits – unsurprisingly, given that (as Panter-Downes noted) 'the majority of its supporters are certainly prominent among those who look at the private-enterprise programs more frequently than they do at the B.B.C.'. Christopher Mayhew, Labour's longest-standing and most doughty opponent of commercial television, suspected an element of dirty work at the crossroads: and in his subsequent memoirs he explicitly fingered George Brown for swaying the shadow Cabinet, with Brown apparently on the payroll of Cecil King, chairman of the *Daily Mirror* and 'campaigning virulently for commercialisation'. Labour's philosopher-king, Anthony Crosland, was torn. Most of his instincts were libertarian, and in articles later in the year he made clear that he did not favour, by 'imposing (à la Reith) a particular view or level of taste', eradication of the 'inane, banal' programmes that apparently 'most of the public currently wants'. Instead, he pinned his hopes on demanding 'a wider range of serious programmes than would be chosen by immediate majority vote; in the hope that over the years the public, having been offered this range, will more and more freely choose it'.[10] At the time, as higher education began to expand its reach and Rupert Murdoch was still only an Australian media presence, this was perhaps not such an irrational aspiration for the direction of cultural travel.

So what actually happened? Given the visceral hostility of Macmillan and most of his colleagues, the answer is somewhat more than one might have expected. Not only did the BBC get its second channel, its monopoly over local radio and the retention of the licence fee, but the 1963 Television Act ('pushed through', notes Jeffrey Milland, the historian of Pilkington, 'by the widely underestimated Reginald Bevins against considerable opposition from both ministers and Conservative backbenchers') significantly weakened the independent companies and strengthened the ITA, giving it responsibility for ensuring 'a high general standard' and 'proper balance on subject matter'. One specific effect was to reduce the quantity of American imports, but it was the fate of the American-style cash prize which was emblematic. Initiated on British television in 1955 on ITV's instantly popular *Double Your Money* (with Hughie Green offering a top prize of £1,000), the very concept of cash prizes on quiz shows was roundly condemned by Pilkington as appealing to 'suspense and greed and fear'. The upshot, observes Joe Moran, was 'more than 30 years of regulation and restraint', as 'quiz show prizes became money substitutes suggestive of a genteel consumerism: canteen and cutlery sets, dining suites, music centres and family cars'. As for the BBC, it would be left to continue relatively undisturbed (emphasis perhaps on 'relatively') the journey it had been on since the unwelcome advent of a competitor: towards a greater professionalism, a less ostentatiously signalled diffusion of sweetness and light, a degree of creative adventure, and a very mild populism, sometimes so mild it could not be discerned at all.

A last word goes to two diarists. 'Much hullaballoo in the papers,' recorded Anthony Heap, 'over the findings of a Government committee on Television which denounces Independent Television in its report as "trivial, vapid, puerile, repetitive, cheaply sensational, sordid & unsavoury". No eight mots could be more juste!' Phyllis Willmott – entering her forties, married to the sociologist Peter Willmott, increasingly re-entering the world as her children got older and very much someone of the moderate but committed left – on balance disagreed. 'T.V. means Pilkington today,' she wrote the weekend after the report's publication:

> Papers are full of it and the influence of Hoggart. Some say good old Hoggart (the anti ITV's at any price), others chant the Kingsley [Amis] line 'Who-wants-Hoggart-wash. Who wants H-G-W-SH, etc'. Although I feel disgust on most occasions I look at most TV – perhaps *rather* more with ITV than BBC – I'm inclined to be with the Kingsley Mob. That puritanical holier-than-*thou*-ness gets me bobbing with irritation. All that guff of his at the Lady C. [Chatterley] trial to prevent censorship of 'literature', and now more guff to create a form of censorship. It's a 'We know bestness.' Who says?[11]

'That's our baby,' exclaimed the *Daily Mail* after the VC-10, Britain's latest challenger for dominance over the world's long-range airline routes, had made on 29 June, two days after Pilkington, its maiden flight: from the Vickers airfield (inside the old Brooklands motor-racing track) at Weybridge to, all of three miles away, Wisley airfield. 'In the field of the big jet,' BOAC's Sir Basil Smallpeice confidently declared, 'the VC-10 is the only really new development between the earliest subsonic jet and the first supersonic airliners, which are not yet in sight.' That same Friday, Elizabeth David grievously offended the manufacturers by mentioning in the *Spectator* that she had given the filling of a recently bought veal and ham pie to her cat, who had turned it down; the panel at a Mothers' Union meeting at Wick, near Littlehampton, was split on the question of whether a marriage should end when the partners hated each other ('never any going back on solemn promises made before God' versus 'sometimes a dreadful necessity'); Jimi Hendrix was discharged from the US Army; and the Bishop of Woolwich, John Robinson, hosted a supper party for friends to discuss his draft manuscript, with his wife suggesting the title 'Honest to God' and Robinson remarking at the end, 'When it's published, I hope you will come to visit me in some theological Devil's Island!' Next day in Pembroke saw local girls throwing eggs at the Labour politician Michael Foot, there to lead a protest march against West German troops being trained at the nearby Panzer camp – whose spokesman afterwards noted that they had been 'very impressed by the discipline and correctness' of the thousand or so protesters; while on Sunday the new month began in Trafalgar Square with the first public meeting called by the British National Socialist Movement, led by Colin Jordan. The meeting's theme was 'free Britain from Jewish control', swastikas and shouts of 'Heil Hitler' featured freely, some 200 vigorous protesters (among a crowd of around 3,000) kept up a torrent of abuse and a hail of missiles at the speakers, and one report was not wrong to conclude that 'the outpourings of hate for Jews were perhaps the vilest speeches made in Trafalgar Square since the 1930s'. Polio was the overriding concern that week in Dundee: a sharp outbreak (fortunately brief in the event), mainly affecting children under six, had started in June in the new peripheral housing scheme at Fintry, one of whose housewives took exception in the *Dundee Courier* on the 2nd to a letter-writer from another district who had not wanted people from polio-affected areas to travel on normal buses. 'I wonder what "Perturbed", Maryfield, would have had to say if it had started in his area of town?' she wrote. 'I should have thought his thoughts would have been for those poor children, who harm no one and have been struck with this terrible disease ... People have to work. Housewives have to shop, so they are entitled to use transport.' That Monday the struggling, middle-aged artist William Halle, living in Wandsworth on his own and working nights at a telephone exchange in Kensington, had the day to himself. He could have gone to Stepney, where Henry Moore's huge bronze sculpture, *Draped Seated Woman*, had been installed the day before on the Stifford housing estate and would soon be nicknamed 'Old Flo'; or to Lower Thames Street in the City, where the magnificent but doomed Coal Exchange was briefly being opened to the public before the wrecking balls did their worst; but instead he chose a day away from the big smoke:

> I am going off to the country. Where I do not know. Where shall I go? Whom shall I meet?
>
> Edenbridge. I went by train, changing at Oxted into the little steam train. A hot sunny day. Went in four pubs in Edenbridge, also the church, where I made a small rubbing in my sketchbook of a brass saint. Also copied wonderful inscription on a tomb of a young girl.
>
> Went into the country, but it was actually hot and I felt lazy. Slept in a field yellow with mustard flower. Watched little steam trains go by. Walked towards Hever, then at a crossroads a car stopped for me & I could not resist offer of a lift back to Edenbridge. Pleasant man.

'One more drink, a fine salad tea & home,' ended the grateful diarist. 'Day well spent.'[12]

For another creative artist, hoping for the world's recognition, the great moment at last arrived. 'I am sure you will be delighted to hear the long period of waiting has been worthwhile,' began the agent's letter, received by the 36-year-old John Fowles on 4 July. 'Tom Maschler tells me that Cape would like to take THE COLLECTOR.' 'One doesn't', reflected Fowles himself, 'quite believe it when it comes. Not that I haven't kept a belief in the book. But I've had no belief in the agency and publishing world.' The competition – for Fowles never aimed low – included Anthony Powell and Iris Murdoch, each of whom had very recently published a novel. *The Kindly Ones* was the sixth in Powell's sequence (called at this point *The Music of Time*), and at least one reviewer, Philip Toynbee, seems to have assumed that it completed the sequence, prompting him to confess that he remained 'hopelessly uncertain about its survival-value'. But another reviewer, Paul Scott, implicitly looked forward ('the most interesting work-in-progress that I know of today'), as did David Piper, who after comparing the series to 'a giant aquarium-scale goldfish bowl' ended by affirming, 'I have every confidence that the bowl is inexhaustible.' This time round anyway, it was less of a warm glow for Murdoch. Ronald Bryden may have talked about *An Unofficial Rose* showing her moving forward 'in mastery', but for Angus Wilson it was 'a vexing disappointment' (not least because 'the surface of the novel is of a grating "gracious living" vulgarity that is hard to bear'), while Francis Hope baldly concluded that 'Miss Murdoch is guilty of writing too much and too fast.' Still, when Fowles went to see Maschler on Friday the 6th, she was the name on the lips of the ambitious young publisher, who had only quite recently become editorial director at Cape. 'He was grim about the fiction situation in general,' reported Fowles. 'Apparently 1,500 copies is a very good sale for a first novel nowadays ... Murdoch's novels, which sell about 10,000 copies, are the bestsellers today, and then only because she is the OK suburban woman's novelist – not too hard to understand, and looks good on the coffee-table.' As for the 'intelligent, frank, tall Jew' himself, Fowles made a perceptive assessment: 'A feeling that all he really wants is a tough, hard, glossy end-product – something that will sell, that will be in vogue. A good shrewd judge of what will sell today; but I wouldn't back him to pick what will be read in 2062.'[13]

On this particular Friday in 1962, the midday concert at the Cheltenham Festival featured the 17-year-old cellist Jacqueline du Pré, partnered by her mother in a recital of sonatas. 'This gifted young player', freely acknowledged the critic Colin Mason, albeit at times, he added helpfully for family harmony, masked by 'a lack of rhythmic definition and impetus' on the part of her accompanying pianist. Accordingly, 'she perhaps now needs to begin playing with partners whose artistry and technique will be a greater challenge for her to match'. Also rather muffled the same day was Eric Hobsbawm's grudging semi-defence of pop music. 'Insofar as it gives people a locus for their dreams or a voice which echoes their own sentiments,' he wrote in the *New Statesman* in response to MacInnes's attack, 'we must respect it.' Over the 1960s as a whole, Hobsbawm's lack of enthusiasm for pop and rock music – and his continuing faithfulness to jazz – would be one of the reasons why he continued to keep a certain distance from the New Left, instinctively keener than he was on new, counter-cultural forms. Not that pop music was likely to get all that much of a look-in in the *New Left Review*, by now under the editorship of the startlingly young (twenty-three), startlingly cerebral Perry Anderson. That weekend, at a meeting at Keele University of the magazine's board – from which both Doris Lessing and Ralph (later Raphael) Samuel had resigned, but with E. P. Thompson for the moment still on it – Anderson set out his bracing editorial plans:

> Articles are to be accepted on a basis of their intrinsic interest rather than for their place in a pre-established socialist framework. Difficulty of language is not to be considered grounds for rejection. The Review must not become ingrown, socialist writers outside the immediate New Left should consider it a natural place to submit their work. Marxism represents the only complete body of socialist theory, and there is a lack of real Marxist study in England. There is further work to be done on building a house of socialist theory for the twentieth century. The vocabulary of the Review is to be internationalised, also the contributions, which will entail an acceptance of new idioms.

Ensuing discussion 'centred mainly on maintaining a balance between readability and a high intellectual level'; and 'in his reply Perry pointed to the need for a balance between existing academic journals and the New Left's role as an agent of social change'. 'Vastly self-assured' (Fred Inglis's words) and 'fluent' with it, Anderson now had the way clear to put his uncompromisingly stringent stamp on the magazine of a movement which had originally been a humanist as well as a socialist response to the Soviet tanks of 1956. 'It tends towards a humourless fixity of theory miles away from the life really lived by those for whom it most seeks to theorize,' Inglis would aptly reflect in 1982, some twenty years after Lessing, Samuel and Thompson had sensed that direction of travel.[14]

'Youth at its worst' was the *Surrey Comet*'s headline on Saturday, in the context of the local council having issued summonses against two youths who had thrown stones at street lamps in Thetford Road, New Malden. 'Nothing seems to be safe nowadays from these hooligans, who roam the streets and parks, wrecking public seats, trees and flower beds, as well as lights, all provided by the ratepayers at considerable expense,' declared an editorial coming from the heart of a suburban England arguably *terra incognita* to Lessing and co. just as much as to Anderson. 'The troublemakers are only a tiny minority, but they do havoc out of all proportion to their numbers and it has gone unchecked for too long.' So too that same day on the south coast. 'I have yet to be convinced that people who live in bed-sitters do not have a communal dustbin provided for their garbage,' complained a letter-writer in the *Bexhill-on-Sea Observer* about public litter bins being used for domestic rubbish. 'It is just sheer laziness and the easiest way out, regardless of other folk who try to keep the town tidy. I am sure our local cinema manager, if approached, would put a slide on his screen to educate the people about the use of litter bins.'

Elsewhere, the centre of Basildon saw the formal opening of Brooke House, a fourteen-storey block of flats welcomed by an architectural critic later in the year for the way in which 'suddenly the drama and scale so conspicuously absent in other New Towns is achieved'; reporting on a production by the Dover Players of *A Midsummer Night's Dream*, performed in the grounds of Kearsney Abbey, the local paper noted that 'never could Dover audiences have seen a more energetic puckish-Puck than Dover College master Jeffrey Archer who created havoc in the wood as he worked for his fairy king Oberon'; Wimbledon (still all-amateur, nominally anyway) ended, with viewer research revealing that Dan ('Oh, I say!') Maskell was the favourite commentator by some way, leaving Peter West, Jack Kramer and David Coleman all bunched behind him; and on ITV, *The Morecambe and Wise Show*, also known as *Two of a Kind*, enjoyed a primetime Saturday-evening slot. Just half an hour long, it included two sprightly numbers by Kenny Ball and his Jazzmen (the trad jazz phenomenon perhaps starting by now to run out of puff), the winsome Beverley Sisters singing 'It's Illegal, It's Immoral or It Makes You Fat', and a cherishable sketch in which Eric and Ernie play two opposing footballers marking each other near the touchline and, starved of the ball, starting to chat. 'I want to prove I'm worth 40 million lire,' says Eric, wearing notably brief shorts and claiming that he is being watched by scouts from Milan. '40 million lire?' asks Ernie. 'Yes.' 'I tell you it's 50 million lire for a newspaper.' 'Ah well, I don't read a lot anyway.'

Their show was perhaps a source of cheer in Newcastle, where according to a report highlighted this day by the *British Medical Journal*, the equivalent of 200,000 amphetamine tablets were prescribed monthly to a population of under 270,000, with the largest group of recipients being middle-aged women. 'The reasons given by these patients for taking amphetamines are relatively few. Depression, fatigue, obesity, and, surprisingly, anxiety are the most common.' Jennie Hill near Winchester would have sympathised. 'Still feel v. depressed,' she wrote in her diary that evening. 'Can't shake it off. There doesn't seem to be any future in anything to me.' But, for the Haines family, a good weekend as Judy, husband John and teenage daughters Ione and Pamela set off from Chingford on a fortnight's holiday, including on the way to Somerset 'a jolly picnic in Savernake Forest', after which 'Pam turfed and buried our debris'. Next day was first full day at a camp in St Audries Bay (where they'd been the previous year). 'A very small attendance at 9.45 a.m. Service in the ballroom,' recorded Judy. 'Six, including Vicar.'[15]

Next morning, at their home in North Tawton, Devon, Sylvia Plath answered a phone call intended for her husband Ted Hughes, realised that the disguised voice at the other end belonged to the predatory Assia Wevill, and furiously ripped the cord of the phone out of the wall – before later on, as Hughes fled to London, consigning his letters and manuscripts to a bonfire in the yard.[16] Tuesday the 10th was Telstar Day. Here, the West Country focus was Cornwall, specifically the Lizard Peninsula's Goonhilly Downs, where amid considerable late-night crowds Raymond Baxter was on point duty to provide commentary as a giant satellite dish sought to pick up the signal from the world's first TV satellite, currently orbiting Earth. 'That's a man's face,' he was eventually able to exclaim at around 1 a.m. 'That's the picture … there it is. It's a man … there is the first live television picture across the Atlantic with rather less than four minutes of available time left.' Holding it all together at the London end was the inevitable Richard Dimbleby, happily and confidently in the course of the long evening referring to 'our friend Telstar'. 'Scanner' for one was unconvinced. 'My own excitement was lost in the B.B.C.'s heavy-handed treatment of the occasion,' reckoned the TV critic for the *Birkenhead News and Advertiser*. 'These days I always have forebodings when Richard Dimbleby is scheduled for jobs like this. I find myself rather like a schoolboy lapping up teacher's bright remarks – and I don't like it as I used to. I want to feel I've grown out of it, even if I haven't.' As for the distantly cordial Telstar, one diarist, the elderly Marian Raynham in Surbiton, was ambivalent: 'Now we, in all the World, will get in each others hair worse than ever. Perhaps all this will make War more difficult.' An altogether low-tech breakthrough occurred the following evening – BBC TV's first *Barn Dance*, coming from Newcastle, hosted by Brian Redhead and starring the wholesome, Aran-sweatered Liverpool Spinners (later the Spinners), the start arguably of the British folk boom – near the end of a day in which Hughes had made very physical love to Wevill. 'You know,' she told a friend soon afterwards, 'in bed he smells like a butcher.'[17]

What sort of urban future lay ahead? On Wednesday the 11th, the same day the press reported Manchester Housing Committee's rejection as impracticable of the suggestion by a councillor (representing one of the oldest areas of north Manchester) that tenants in blocks of slum houses should be moved together to new dwellings in the inner-city districts where they had lived for years, the latest issue of the *Architects' Journal* included two noteworthy items: not only the photo of a model of the proposed Gateshead shopping centre (featuring above it Owen Luder's multi-storey car park, to be immortalised in *Get Carter*), but also a major survey, 'Coping with Cars', to mark the start that day of the RIBA Conference in Coventry that was aiming to tackle the ever-thornier subject. No big city was instinctively more pro-car than Birmingham, and the main article explained how it planned 'to forge ahead with a ten-year programme costing £43,000,000 which includes the completion of the inner ring road and its spurs and the construction of thirty-nine underpasses and flyovers plus one or two lengths of new road'. But the writer also quoted Maurice Ash's description of the motor car in a recent Town and Country Planning Association pamphlet: 'The symbol of our civic crisis as well as the very vehicle of our freedoms.' On the first evening of this Coventry gathering, the assembled architects went, on the invitation of the Lord

Mayor, to see David Turner's recently opened play, *Semi-Detached*, at the suitably modernist Belgrade Theatre. 'Sour stuff ... not an ounce of honesty,' reckoned the *AJ*'s columnist 'Astragal', perhaps not altogether doing justice to a self-consciously Jonsonian satire on the human-cum-ethical price of social ambition. 'Rather boring to listen for two hours to this one-stringed lower middle-class fiddle, one would have thought, but our sophisticated profession applauded with embarrassingly undiscerning enthusiasm.' Which arguably raises the question: as urban redevelopment of one sort or another gathered pace by the day, were Britain's architects of the early 1960s made of the right stuff (including the necessary humility) to create a legacy which over the ensuing years would nourish rather than damage the human spirit, however such imponderables are measured?

The stakes could hardly have been higher. 'Lancashire Mill Towns' – specifically, Blackburn, Bolton, Burnley, Bury, Preston, Rochdale – were the subject for Ian Nairn, most humane and understanding of architectural writers, in that month's *Architectural Review*. 'All of them', he noted, 'have big renewal schemes at varying stages of negotiation, mostly done with London money by London architects.' But his explicit worry was that 'the architects of Britain may fail these noble, genuine places':

> One of the things that they all have in common is a vivid market life. Where precincts may stay glum, the market hall and the stalls around it sell everything and are full of life. They work best of all when they are bang in the centre. The Town Hall still means something here, in a personal way, and sometimes market hall and town hall have remained close together and react on each other as vividly as an Ypres or Arras. The best example in the six towns is at Blackburn; yet the very first stage in the redevelopment of Blackburn's centre is to demolish the market and put it two hundred yards away.
>
> And, naturally enough, the progressive supporters of such a scheme are led by its undoubted virtues into a kind of brave new world hubris ...

'All of the mill towns', Nairn did not deny, 'have parts of their centres which really are outworn. Rebuilding in some kind of partnership between town and developer is a good way of doing it.' What he dreaded, however, was not just the destruction of an old, intimate, local way of daily life, but its replacement in these towns with what he called 'a hack assembly of slabs and curtain walling plus a piazza put in for amenity's sake', not to mention the displacement of local shops by every high-street multiple. 'There is', he concluded perhaps half-hopefully, 'a marvellous chance to match the nineteenth century's achievement in buildings which the town will be proud of in fifty years, instead of being fed up with in five. But to do so, the far-from-poor property companies and their architects will have to get their fingers out.'[18]

On the same day that the architects began their discussions in Coventry, the aggressively visionary banker Sir George Bolton sent an important letter to Lord Cromer, Governor of the Bank of England. Since the guns of August 1914, the City of London had largely stagnated as an international financial centre, though the emergence from the late 1950s of the Eurodollar market, strongly encouraged by Bolton, had begun to point the way towards a less UK-oriented future. Some weeks earlier this summer, he had spoken to Cromer about 'a certain exchange of ideas that is currently taking place regarding the opening of the London market to a wide variety of borrowers for loans denominated in foreign currencies'; those in the know comprised representatives of the merchant banks Barings, Samuel Montagu and Warburgs as well as Bolton's own bank, the Bank of London and South America (BOLSA). Now, on 11 July, Bolton informed Cromer that Hambros had joined the party and outlined various specific plans, including a possible $15–20 million loan for the Kingdom of Norway, aimed at 'helping to restore London's function as a capital market and for finding some alternative to the greatly weakened New York market'. He and the others still needed Cromer's blessing, but these were the first steps in what would become the flourishing Eurobond market, most visible symbol of a largely glittering future for the Square Mile. Sadly, a less glittering prospect far away in Scotland, where on this Wednesday the National Coal Board's Scottish Division announced a five-year review listing twenty-seven collieries likely to be closed by 1966, at a loss of up to 20,000 jobs. 'This is not the death knell of the coal industry,' promised R. W. Parker, the divisional chairman; but in the context of intensive competition from oil, gas and electricity, as well as the railways requiring less coal, few would seriously have quarrelled with the reaction of a Fife councillor, John McWilliam, that the outlook was 'grim'.[19]

Next day, several hundred members of the Exclusive Brethren ('one of the most reclusive and savage Protestant sects in British history', in the words of Rebecca Stott, daughter of one of its ministering brothers) gathered at Alexandra Palace, convinced that the Lord was working fast and the Rapture was imminent; nearby, a special court at the Royal Free Hospital in Hampstead heard evidence of a forbidden activity; and *Steptoe* ended its first series on a creative high. The evidence that the court heard came from four young women in their early twenties, who related how a 29-year-old French film producer called Bernard Larroque, living at Leinster Gardens in Bayswater, had (reported the *Ham & High*) 'carried out operations on them with intent to procure abortions' – a practice wholly illegal unless licensed, which was the case only in a minority of abortions. The amount they paid varied but was between £20 and £40; one of them was admitted to hospital soon afterwards suffering from peritonitis, with a doctor explaining that it was 'too early to say whether she will suffer any permanent injury'; and Larroque, reserving his defence, was sent to the Old Bailey for trial, with bail refused. That Thursday evening, the Steptoe storyline of 'The Holiday' was harrowing in its own way. Harold desperate to go to Greece without Albert, as opposed to their usual twosome at Bognor; the tearful old man (a stranger to Europe since his First World War experiences) staging a perfectly timed psychosomatic heart attack; and the doctor coming up with the killer lines 'There's no cure for loneliness, Harold' and 'We're all trapped by something.' '*Steptoe and Son* virtually obliterates the division between drama and comedy,' Maurice Wiggins justifiably claimed in the *Sunday Times* soon afterwards. 'Messrs Simpson and Galton have struck a vein so rich that one can almost speak of a major breakthrough in television comedy.'[20]

The most powerful unfolding drama on the 12th was political. The catastrophic defeat of the Tories by the Liberals at Orpington in March (the biggest by-election swing in history), Selwyn Lloyd's lacklustre Budget in April, a string of poor by-election results since then, the pay-paused economy palpably stagnating even as inflation increased – Harold Macmillan's government was by early July pinned firmly on the back foot, not helped by Macmillan's own carefully cultivated 'Edwardian' image starting to look increasingly anachronistic. On Sunday the 8th, the same day that the *Observer* published opinion-polling evidence from nineteen suburban constituencies that over half of Conservative supporters agreed that Macmillan was 'tired' and almost a third 'think that the whole Conservative Party leadership is tired, played out, complacent and out of touch', the PM reflected in his diary that he was going to have to replace his Chancellor, that Lloyd was 'by nature, more of a staff officer than a commander'. In truth, no one could deny that the dogged, ultra-loyal Lloyd was an uncharismatic politician, severely orthodox in his thinking and unswayed by public opinion. But there was also on Macmillan's part an element of social snobbery, even calling Lloyd to his face 'a middle-class lawyer from Liverpool', or alternatively (though perhaps not to his face) 'the Little Attorney'. Things now moved quickly. On Tuesday the 10th, an opinion poll revealed that the Tories were likely to be trounced at the Leicester North East by-election on Thursday; before then, on Wednesday, the Home Secretary, Rab Butler, revealed to Lord Rothermere, owner of the *Daily Mail*, that his chief had in mind a major Cabinet reshuffle after the summer recess; next morning, while the *Guardian* ran the headline 'MR LLOYD TO KEEP A TIGHT GRIP', the *Mail* splashed with 'MAC'S MASTER PLAN', in effect forcing his hand; and that Thursday at 6 p.m., after being summoned to Admiralty House (where Macmillan was staying while work was being done on No. 10), an utterly shocked Lloyd – who had refused to countenance the *Mail* story – was told by an emotional PM, talking about plots against him, that the Chancellor's services were no longer required. During the rest of the evening, Macmillan made one other sacking (like Lloyd's, not instantly made public), before a few minutes ahead of midnight an entirely predictable result came through from Leicester: Labour increasing its majority, a strong showing from the Liberals, and the Conservatives coming comfortably bottom of the poll, with a vote share some 24 per cent down on the 1959 general election. The party's candidate was Robin Marlar, the Sussex amateur cricketer, and he promised that 'We shall be back.'[21]

This Thursday evening was not just about waiting for the Leicester result or watching the Steptoes. 'Mick Jagger, R & B vocalist, is taking a rhythm and blues group into the Marquee tomorrow night,' *Jazz News* had announced in its 'Stop Press' column the day before, adding that the group was called 'The Rollin' Stones' and quoting Mick: 'I hope they don't think we're a rock and roll outfit.' It was debut time for a new combo – Brian Jones as main man, Jagger and Keith Richards as main accomplices – which in the basement of Oxford Street's Academy Cinema played, as support for Long John Baldry, a fifty-minute set liberally laced with the blues. 'Jagger barely moved throughout,' notes a biographer. 'He wore a striped sweater and corduroys, Jones a fringed jacket, Richards a suit of funereal darkness.' The reception was mixed, with the odd mutter being due to length of hair at least as much as to quality of performance. And a performance – a live performance – it was. 'That feeling is worth more than anything,' remembered Richards almost half a century later. 'There's a certain moment when you realize that you've actually just left the planet for a bit and that nobody can touch you. You're elevated because you're with a bunch of guys that want to do the same thing as you. And when it works, baby, you've got wings ... It's flying without a licence.'[22]

'There is stagnation in Britain,' declared Anthony Crosland on 3 July at the start of a state-of-the-nation discussion on the Third Programme,

> in the sense that in many spheres of our national life – in economic growth; in the public service; in industry; inside the Labour movement; even, if it comes to that, in sport – there is a failure to move in as progressive a manner as other countries are doing. This extends far outside simply the question of economic growth on which everybody concentrates. It extends to almost every aspect of the national life at the moment, and its most obvious symptom is the lack of a willingness to innovate and to get things changed and moved. There is a certain paralysis of the will, a certain refusal to grapple with problems and to find new solutions for them.

A significant cause of this state of stasis was, he argued, the way long-term decline had been masked by the fact of having won, albeit at huge cost, two world wars. 'We never had what, in terms of history, might ironically have been the lucky accident of a proper defeat which everybody recognized.' And as a result:

> The trouble with many of our rulers at the moment – in very different spheres of national life – is that they have the attitude that we can get away with things still as we could in the past. In the past we could get away with certain attitudes of mind which we certainly cannot get away with now; it was possible, unattractive, to sneer at the professionalism of the 'Huns' and the 'Yanks' and the 'experts' and the 'technocrats' and all the rest of it. The trouble is that this attitude of mind persists now, and we still have a cult of the amateur, of the all-rounder, of the dilettante, an emphasis on character and on manners, and a strong basic hostility to professionalism and expertise and technocracy.

Crosland cited as his prime example the Civil Service, an institution which 'we all assume is the most marvellous in the world', but where in fact 'real professionalism is heavily discounted'. As a consequence, the Treasury was 'hopelessly behind in the field of long-term planning', while ministries like education, pensions and housing 'also lack a professional attitude to problems of planning and problems of long-term research'.

Nor of course, he went on to emphasise, did 'our whole inherited social class system', which 'divides the country up into broad classes according to education and social background', help matters. 'One notices the contrast with many of the European countries, where even though, say, the income differences are the same as they are in this country, there is a sense of people roughly speaking the same language and belonging to the same cultural tradition.' Near the end, his fellow discussant, the sociologist Donald MacRae, reflected on how Britain was 'the only country where calling someone clever is to abuse them': 'I do think that we do lack common understanding and a common image of the diversity and virility of our society. That is a bad thing: we do not want the unity which normally tends to end up in conformity, perhaps even in some sort of tyranny of one kind or another either social or political or both, but we do lack unity in the sense of a common understanding.' 'That is the crux,' agreed Crosland. 'One must be careful about words like unity and community because they can, as you say, lead to conformist and even authoritarian pressures. But still what is lacking in Britain is a common understanding, an ability to communicate freely, a sense of a national pattern.'[23]

Perfect timing, then, for Anthony Sampson's pioneering *Anatomy of Britain*, which was published very soon afterwards, with the bulk of the reviews appearing in mid-July. 'This', he stated at the outset, 'is a book about the workings of Britain – who runs it and how, how they got there, and how they are changing.' 'I have concentrated', he explained, 'on the basic anatomy – the arms and legs and the main blood stream ... Basically this is a book about the managers – in government, industry, science or communication.' Based on almost 200 interviews with leading people (almost entirely male) in those fields, the result was a hugely readable panorama, with a journalist's eye for the telling detail or remark. 'The Stock Exchange has the atmosphere of a superannuated schoolroom. On an afternoon when I was there [presumably viewing proceedings from the public gallery, which had only opened in 1953, a full three-quarters of a century after a Royal Commission had recommended it], one lugubrious-looking broker was walking round the room with a feather duster, tickling the other side of men's bald heads, so that they looked round to discover nobody; another broker was kicking a newspaper, crunched into a football, round the hall; another was throwing paper-pellets, with careful marksmanship, at his colleagues.' Or on the next page about stockbrokers generally: 'The big firms have become regarded as intelligence service for the City, at the centre of the telephone network of mmms and wells and meaningful grunts. "Better ask Cazenove's," a banker will mumble, and the answer will come back with the authority of the market-place.'

Perhaps unsurprisingly, Sampson's overall conclusions about what he saw as a serious failure of leadership were not so different from Crosland's:

> The old privileged values of aristocracy, public schools and Oxbridge, which still dominate government today, have failed to provide the stimulus, the purposive policies and the keen eye on the future which Britain is looking for, and must have. The old ethos was moulded by the success of an invincible imperial

machine. Its style was to make big things seem small, exciting things boring, new things familiar: but in the unconfident context of today this bland depreciation – and the assumed superiority that goes with it – merely succeeds in dispelling enthusiasms, blunting curiosity and dulling experiment. The groove-outlook, the club-amateur outlook, the pragmatic outlook are all totally out of keeping with an age which suffers, unlike the Victorians', from an oppressive lack of innovation and zeal. The old fabric of the British governing class, while keeping its social and political hold, has failed to accommodate or analyse the vast forces of science, education or social change which (whether they like it or not) are changing the face of the country. The new and potentially exciting institutions which control large areas of the future – for instance nationalised industries, insurance companies, redbrick universities – have grown up in a separate and unacknowledged sector, and the resulting rift has cut off the old from the new. Britain's malaise, I suspect, is not primarily a malaise of the ordinary people, but a malaise among the few thousand managers of our society who have failed to absorb and communicate new challenges and new ideas.

In short, 'the institutions and the men who work them have, I believe, become dangerously out of touch with the public, insensitive to change, and wrapped up in their private rituals'. Sampson ended his *tour de force* – which it was, whatever the sneers of subsequent academic historians – by quoting the solemn words of Walter Bagehot: 'The characteristic danger of great nations, like the Romans or the English, which have a long history of continuous creation, is that they may at last fail from not comprehending the great institutions they have created.'[24]

Sampson's core thesis – country-going-to-the-dogs inadequacy in the modern world of Britain's key institutions and their leaders – wholly convinced Bernard Levin. 'We can only hope', he ended his *Spectator* review, 'that enough of us will see the danger in time, that the tempo of change and reconstruction will quicken, that some serious long-range looking into the country's future will take place, and that the results will start to become apparent before the bloody dogs get us all.' By contrast, the political journalist Norman Shrapnel was less certain that a dedicated programme of modernisation and professionalism necessarily represented the best way forward: 'Just conceivably – so the mixed-up British may be thinking deep down, without ever daring to put it into words – one can be efficient without being ruthless,' he reflected in the *TLS*. 'Certainly the heretical thought occurs to some, late at night in the privacy of their homes, that one can fail to export and still not die.' No other reviewer went as far as the novelist Simon Raven – caustically dismissive of the Sampson thesis and holding out instead for the virtues of 'complacency, nepotism, charm, the amateur spirit' – but the young David Marquand also had his doubts, arguing in the *Guardian* that Sampson's prescription of 'a kind of tough-minded, forward-looking elitism' (Marquand's words) 'seems to me almost as unpleasant as the attitudes which prevail now'. 'Mr Sampson's Britain would be much harder, more ruthless and more prosperous than the present one; but I am not sure that it would be more democratic or more humane.' Marquand then went on to take even more fundamental issue: not only was the 'fashionable' doctrine (in the form espoused by Sampson too) that inefficiency not inequality was the main defect of modern British society 'a hopelessly barren one', ignoring as it did the question 'efficient for what purpose?'; but he also found 'disturbing' Sampson's 'apparent admiration for the "meritocrats and technocrats"': 'If we have to have an élite, then I agree with Mr Sampson in wanting a dynamic élite, open to talent rather than the present exclusive and unadventurous one. But I would prefer to have no élites at all – and if that led to a loss of power or prosperity, it would seem to me that the price had been worth paying.' As to whether the British people would *really* choose such priorities – well, that lay outside the remit of Marquand's review. As indeed did public opinion generally lie outside Sampson's own self-imposed remit, with Timothy Raison noting in *Punch* that the survey 'frankly excludes art, provincial culture and the life of the ordinary people'. And, less than three months before this future Conservative politician was due to edit a new weekly magazine that *would* seek to describe the lives and elicit the views of society at large, he reflected that Sampson 'does not for a moment admit the possibility that it could be the few thousand managers who keep Britain moving, and that the malaise is among the ordinary people'.[25]

As it happened, the paper for top people was now at last trying to find out what 'ordinary people' *did* think about things. Running during the second half of July, 'The Pulse of England' was the title for a series of articles by *The Times*'s Midland Correspondent (MC), who between roughly late May and early July had left his usual patch and spent six weeks travelling around England seeking to gauge opinion and sentiment.[26] The inspiration had apparently come from lunch with an 'affable and senior' Tory:

> Over soup we agreed that things had gone very wrong with the Government's image lately. While dispatching some excellent ham we tried but failed to hit upon the exact reasons. In a mellow moment when coffee arrived this pleasant chap said suddenly: 'You know, this country wants something; it is trying to tell us something through these by-elections. The whole difficulty is to discover what that something is.'

Thus the six-week trip, involving conversations with over 150 people. 'The public opinion poll can take a snap photograph of the political landscape: I was after the underlying geology.' If not in the class of say J. B. Priestley's classic quest (*English Journey*) of three decades earlier, the result was far from negligible as a kind of portrait of a civilisation and its – on the whole – discontents.

First stop for the MC was Blackpool, by far the country's most popular seaside resort, where 'talking over best bitter, late at night, at a room filled with smoke', a group of Tory supporters – presumably all of them men, probably on holiday – did not hold back:

> The Government have been too weak. I should not mind some unemployment if it would get us some waitresses here.

> I think the Government have been scandalous lately. We used to have an Empire in my young days, but now we are crawling on our bellies to the little countries and asking them to let us into the Common Market [that is the European Economic Community, which Britain the previous autumn had applied to join].

> I cannot say I disapprove because Jews are not admitted to a local golf club. I know the answer to the staff shortage would be

to get West Indians here, but if I saw a big, buck nigger serving behind a bar I would walk straight out of the place. I would not drink there.

No such bile, but little optimism either, 'among Blackpool young people' on a Saturday night in the Empress ballroom. Fifteen of the nineteen girls who spoke to him revealed that they did not expect, overall, a happy future. 'The future is going to be lousy, isn't it? What is there to look forward to?' And 'I feel hemmed in. There's no getting out of it somehow.' 'At first,' reflected the MC, 'I doubted the accuracy of the interviewing, but these results have been accepted in expert assessments of young people elsewhere in the country.'

Then on to Ullswater in the Lake District. 'The trouble is that young people have got away from the basic things today,' the man from the Outward Bound school told him. 'The 900 boys we take here every year are better fed than before the war but not so fit. I should say that usually only the country boys could walk five miles across this country when they arrive. The boys are often absolutely reliant on mother, and she is often the only woman they treat with respect.' Even more emphatic was 'the small lady in the hotel' at his next stop. 'I was born in Carlisle, baptised in Carlisle, married in Carlisle, and I'll die in Carlisle. There ought to be more for young people to do, but I love Carlisle. Don't you write anything against it.' From there he drove to the Cumberland coast and Whitehaven. 'The name is totally misleading. What Whitehaven needs is paint – a good deal of it and then a dingy town centre could be turned into something quaint and gay.' Finally, to complete this leg, the road south, 'until there appears a cloud of steam from cooling towers and a great cluster of eccentric buildings between the road and the sea. This is Windscale and the Calder works, where electricity is being produced by nuclear power.' There he listened to the views of some of the scientists, those men who at the time of Calder Hall's royal opening in 1956 had absolutely seemed – and to some extent still did – the new men of a dawning age:

I sometimes wonder at the moment if we can afford democracy. One feels we must put through a certain number of policies which might be distasteful to more than half the population.

After all, this country did wonders during the war when it was a question of doing something or going under.

I am against organized religion. Karl Marx may have said that religion was the people's opium, but now they have another drug. Put them down in front of a television set all day, switch it on, and most of them would be perfectly happy.

The trouble with this country now is that people are always ducking the difficult decisions. The people have got to be told that unless they work harder we are storing up trouble for the future. The people who should be telling them are frightened to stick their necks out, but it can be done with the right approach.

'It is easy to give an impression of brashness or intemperance,' the MC helpfully glossed. 'These are intelligent and pleasant people speaking.'

Later that day, through 'sweeping and splendid' countryside across the top of England, he drove to Newcastle, where next morning – half expecting 'a pall of smoke from which, on occasion, will emerge the figures of stunted natives, most of them wearing cloth caps and mufflers, gabbling strangely about the beer, the dogs, and gangin'' along the Scotswood Road' – he encountered instead 'a town of which people can reasonably be proud': 'Its folk are well dressed and they are friendly (but it helps to explain that one comes not from London but from Birmingham).' In short, 'Newcastle was obviously a good deal too smart to harbour the working man as he used to be,' so accordingly he picked a town almost at random and headed off to North Shields. 'It turned out to be a fishing port with some grimly friendly people, two Chinese restaurants, and a sign outside the General Havelock Inn which says: "No ladies supplied".' In the event, it was not on the banks of the Tyne but near those of the Tees that the urban explorer at last found what he had been looking for, the authentic face of the past. Namely, 'in those unfortunate towns of Hartlepool and West Hartlepool':

'This place has stood still since 1935,' said one resident. Another claimed it had as certainly slipped back. West Hartlepool has at least one superb hotel, but why else should there be that proud

and complacent stare on the statue of the town's founder?
I walked through unlovely streets to the sea front, where
groups of grey men in cloth caps stood aimlessly looking out
at the waves. More men were sitting or standing about in the
untidy goods yard by the docks. Their minds seemed closed to
strangers; they would not open out. It was the low point, the one
dreadful day of the tour. If this was the thirties as they were, then
we are well rid of them. I went to the art gallery and museum and
looked at the stuffed lion there and Victorian paintings telling
stories. I gave half-a-crown to the picture fund. One should try
to do something …

That act of charity performed, the MC did finally manage to get a
local to talk at some length. 'We have very few communists here but
those stupid clots in Whitehall are doing their best to encourage them,'
asserted a trade unionist. 'It is unfair to introduce a pay pause if you do
not try to control the cost of living and members of the upper middle
class can go on feathering their nests. What this country needs is a
call. At the moment we are just like a crowd of people milling about
outside a football ground without anyone to show us inside. At the
moment we are a mob, and I should not like us to enter the Common
Market in this haphazard state.' Presumably that milling crowd was
not outside the Victoria Ground, home to Hartlepool United, which
at the end of each of the previous three seasons, coming at or near
the bottom of Division Four, had had to apply for re-election to the
Football League.

For the MC it was now down to the West Riding, where in Leeds
he went to a small variety theatre (originally the singing room of the
White Horse Inn) and watched 'an old-style variety artiste', who had
been on the boards since she was eleven, 'putting over old songs with
fire, skill, and almost every trick in the book'. 'It is very difficult', she
told him afterwards, 'following a stripper; a sort of coldness comes
up from the audience when you go on. Nevertheless, this is the only
place in the country where they still have twice-nightly variety: it is
a tragedy the way the theatres are closing now. Where are the young
performers going to learn their business?' No such concerns at the
hugely popular, family-friendly 'bowling emporium' he went to
next: 'The balls trundling down the brightly lit alleys, the rows of

men in coloured sweaters bowling away, the pins tumbling, the whole thing seeming jolly, unexceptionable, and highly organized'.

Then it was on to Bradford, which for an hour or two he positively 'hated': 'The town centre is being redeveloped, but nothing much is happening in many of the back streets except that the accretion of industrial grime grows daily thicker.' But the rest of his visit proved an experience in revisionism, helped by 'a man in the wool business' being 'one of the most civilised people' he spoke with during his entire tour. 'I am filled with regret at the end of our empire, but I consider what is happening is right and inevitable,' reflected this interviewee. 'Although I believe it will be to the wool industry's benefit to enter the Common Market, I personally hope we do not. The British way and purpose might be better preserved by staying out. I believe we do need a sense of direction and it might be possible to reawaken something of the Dunkirk spirit if we did not go in.' Still in Bradford, amid 'the smoke-blackened buildings' and pervasive griminess, the MC then spotted a poster and discovered that, 'amazingly', it was also 'the world of the Bradford Gilbert and Sullivan Society'; and that evening he was one of more than a thousand at the Alhambra to help 'cheer on the cast with justified delight' as local amateur enthusiasts performed *The Pirates of Penzance*.

This particular leg ended at Batley and, almost inevitably, a visit to a working men's club, well appointed and profitable. Even so, he and the group he was sitting with 'wondered about the future of Batley and of clubs':

My expert guide said that club life did not have the same appeal to the man on the new estate: he had not so much money to spend, he watched television more.

A ventriloquist mounted the stage. His question of the moment was whether a woman with one leg would have change for a £1 note. The Common Market faded into a proper perspective. With a cackle of triumph the dummy supplied the answer: a woman with one leg does not have change for a £1 note – she has only half a knicker.

Everybody roared joyfully (it was fairly late). A few minutes later a plumpish woman, wearing long white gloves, was singing Charmaine, and so was everybody else, and suddenly it seemed

unlikely that Yorkshire would give in to the wiles of mass
entertainment just yet.

A good moment for the well-disposed MC, as suddenly it occurred
to him that 'the wheel has gone full circle and although this was a
Batley club it was also, in its happy, beery way, exactly like the singing
room of the White Horse Inn, Leeds, as it must have been well over
100 years ago'.

Across the Pennines, a Sunday afternoon in Manchester's Piccadilly
presented a less invigorating picture. 'The sound of recorded hymns
wafted through the square by loudspeakers,' while 'old and tattered
men, lonely youngsters, and aged couples' sat in the sun 'reading
papers or staring into space and allowing the music to wash over
them'. 'One shabby young man sitting on a bench', added the MC,
'was still there 90 minutes later when I returned. He was in the same
awkward position, looking dully out on the world. The hymns went
gently on with never a strident moment; a few old people tapped their
fingers in time to the music.'

The next two days were devoted to sounding out the views of
local industry, including from the hard-hit cotton industry the
usual complaints about government's apparent refusal to do more
for it – complaints, noted the MC, similarly to be found 'among
Bradford wool men, Midland car men, and Lancashire engineers', all
of whom saw the government's trade negotiators as 'well-meaning
innocents abroad in a wicked world'. Then it was a short journey
west. 'What one remembers about Manchester is an impressive
centre and the rows of dark, stained, and awful streets branching
from the roads leading into the city. The Liverpool city centre would
impress nobody, but one sees a great many new houses. This seems
an excellent order of priority.' The MC concentrated his attention
on Liverpool 8, 'an area of poor houses and redevelopment schemes,
where new things are happening'. In particular, 'local churches, clubs,
community centres, missions, policemen, councillors, residents and
shopkeepers' were due in September to set up 'a community council
aimed at coordinating work on the district's human problems'. 'In
this area crime was once normal,' reflected an optimistic, actively
concerned local resident. 'I think the function of a youth club, as
much as anything, is to contain the youngsters and go on believing

in them, knowing full well that 99 per cent of them will be perfectly good citizens in a few years' time.'

That was the last of the north, and the rest of the MC's English tour had a rather scattergun feel to it. In Devon's Torbay, with its many 'rusticated colonial administrators trying to exist on half-pensions and too proud to seek help from the welfare state', a middle-aged housewife lamented that 'the government hasn't any force behind it somehow'; in Exeter, a resident explained how the post-war planners there had consciously tried to reconstruct the bombed city on a human scale ('we are not going for the wide open spaces, the circuses, and so on, for this is after all a market town'), with the comparison with Plymouth left unstated and the MC himself noting that 'local people seem to like the result'; in Bristol, he heard diametrically opposed views about the value of town planning, including those of one man – as they sat 'in scented and languid air' in a Kashmiri restaurant eating 'good curry' served by 'a willowy waitress' – who thought future trends of travel and shopping so uncertain to predict that he wanted to hand the task over largely to a mixture of sociologists, psychologists and computers. Then it was off to East Anglia, where he came across farmers worried about the Common Market and the future of small towns; a motor cruiser's crew member who (as they chatted over a pint at Acle) declared that he would be 'totally opposed to an election on the issue of the Common Market', because 'you cannot let the masses decide an issue like that'; an Anglican rector unhappy about the social divisiveness, within families and beyond, of the eleven-plus exam; young people preoccupied by 'the Bomb', a subject 'rarely raised by middle-aged folk'; and four notably articulate young accountants on holiday from the Midlands. 'Those other people you have been talking to sound pretty priggish to me,' said one to the MC. 'My father is a factory worker and he has a down-to-earth common sense which a lot of better-educated people lack.'

The last area, before heading back to Brum, was south and west of London, most of it Tory heartland. 'Sitting on a hillside five minutes' walk from the centre of Dorking, listening to the breeze in the grass and watching the lights go on in the comfortable houses below, one realizes the Home Counties are beautiful,' he reflected. 'Here is good living in a superb setting. The advertisements for armouries of barbecue equipment, the pictures of sleek women leaning against potent sports cars makes sense. These dream people really exist. They live here.' Even so, the MC then went on to quote the 'salutary views' of a young executive who had quite recently moved to 'a good modern house in a splendid garden', perhaps somewhere like Epsom or Leatherhead. After noting that he knew of people there 'beggaring themselves to send the boys away to school', and that 'few local people discussed politics much', he continued about those living in southern comfort around him:

> A lot of people live a surface life: they never get to grips with realities. It would do a lot of them a great deal of good to drive through the slums of Lancashire. I am always appalled by the ignorance of those people who have grown up in these sort of surroundings and have lived in this sort of place all their lives. They have not the faintest conception of the difficulties and problems and tribulations of the ordinary man in this country. There is an awful lot of claptrap talked about the working man not working hard today. He does work. If I had to go into our factory and carry out some of the processes there, it would just about kill me. I think it is reasonable to ask just how much work some people in this area do.

The MC could not but sympathise. 'Remembering the slums and smoke of Manchester or Birmingham, the groups of unemployed hanging about at West Hartlepool, life here looks a little too soft. It has not all that much in common with the existence of the nation as a whole.' And after noting the preponderance in the Cabinet of ministers representing Home Counties constituencies, he pondered on the larger implications. 'The most common complaints against this Government are that it lacks authority, resolution, and a sense of direction. How long, one wonders, have these qualities ever managed to thrive or even maintain themselves in an atmosphere so unSpartan as that in the Home Counties today?'

At which point, his tour for better or worse completed, 'I drove gladly off home.'

———

On Friday, 13 July, the day after the Stones had not quite yet set the world alight and as the Varsity match (centuries for Mike

Brearley and Tony Lewis) ground to a familiar draw at Lord's, the Home Secretary, Rab Butler, signed a deportation order relating to Carmen Bryan. She was a 22-year-old Jamaican who had come to live in London in 1960 and had worked as a machine operator in a welding factory before becoming ill (involving an operation) and unemployed, despite attempts to secure an office job. On 2 June, committing her first offence, she had stolen five pairs of nylons, a heatproof glass bowl, a packet of tomatoes, four tins of milk, two pairs of hand-tongs and a clothes-line – goods valued altogether at £2 4s 7d – from a shop in Church Street, Paddington; she also stole from a shop in nearby Edgware Road goods valued at £1 8s 9d, comprising a tin of milk powder, a tin of starch, a jar of Vaseline, a cover for an ironing board, a bottle of shampoo and one tin of Body Mist. The upshot – despite being given a conditional discharge at Paddington magistrates' court, along with the recommendation that it would be better for her if she returned to the Caribbean – was almost six weeks' detention at Holloway Prison, with no opportunity to appeal against the recommendation, until at last Butler signed the piece of paper. The Commonwealth Immigrants Act had come into force at the start of the month, seeking (through a mixture of vouchers and quotas) to restrict the flow of non-white immigrants; and this would be the first deportation under the new legislation. But whether Bryan's case fulfilled the government's specific assurances to Parliament, ahead of legislation, that deportation orders 'would not be made in the case of Commonwealth immigrants for relatively trivial offences', and that 'the powers sought were for only serious offences', seemed at best open to doubt.[27]

Signing the order was more or less Butler's final act as Home Secretary, for early that evening it was announced that seven members of the Cabinet (including of course Selwyn Lloyd) would be departing, while Butler himself became First Secretary of State and in effect Deputy PM. The new man at No. 11 was the more expansion-minded and image-friendly Reginald Maudling; Dr Hill was replaced at Housing by Sir Keith Joseph (a 'clever young man', noted Macmillan in his diary next day); and Sir Edward Boyle (a *very* clever young man') succeeded Sir David Eccles at Education. Altogether, one-third of the Cabinet had been summarily sent packing by Macmillan – the instantly fabled 'Night of the Long Knives'.[28]

One minister not moving was the War Secretary. 'My Darling
Darling – I suppose one thought hasn't occurred to you,' John
Profumo scribbled in red pencil to his wife (the former actress Valerie
Hobson) immediately after the announcement. 'The reason I haven't
gone with the wind of change is largely because Mr Mac also didn't
want to be without *your* side of our team, it's the sort of image he
wants. I have my darling wife to thank ...' Among those departing
there were some severely bruised feelings: not only did Lloyd feel
understandably betrayed, given all the assurances of support he had
received, but Eccles complained afterwards to friends that he had
been dismissed with less notice than a housemaid. One of the more
surprising new appointments was William Deedes (*Daily Telegraph*
journalist doubling as an MP) to be Minister without Portfolio; and
later that day he recorded the meeting in the Cabinet Room, where
the PM had sat with 'a strong whisky and soda' in front of him:

> Macmillan was sucking a pipe, looking weary and watery of eye.
> 'No idea how you are placed,' he said, 'but wondering if you
> could help me. Want a Minister, in Cabinet of course, who will not
> only take over the Information Services, but without department
> and can do some of the many jobs that fall to Cabinet Ministers.'
> My heart sank, but I managed a sympathetic smile. 'Political
> situation very serious. Considered my own position. Discussed
> with the Queen. Wishes me to stay. But willing enough to go.'
> I began to feel like Alice in Wonderland.

Macmillan then outlined the dimensions of the shake-up. He was
clearly distressed by the departure of Selwyn Lloyd. 'Had to go.'
Then, 'Hill gone. Maclay gone ... admirable young men coming in ...
Joseph, Noble. Will you help? Will you return to the sinking ship?'
'What on earth', reflected Deedes, 'is one left to say to that? A sinking
ship is my spiritual home. I nodded.'

The media had plenty to work on. Warm-up act that night was a
Panorama Special, featuring the *Sunday Times*'s political editor. 'Mr
William Rees-Mogg surveyed the battlefield with the gloomy relish
of a high-class undertaker,' observed one viewer. 'I kept expecting
the ham and sherry to be brought on at any moment.' But it was the
press over the next few days that really counted, and broadly speaking

Macmillan took a hammering. The *Daily Telegraph* was loyal enough, but *The Times* was distinctly sceptical: on the Saturday a stern editorial insisted that if the Cabinet purge had been done 'with any thought of buying the Conservative party out of its electoral troubles, it will deserve to be remembered as an act of collective political cowardice'; on the Monday, the paper's tone was frankly ominous:

> He has been ruthless. His followers will admire this if it proves to have done the trick. The Tory Party also has its loyalties and sentiments. Ruthlessness that proved ineffective would not be admired. If Mr Macmillan cannot bring about a change with so largely reconstructed a team, the question will not long be burked whether he could win with any other.

In between, the normally ultra-supportive *Sunday Express* featured a cartoon of a listing SS *Never-Had-It-So-Good* firmly aground. 'Members of the crew! I have driven the ship on the rocks,' the captain announced from the tilting bridge. 'For such shocking incompetence YOU'RE fired.'[29]

In long-term retrospect, the most significant commentary came from the increasingly influential *Financial Times*, where the staunchly free-market, small-state Harold Wincott had a regular Tuesday column which was swimming against the larger Keynesian tide but still enjoyed a very considerable City following. In his first column after the bloodbath, 'The Betrayal of Selwyn Lloyd', he berated the PM: 'The truth is that Mr Macmillan is and always has been an inflationist ... The truth is that Mr Macmillan still lives and thinks in the atmosphere of Stockton-on-Tees [where he had been MP] in the early thirties.' As for the new Chancellor, 'If Mr Maudling thinks we can go back to indiscriminate expansion, to flooding the economy with credit, and without tackling the fundamental maladjustments which still obtain in many of our basic industries, he will find he has created the same sort of mess that Selwyn Lloyd inherited.' As when Peter Thorneycroft and his fellow Treasury ministers (including Enoch Powell, from whom not a murmur now) had resigned four and a half years earlier in protest at Macmillan's big-spending instincts, battle lines were being drawn for the future. Still, the relationship between economic purity on the one hand and political reality on the other is always a shifting and complicated one. 'NOT A MOMENT TOO SOON' was, after all, the *Sunday Telegraph*'s take on the sacking of Lloyd; and the author of the accompanying piece was the paper's City editor, Nigel Lawson.

Irrespective of whether the wholesale reconstruction of the Cabinet had improved its overall quality – and almost certainly it had – perceptions at large were mainly negative, not least because Macmillan over the years had traded so much on his unflappability, putting him somehow above the daily rough and tumble. 'The government – or at any rate, the Prime Minister – has got the wind up with a vengeance!' recorded Anthony Heap, a verdict with which on the evidence it was hard to quarrel. Later in the month, Mollie Panter-Downes reflected on how there was particular sympathy for Selwyn Lloyd, with his 'dogged sincerity and loyalty':

> This may perhaps turn out to be Mr Macmillan's major mistake – a curious miscalculation of the British character with its elephantine memory for old friends and its apparent inconsistencies, which can throw a Churchill out of office but retain him gratefully planted forever in its deepest affections. Vast numbers of the public, no matter how unfair they considered Mr Lloyd's wages standstill after he became Chancellor, still remember him as the Minister who [as Foreign Secretary] stood most of the gruelling heat of the day in the Suez episode [the 1956 crisis that had split the country]. Many Conservatives feel that his receiving an excessively raw deal now over a policy for which the whole Cabinet presumably carried collective responsibility will deal a further damaging knock to Mr Macmillan's popularity in the country, which recently flashed its latest laconic signal from the voters in the Northeast Leicester by-election ...

Was the whole episode, undeniably important in the political narrative of the early 1960s, also historic in some more fundamental sense? 'We can see now', argued Ferdinand Mount in 2008, 'that just as Suez marked a watershed in the conduct of British foreign policy, so the day Macmillan sacked Lloyd and the others marked a watershed in domestic policy. Before that date, the actions of the British government, though they might often be mistaken, seemed to have some kind of weight behind them. After, they appear more like gestures of impotence, with no settled purpose, dictated by the last by-election or opinion poll.'[30] It is a plausible case. Good days to bury bad news were still a long way off, but politics was now on that cynical, damaging path.

Perhaps the weather was to blame. 'All this week it has been foul,' noted Kenneth Williams on Saturday the 14th, 'wet sticky heat hanging like a blanket of doom over the city ... Today it was so heavy & still that it was putrid, & felt like a plague-ridden town. I'm amazed to see that people aren't covered in spots & sores: but they look incredibly healthy on the whole.' The Queen that day was wisely out of town, at Lingfield Park for a charity race meeting. She lunched with the much publicised washing-machine tycoon John Bloom, sponsor of the Rolls Rapid Handicap, won that afternoon by Spartan General, whose owner was the ambitious airline entrepreneur Freddie Laker. On *Juke Box Jury* the panel was a nice mix of the old and the new – the ineffable Godfrey Winn at one end of the spectrum, the *Evening Standard*'s pop writer Maureen Cleave at the other, Katie Boyle somewhere in between, and 56-year-old disc jockey Jack Jackson making up numbers – while in the south-west the Haines family began near Brixham the second week of their holiday. 'Homelea Camp [self-catering, and where like St Audries Bay they had been the previous year] is taken over by Pontin's, as are Dolphin and St Mary's Bay Camps,' recorded Judy from their chalet. 'We felt a slight improvement. More substantial curtains and closed in sink, gas rings and cutlery basket, making one long table. Still no springs for double bed. Lounge has more easy chairs and some very pleasant uprights, too. The grounds look better kept, too.' And it was also a plus that 'Daddy managed to get Luxemburg on Transistor Radio we have hired for the girls.' New-fangled trannies in Oxfordshire too, as next morning Henry St John caught a train from Henley-on-Thames (where he'd been staying overnight) to Oxford, involuntarily accompanied by 'a few young people' who 'switched on what must have been a transistor radio broadcasting "The Archers"'. Even so, old habits in relation to the new continued to die hard. 'With the exception of Michael Frayn and his wife, architects, and people who have married Americans, my husband and I are the only London couple we know who have modern furniture,' regretfully wrote

Katharine Whitehorn in the *Observer*, adding on a defiant note that 'I will eat my shroud if my great-grandchildren do not treasure my simple, beautifully made Danish teak desk.'[31]

Guests at lunch that Sunday at the Duke of Wellington's house at Stratfield Saye included Lady Cynthia Gladwyn and the Duke's grandson, Jeremy Clyde (becoming around this time part of the folk-inflected duo Chad & Jeremy). 'He is typical of the rising generation in a conventional family,' she noted of the 21-year-old Old Etonian. 'He is a beatnik, and wears his hair long ...' But the main event of the day, at least in retrospect, was the ponderous, two-and-a-half-hours-long first pilot for what would become *That Was The Week That Was*. To judge by the recollections of its front man, David Frost (not first choice), the putative satirical programme would have sunk without trace but for a thoroughly testy interchange between Bernard Levin and an invited group of Conservative ladies:

First Lady: Mr Macmillan has always satisfied *me* ...
Second Lady: It seems to me, Mr Levin, that anyone is rational if
                they agree with you ...
Levin: That's one definition of rationality certainly ...
First Lady: Mr Macmillan has always satisfied us ...
Third Lady: Mr Levin, how would you like your daughter to be
                walking along a dark street at night ... and nothing
                done about it?

The *coup de grâce* came at the end. 'Because of the letters you write to them,' declared Levin, 'the Conservative Party's Central Office has bigger waste-paper baskets than anywhere else in the world' – prompting one of the ladies to rise to her feet shouting, 'And they need them, Mr Levin! And they need them!' The fortuitous upshot was that the ladies complained to Central Office, which in turn complained to the BBC that they had 'been made a laughing stock of'; and two BBC high-ups then watched the pilot, deciding not only that the complaints were absurd but also that perhaps, after all, the show did have something going for it; and another pilot was scheduled for late September.[32]

Monday was the first day at the Commons since the great purge. Business began with questions to the Minister of Pensions, an office temporarily unfilled as Macmillan made a series of changes below Cabinet level, so instead they went to the two joint Parliamentary secretaries. Richard Sharples, an MP since 1954, answered one of the fifteen questions; the other fourteen were handled by Margaret Thatcher, an MP for less than three years. Even though the government front bench looked in its transience 'rather like that of a waiting-room at an airport', Norman Shrapnel in the press gallery could not but admire 'the gay fortitude with which she freighted the Government's gloomy cargo'. 'The cheerful Mrs Thatcher did not falter at her dangerous controls, or wince at the double-edged supplementaries [questions additional to the ones that had been tabled] that were flying around,' he went on. 'She promised one of her own back-benchers to pass on his message about the plight of pensioners "to my right honourable friend when I have one". There was a fierce hilarity on the subject of pensions and retirement in general but Mrs Thatcher refused to be thrown off course by a suggestion from Mr W. W. Hamilton, of West Fife, that the Prime Minister himself would soon be qualifying for her department at the receiving end.' In all, reflected Shrapnel, 'quite an achievement'. Monday was also of course *Coronation Street* – Gamma Garments holding its summer sale, despite the manager Leonard Swindley (played by Arthur Lowe) forgetting the door key and having to go home to fetch it; Ken Barlow proposing (at his mother's grave) to Valerie Tatlock, despite Val fearing that Ken was only looking for a mother figure – as well as later on this particular evening a one-off BBC TV drama, *The Playmates* by Johnny Speight. 'Disgusting – looking at idiots through a peep-hole – it made me feel ashamed,' was one typical viewer reaction to an unsettling two-hander about a strange young man arriving at the home of an unmarried middle-aged woman and proceeding to menace her; 'mental sickness and loneliness do not make good entertainment' and 'I thought it degrading to see human beings acting in this manner' were two others, contributing to an unsurprising Reaction Index of only 47, well below average. Still, it was another notch up the ladder for a relatively unknown working-class actor, with one critic praising the 'marvellously edgy performance by Michael Caine'.[33]

Next day, being Prime Minister's Questions, was the first sighting of Macmillan himself. 'No applause from our side, jeers from Opposition,' he noted about his much awaited entrance. 'During my answers, a lot of laughter and barracking from Opposition. Our side quiet, except for one or two who tried to come to my help but did (as so often) more harm than good. It was clear to me that the storm is going to be quite hard to ride.' Among those 'one or two' was presumably (giving him the benefit of the doubt) the 60-year-old Tory backbencher Gilbert Longden, instinctively on Macmillan's one-nation side of the party. *The Times*'s Parliamentary correspondent recorded a scene that Kipling himself, albeit probably not a one-nation Conservative, might have enjoyed watching:

> 'May I take this first opportunity', Mr Longden said solemnly, 'of congratulating my right hon. friend on having kept his head, whilst all about were losing theirs …'
>
> Mr Selwyn Lloyd kept a carefully straight face as general laughter burst out, increased in volume, and continued for so long that the Speaker was compelled to call for order. Mr Macmillan seemed to have some answer on the tip of his tongue, as he rose during the crescendo, but never delivered it. Mr Longden was waving agitatedly to indicate that he had not finished.
>
> Silence fell, and Mr Macmillan's supporter (better late than never) added: '… and blaming it on him.' The Prime Minister was not looking pleased by this time, and Mr Grimond caused the ruthless brow to darken a little more by congratulating Mr Macmillan on 'this first demonstration of support he has received from his back benches'.

The same day, one of Grimond's younger colleagues, Jeremy Thorpe, made his mordant stab for immortality, reflecting aloud that 'greater love hath no man than this, that he lay down his friends for his life'; while at the Old Bailey, a fellow homosexual, the war hero and former Tory MP Sir Ian Horobin, received a four-year prison sentence after he had pleaded guilty to ten charges of indecency and to offences with boys and young men at the Mansfield House University Settlement in Canning Town where he had been warden since 1923. 'Us poor devils who are born like this,' Horobin was reported as having said to the secretary of the settlement. 'Nothing can change me. It is natural for us to love boys in this way.' Light relief, by contrast, from this evening's debut episode of the sitcom *Hugh & I*, starring Hugh Lloyd and Terry Scott as the socio-economically contrasting residents of 33 Lobelia Avenue, Tooting, with the Crispins (Mollie Sugden as Mrs C) and the Wormolds (Patricia Hayes as Mrs W) as neighbours. Again, the contrast was between critics and viewers. 'A few incidental lines and situations were agreeable enough, but everything to do with the plot, a limp affair about insurance salesmanship, was sadly inept,' thought the *Listener*'s Derek Hill, whereas 'a bit slow, but fair entertainment' was the typical reasonably positive response (part of an RI of 58) of one viewer. Indeed, he/she added, 'I have seen a good deal worse. It has prospects, I think.'[34]

Wednesday the 18th was wet in the north, bright but windy in the south. The Lord Chamberlain announced that the Queen's Gallery in Buckingham Palace would, for the first time, be open later that month to show 'Treasures from the Royal Collection', an announcement accompanied by the stern warning to rubberneckers that 'NO OTHER PART OF THE INSIDE OF THE PALACE WILL BE SEEN'; the House of Lords debated Pilkington, with the speech from Labour's Lord Morrison of Lambeth (the former Herbert Morrison) veering between 'Perry Mason I adore' and 'we're in danger of going television mad'; prizegiving at Collingbourne Ducis Primary School in Wiltshire featured accolades for 'keenness and general knowledge', for 'cheerfulness and progress in spite of illness', for 'constant effort' and for 'general effort'; Macmillan attended the Royal Tournament to a gratifyingly positive reception; and John Osborne's *Plays for England*, including *Under Plain Cover* directed by Jonathan Miller, had their dress rehearsal at the Royal Court. 'I'm glad I've kept away from J. Miller,' disobligingly reflected the playwright. 'The striving fluency of the Hampstead nanny's boy is deceptive and occasionally plausible. With its cultural allusions and cross-references to other disciplines, it is the gab-gift of someone to whom English is an adoptive tongue. Intellect does terrible things to the mind. As a director, he's an Armenian carpet-seller ...' It was also the day that Salford's planning committee approved plans to rebuild the centre over the next five years as (in the words of a Manchester paper) 'a super city of the space-age', including a shopping precinct and a civic centre, as well as 2,800 multi-storey flats and maisonettes 'to replace the now demolished Ellor Street slums'. 'This', declared Councillor Albert Jones, the committee's chairman, 'will be a bigger centre even than Coventry's, which is at present the largest in Britain.

It will, we hope, avoid all the snags that were inevitable in Coventry's pioneer scheme.' Indeed, went on Jones, 'this will be the largest development in Europe', possibly even 'the largest project which has been undertaken in one place'.[35]

The historic cricket fixture Gentlemen versus Players – or, put more prosaically, amateurs versus professionals – would not be part of the brave new space-age world. Back in 1958, a committee set up by MCC (Marylebone Cricket Club, the game's ruling body) had rejected abolishing what was inevitably a very class-conscious and by this time increasingly hypocritical distinction. This was on the grounds that 'the distinctive status of the amateur cricketer is not obsolete, is of great value to the game and should be preserved'; but, almost certainly, few believed that the writing was not on the wall, with even the *Daily Express* labelling the committee's report 'The Shamateurs' Charter'. Piquantly enough, this particular July 1962 iteration of the fixture, beginning at Lord's on the 18th, had an emblematic sub-plot, with an announcement expected during the match about which of three likely participants would captain the forthcoming tour of Australia. Emblematic because they were all of them – Colin Cowdrey, Ted Dexter, David Sheppard – public school and Oxbridge amateurs seemingly out of central casting. In the event, Cowdrey had to withdraw from the match because of illness, but Dexter and Sheppard were present and correct, albeit Sheppard having (because of his missionary work in the East End) played perilously little first-class cricket in the previous five years. Both men batted well on the first day (Dexter an almost violently aggressive half-century, Sheppard a more careful century), as the Gents compiled a respectable 323 against an attack led by the unashamedly below-the-salt Fred Trueman, also doubling as the Players' captain. Three run-outs featured in the amateurs' innings: ultimately, and arguably through no fault of their own, they were not quite business cricketers.[36]

3

Things They Do Change

That same third Wednesday in July also saw – far away from the mansion blocks of St John's Wood and all the urban amenities – a handful of glimpses of a different sort of Britain. Starting at the auction offices of Tilley & Culverwell at 14 Market Place, Chippenham, where prompt at 10.30 a.m. the sale began ('light refreshments available') of the entire stock of Horwood Farm, Ansty, between Shaftesbury and Salisbury. Not only were 248 head of cattle and 250 head of poultry on offer, but also a 'comprehensive collection of modern implements and machinery':

3 Diesel Tractors (2 Fordson, 1 Nuffield); New Kools Silage Dump Box; New Kools Silage Blower; Hurricane Forage Harvester; Allis Chalmers '60' Combine Harvester – Tanker model; 2 Complete Silage Trailers; B/45 Bailer; Denning 6ft Mower; International 5ft Mower; Vicon Acrobat; Lister Bale Elevator; 2 Buckrakes; Commer 3-ton flatbed Lorry; Wrekin P.T.O. Saw-bench; Ransome 4-furrow Mounted Plough; Disc, Drag, Seed and Chain Harrows; Set of Tandem Cambridge Rolls; M/H Combine Drill; Teagle A/M Spinner; David Brown Dung Spreader; Rubber Tyred 4-wheel Trailer; Christie and Norris Automatic Corn Mill; Bentall Roller Mill; 6-unit Alfa-Laval In-Churn Milking Parlour with Weycroft Macford Pulsator and Clusters; Diesel Land-Rover, etc etc.

The day's centrepiece in East Anglia was the Ipswich and East of England Horticultural Society Summer Show, with some six to seven thousand people milling in Christchurch Park in fine weather. As usual, the Royal Horticultural Society's Banksian Medal was awarded to the winner of the largest amount of money prizes; and this year it went to Dr A. H. Morris, better known as the Bishop of St Edmundsbury and Ipswich, who had won seven prizes (three firsts and four seconds) in the classes for pot plants and vegetables. In Shropshire, prizes too at the annual Rectory Fete of Church Stretton Parish Church, held in the Old Rectory Field and opened by the Countess of Plymouth. Roll-a-penny, skittles, rolling ping pong, hoop-la and wheel of fortune were among the various sideshows, as well as a fortune teller, bean bags and (put in suitably mysterious inverted commas by the *Shrewsbury Chronicle*'s local reporter) 'Escalado', in fact a table horse-racing game. It was also a day of pronouncements about the future of rural Britain. 'Farming today is a great industry in which you have also to be something of an accountant, a scientist and, perhaps, an electronic engineer,' Sir Thomas Bland (chairman of Barclays Bank) warned those attending Kesteven Farm Institute's speech day at Caythorpe Court in Lincolnshire. But, provided the National Farmers' Union maintained the quality of its leadership, he was still confident that 'over the years a decent living for the decent farmer is fairly certain'. Similarly optimistic noises from Mr F. H. W. Swallow, addressing a meeting in Nottingham of the Institute of Corn and Agricultural Merchants, in his capacity as a past president of those merchants' National Association. He was sure, he told them, that Britain could look forward, once it had joined the European Economic Community, to increased sales of feeding barley and seed grain; but at the same time he insisted that, as far as quality was concerned, 'only the best will be good enough'. No such matters weighed on the mind of Sidney Jackson, keeper of Cartwright Hall Museum in Bradford. After noting in his diary that during the day he had done 'more work on cruck exhibit', he went on:

Archaeology Group [Yorkshire Archaeological Society?] excursion this evening, to Reynard Ing Farm, Ilkley, home of Mr and Mrs Thomas Mason. In the motor coach went 41, while a further 25 went there in cars. Rain – not heavy – rather spoilt things, but everyone appeared to enjoy the event. We saw querns, old millstones, bee boles, cheese press stones and other old things, and partook of tea and cakes provided by Mrs Mason, eating in a crowded farmhouse parlour. This was one of the pleasantest events we have ever had, in spite of the rain. Eating and drinking in company, crowded and in a warm, well-lit room, always produces pleasant feelings, though.[1]

A decade and a half after the Agriculture Act of 1947, British farming was still essentially – for better or worse – in its grip. On the one hand, cheap food for urban consumers without a heavy reliance on imports; on the other hand, price-support manipulation, capital grants, subsidies and so on for the farmers – altogether, the rural historian-cum-sociologist Howard Newby would declare, 'the Act was an ingenious piece of legislation which, with some justification, has since been revered as a model of how to harmonize and transcend the conflicting interests in the support of agricultural production'. Such was the legislation's immediate success, he adds, that for the next three decades, against the background of a stable and efficient agricultural sector in marked contrast to its struggles between the wars, 'agriculture was elevated above the everyday controversies of party politics and discussion limited increasingly to arcane and somewhat mystifying policy minutiae among a closed circle of ministry officials, academic observers and the representatives of farming organizations'.

Undoubtedly, the consequences of the Act, the defining framework for so many years, were profound, fourfold at least. First, rapidly increasing mechanisation, above all tractors (up from 180,000 in 1946 to 417,000 in 1963), combine harvesters (up from 3,000 to 55,000) and milking machines (no precise figures, but whereas in the 1940s one person hand-milked fifteen cows, by the 1970s one person and a relief worker would machine-milk more than seventy cows). Second, a sharply reduced need for manpower, down from 553,000 full-time workers on the land in 1951 to 333,000 by 1964. Third, an ever more relentless emphasis on size (holdings over 300 acres increasing by 15 per cent, to nearly 15,000, between 1947 and 1964), not least because of direct government incentives: by 1960, it was estimated, a mere one hundred 1,000-acre holdings in England's eastern counties received more in subsidy than all 7,000 farms (most of them small) in Carmarthenshire. And fourth, again much incentivised, the application of science in many and varied forms, including genetic, nutritional and chemical. Increasingly reliant on economies of scale, increasingly capital-intensive, increasingly specialised, British agriculture by the early 1960s was firmly on its way, though still only at a relatively early stage of the journey taking the sector as a whole, towards a fully fledged industrialised future. The achievement, whatever the collateral damage, was undeniable: according to a Labour Party policy paper in January 1963, overall output was up by 50 per cent since the war, output per worker up by 130 per cent; or, expressed more comparatively, output per head of the agricultural population was, by the early 1960s, higher in Britain than in all West European countries except the Netherlands. Who on the face of it – especially in the context of seemingly inexorable relative decline in almost every other area of national economic performance – could quarrel with that? Certainly not the scriptwriters for *The Archers*, that everyday story of country folk which, through the 1950s and 1960s, systematically wove in government propaganda about best farming practice.[2]

Change during the quarter-century after the war was probably greatest in arable farming, especially wheat and barley, where yields by the early 1960s were often 50 per cent higher than in the immediate pre-war period. Weed and pest control (nearly 200 pesticides in common use by the mid-1960s), artificial fertilisers (a fourfold increase in their use between the late 1930s and late 1960s) and of course mechanisation (not just tractors and combine harvesters, but a range of new devices to solve particular problems) all played their parts, as did plant breeding and increasing specialisation. 'Cornucopia' was the title of a survey in 1963 by one agricultural correspondent of the latest scientific advances in new varieties of wheats and barleys, normally led by the Cambridge Plant Breeding Institute, but whose popular Proctor variety (short-strawed, high-yielding barley with a very high malting quality) was increasingly under challenge from 'the variety Pallas, an X-ray mutant from Bonus, bred in Sweden'. As for specialisation, it was the cereal-growing eastern counties (flatter and dryer) which were conclusively leading the trend away from traditional mixed farming. 'In the old days the only means of fertilizing land was by carting out dung made in yards by cattle or keeping sheep on the land eating crops like turnips and swedes,' noted in the mid-1960s a guide to East

Anglian farming. 'Though these practices are still sound and persist to a degree, the use of artificial fertilizers has developed to such an extent that the chief method of replenishing the soil is the use of artificial product.'[3] In the old days ... Or put another way, the 1950s and 1960s were the decades in which, across huge swathes of eastern England, livestock simply disappeared from the scene.

Even so, across Britain as a whole, there had perhaps never been so much livestock as in the early 1960s. Take the census figures for June 1962: 10.8 million cattle (compared to 8.7 million in 1945); 3.1 million dairy cows (2.7 million); 28.3 million sheep (19.5 million); 5.6 million pigs (1.9 million); and 97.9 million poultry (41.3 million). The livestock production figures were even more telling of a flourishing sector: milk (million litres) up from 8,137 in 1946–7 to 11,892 in 1960–1; eggs (million dozen) up from 460 to 1,080; and as measured by thousand tonnes, poultry up from 56 to 312, pigmeat from 170 to 657, beef and veal from 584 to 821, and sheepmeat from 153 to 227.[4]

Egg and poultry production undoubtedly set the pace, with egg production per bird per year increasing from 150 in the first half of the 1950s to 195 in the first half of the 1960s. Some birds, of course, laid more than others: in 1961 it was calculated that whereas hens in free-range systems produced on average 167 eggs per year, battery hens produced on average 40 more; and inevitably, by the mid-1960s, more than 50 per cent of laying birds were kept in batteries or small cages, fed automatically, and their droppings removed mechanically. 'When the battery cage was first developed it held one bird, and the idea was that each bird's eggs could be individually recorded,' the *Financial Times*'s agricultural correspondent, John Cherrington (himself a farmer), reflected in 1964. 'That can no longer apply. Birds are kept several to a cage and so tightly confined that they can no longer either stretch their wings, their legs or their necks without trampling on their companions. Their lives are spent crouched on a sloping wire floor ...' Increasingly, scale and factory-style methods were everything. 'It was soon clear that very little stockmanship was necessary on the battery system and that, with a small amount of supervision, girls from the village could do the work,' the writer Frances Donaldson recalled about the egg farm in Buckinghamshire that she and her husband ran for eight years from 1960. 'It then became merely a matter of having sufficient capital to do the thing in

a really big way, and, whereas when we first went to Kingsbridge the
6,000 hens we kept seemed a perfectly reasonable unit, we realised
in time that we should not be able to compete with units five, six
or even ten times as large.' Two kingpins stood out: John Eastwood,
who from his base in Nottinghamshire developed in the course of the
decade the largest integrated chicken-and-egg-producing company in
the world, transforming chicken from the dearest of common meats
to the cheapest; and Antony Fisher, whose Sussex farm had in the
1950s pioneered 'broiler' production in this country and enabled
him to fund the Institute of Economic Affairs in order to propagate
his free-market beliefs. But at least, commented Cherrington, these
broiler chickens usually had a chance to scratch themselves, unlike the
truly unfortunate battery hens.[5]

The generally acknowledged 'cornerstone' of British agriculture,
especially on most small and medium-sized holdings, remained the
dairy cow, whose average yield increased from 2,300 litres of milk
soon after the war to almost 3,400 litres by the start of the 1960s
and over 3,700 by the end. Within the British dairy herd over these
years, the popularity of the Ayrshire gradually declined, increasingly
superseded by the higher-yielding Friesian, which also scored
through bequeathing, at the end of its milking days, an excellent beef
carcase. Elsewhere across the livestock range, sheepmeat production
not only had to respond to consumers moving away from the large
mutton joints provided by mature sheep killed during the winter
and instead towards smaller, leaner joints derived from young
lambs, but also organised itself in an increasingly rationalised way,
with far fewer breeds and crosses; as for the provision of pork, that
traditional working-class mainstay, one textbook in the 1960s noted
that 'pig keeping is following the poultry industry into becoming
a concrete-based factory enterprise with land required only for the
disposal of effluent'. Never far out of the picture were the scientists,
not least when some 550 livestock breeders and geneticists assembled
at Harrogate in November 1962 for a conference organised by the
Ministry of Agriculture's Advisory Service. 'We are here', declared
Dr H. P. Donald, director of the Animal Research Organisation in
Edinburgh, 'because we do not believe that our animals are perfect
and we want to consider what can be done to adapt them more closely
to our needs.' As he explained:

Animal breeding today has only a superficial resemblance to animal breeding in 1939. An extended and consolidated genetic theory now provides a comprehensive theoretical background against which to judge probable results. Another change is due to developments in nutrition, the arrival of better grasses and cereals, advances in disease control, fertiliser practice, and machines. Market requirements have changed and will change further today. The habits of shoppers, the tastes of people: technical advances in killing, storing, and selling meat.

Yet clearly there were still tensions between the boffins and the breeders, at least to judge by the reported remarks of Cyril Thornber, described as 'managing director of the Yorkshire firm which last year produced more than 21 million day-old chicks' and which was now spending £150,000 a year on upgrading its stock. ' "The sooner you get rid of this myth about divergence of opinion the sooner you will make positive progress," he said. Neither side was always right. The important thing was for free exchange of ideas and information between the two, and this was something that had been achieved in the poultry industry and which the larger livestock industry might do well to follow.'[6]

The consequences of Britain's second agricultural revolution, predicated on farm-price protection by the state, were momentous. 'A production juggernaut with a blind and seemingly insatiable urge to homogenise the landscape' would be the characterisation by the campaigning writer Graham Harvey of the three decades after the war. 'Throughout lowland Britain, hedges were being grubbed out, ponds and ditches filled in, marshes drained, meadows ploughed and woods and copses felled, all in the name of higher output.' That output was above all arable, as the overall area devoted to grassland substantially contracted and that devoted to cereal cultivation substantially increased, so that in the course of the 1960s it was not just Lincolnshire and East Anglia where arable production was concentrated on, but also to a significant extent traditionally more pastoral counties like Nottinghamshire, Northamptonshire, Derbyshire, Wiltshire and Hampshire, especially as the spread of intensive feeding systems enabled animals to be brought inside and their land freed up for arable purposes. Inevitably, the pressure on farmers to maximise the size of their fields became ever more irresistible. 'It is impossible to get full value from investing in large machines like combine harvesters with a 12-foot or a 16-foot cut when they have to operate in 5- and 10-acre fields,' noted the agricultural writer John Young in 1967. 'Likewise the large modern tractor that can plough 10 to 15 acres a day wants space to be operated to the full economic extent. So much time is wasted turning on headlands.' Equally inevitably during these post-war years, hedgerows disappeared at an alarming rate: according to one estimate, a quarter of all hedgerows in England and Wales were removed by farmers between 1946 and 1974 – a loss of some 120,000 miles in all, with the highest losses being recorded in Norfolk and Cambridgeshire, those counties of huge and enervating prairie-like fields. So too with farmland trees, as roughly two and a half trees per acre in England in 1951 (some 60 million trees in all) declined by 1971 to roughly two trees per acre. There were of course other losses across the rural landscape: in heathland (45,000 acres in Dorset in 1934 almost halved by 1960), in wild grassland (by the mid-1960s, barely 35,000 acres of chalk downland left in the whole of England outside Wiltshire), in woodland (between 1950 and 1973, a third of Essex's ancient woods destroyed). 'I have', reflected in the mid-1960s the Essex-based countryside writer and broadcaster Henry Warren, 'lived in the same parish now for more than twenty years; and during this time I have watched our trees felled by the hundred, if not by the thousand, for timber-merchants, airfields, and farmers.' Warren especially despaired of the farmers. 'Bound to the economic treadmill, they can see no merit in anything that does not yield obvious and immediate returns. To plant trees would be a concession to sentiment. They do not see the ecological necessity for trees on a farm, and in this they are less wise than their fathers. Indeed, the arable farmer of today seems altogether to have lost the attitude towards trees that was formerly part and parcel of good husbandry.'[7]

Yet why by this time, the question implacably arises, was so little being done to stop the destruction of the familiar rural landscape? In part no doubt because farmers were still generally seen in a positive light, unsurprisingly so given their sector's phenomenal success in delivering the goods; in part no doubt because the National Farmers' Union operated as a highly effective industry body; but perhaps also because by this stage, certainly by the early 1960s, representatives of the progressive-minded and socially concerned middle class were still relatively thin on the ground (whether as residents or visitors) in rural Britain.[8] Once they got their wellies on, and started gathering nuts in May, all that would change.

Which is not to say that in the early 1960s there was *wholesale* urban indifference. 'Say what you will, / the countryside is still, / the only place that I can settle down,' began the aspirational lyrics to 'Out of Town', sung by Max Bygraves and from 1960 the theme song of the popular weekly TV magazine programme of that name, presented by the largely genial but not uncritical Jack Hargreaves. In two specific ways, moreover, some kind of pushback was under way, the first being in relation to what one might call the spoliation of the rural landscape. A key text was *The Making of the English Landscape* (1955) by W. G. Hoskins, father of English landscape history. 'England of the Nissen hut, the "pre-fab" and the electric fence, of the high barbed wire around some unmentionable devilment; England of the arterial by-pass, treeless and stinking of diesel oil, murderous with lorries', he wrote in despair about 'The Landscape Today'. There were few causes of despair greater than industrial dereliction, epitomised by the appalling state by the end of the 1950s of the 1,200 acres comprising the Lower Swansea Valley after being enveloped for nearly a century by the fumes of copper-smelting, zinc, steel, tinplate and coal operations. 'The indigenous sessile oak and birch woodland of Kilvey Hill and all grass and heather in the area disappeared,' noted a report in 1967 after an investigation begun in 1960 aiming at reclamation and rehabilitation. 'The topsoil, no longer held by plant roots, was washed off the valley sides leaving the subsoil to be eroded into gullies. The area became a virtual desert.'[9]

Two individuals on the larger 'spoliation' case by the mid-1960s were James Lees-Milne (travelling the country in his work for the National Trust) and Lionel Brett. 'Who cares for England?' asked the former on the Home Service in March 1964, as he prepared to let rip:

Since there are acres of blasted heath completely deserted in the Potteries and industrial Lancashire, why sacrifice what little of England's green and pleasant land is left? Pylons, higher and higher, straddle the land, their fat and ugly cables cutting a straight swathe through woods and across hills and dales.

Electricity transformers, those offensive black radiators on gibbets, and ungainly low-tension poles sprout from the ground wherever two or more buildings are gathered together. Wires come thicker and thicker, drooping, dangling everywhere, so that in the outskirts of towns and in villages you can barely see the blue sky through them ...

Consider the condition of our streets and roads: the revolting, outsize, concrete lamp-standards, stretching from Land's End to John o'Groats; the grass verges scorched black by diesel-oil fumes; the lay-bys used as refuse dumps, and worse – and everywhere the litter. With all our prosperity we have become an unaesthetic and squalid people.

Brett, a man enduring as architect and architectural writer a painfully fraught relationship with the modern, provided chapter and verse in *Landscape in Distress*, a detailed study of the state of the countryside in the summer of 1964 in some 250 square miles of south Oxfordshire. Near Watlington, 'the most exposed crest in the parish chosen for a smoking and wind-blown rubbish dump'; driving out of Benson, 'some unpleasant conversions, a row of bungalows, a knacker's-yard-cum-scrap-dump of exceptional horror even in this landscape, and a decayed great house'; on the Thame–Oxford road, 'a malignant new bungaloid growth in the area of the Draycott–Tiddington cross-roads'; lining the Wheatley bypass, the even worse 'subtopia' of 'council houses to the left, lorry drivers' caffs and general muddy dereliction to the right, as though an army corps had passed through'; and so on. Brett at the end of his survey explained how inadequate were the forces of conservation, whether in terms of legislative or planning or economic clout, to prevent continuing spoliation. Would, he asked in his last paragraph, 'public opinion' begin eventually to catch up with 'the tiny minority that cares about the man-made environment'? Perhaps at some point. Meanwhile, he concluded stoically enough, 'the task for us is to hold the ship off the rocks until the tide comes in'.[10]

The other area of pushback also involved a text, in this case not just key but over the years semi-sacred. 'She writes most persuasively, for she is both intelligent and imaginative,' declared Cyril Connolly in the *Sunday Times* in February 1963, noting that her great theme 'is the toxicity of modern methods of spraying fruit and vegetables, weed-killing, pest-destroying and insect-removing'. The author was the American biologist Rachel Carson and her new book, *Silent Spring*, was poised to become the best-seller in Britain that it had already been in the States since the previous autumn. 'The silence of Rachel Carson's spring is the silence that will come to the world when we have killed off all the singing birds with insecticides,' one of the *Guardian*'s country diarists, writing from Machynlleth, had already explained ahead of publication. 'It is a silence that symbolises all the horrifying effects on nature and on ourselves by the mass onslaught by poison that man is now launching on the earth. So far we have seen only a shadow of what could come unless the reckless madness that has got into our scientists, our agriculturists, our horticulturists, and our forestry experts is checked pretty soon.' On publication day itself, the paper reflected the book's controversial character by counterpointing the views of Dr Bruce Campbell of the Royal Society for the Protection of Birds with those of an unnamed representative of the Association of British Manufacturers of Agricultural Chemicals. For Campbell it was case proven, not least because Carson's 'remarkable documentation', although American-based, also included convincing treatment of 'the outbreaks over here of animal deaths attributed to [poisonous] seed dressings in 1960 and 1961 [some 6,000 birds on one Lincolnshire estate that spring]'. By contrast, the industry rep detected 'a considerable element of poetic licence throughout the book'; argued in essence that there was little to worry about ('Improved chemicals will eventually further decrease the hypothetical risk, and education of farmers, by Government, agriculturists, and pesticide manufacturers, will steadily improve that which already has every appearance of being safer than many aspects of modern existence'); and finished by calling on readers 'to retain their sense of perspective', especially given that 'problems of world health and world hunger form greater and more imminent challenges'.

Some six months later, penning his weekly 'Farming Notes', *Country Life*'s 'Cincinnatus' sought to steer a sensible middle course. Yes, it was surely right that the Agricultural Research Council had set up an interdepartmental Research Committee on Toxic Chemicals, recently reporting that more attention should indeed be given to ecological studies of wild animals and birds and of the interdependence of animals, plants, insects and other organisms. 'This is the aspect of the modern use of

toxic chemicals that has caused most anxiety among the general public,'
commented this latter-day man of virtue at his plough. 'Something that
will get rid of one pest may set off a chain reaction affecting birds that are
quite harmless, foxes and, indeed, human health. So it is important that
top-level scientists should keep a close watch on what is happening.' But
then came the rub: 'We need to use toxic chemicals in farming today to
grow better crops and to keep down the cost of weed control.'[11] Whether,
he did not need to add, two such opposing camps could conceivably
square the circle remained to be seen.

Among *Silent Spring*'s early British readers was the remarkable
ornithologist J. A. (John) Baker. Every winter since 1954 he had been
making sightings of peregrines on the Essex marshes, around the
Chelmer and Blackwater rivers, and taking diary notes for what would
become his 1967 classic of lyrical nature writing, *The Peregrine*. The
British peregrine population was (like the sparrowhawk population)
in sharp decline – about 80 per cent, it was estimated, wiped out by
1964 despite the Wild Birds Protection Act of ten years earlier – and
an early draft identified the peregrine falcon's (and Baker's) enemies
as 'armed men, those who carry guns, who set up traps, who scatter
poison on the fields'. The best known of the poisons, in terms of
destroying wildlife, was DDT, but the most pernicious in its immediate
effects was probably the insecticide dieldrin, withdrawn from the UK
market in 1962 but only – crucially – on a voluntary basis. 'For ten
years,' he would write in his book's opening chapter,

> I followed the peregrine. I was possessed by it. It was a grail to
> me. Now it has gone. The long pursuit is over. Few peregrines
> are left, there will be fewer, they may not survive. Many die on
> their backs, clutching insanely at the sky in their last convulsions,
> withered and burnt away by the filthy, insidious pollen of farm
> chemicals. Before it is too late, I have tried to recapture the
> extraordinary beauty of this bird and to convey the wonder
> of the land he lived in, a land to me as profuse and glorious as
> Africa. It is a dying world, like Mars, but glowing still.

The main body of *The Peregrine* was written in diary form across an
undated winter, with entries drawn from his original entries over the
years. Perhaps none more resonant than this for 22 December:

Till long after sunset I waited on the hillside, thinking of peregrines. Few winter in England now, fewer nest here. Ten years ago, even five years, it was very different. Peregrines were seen almost every winter then: on the North Kent Marshes, from Cliffe to Sheppey; in the Medway valley; over the chain of artificial lakes in the Colne valley, and on to the sterile plain of Middlesex; along the Thames from London to Oxford, and beyond; over the Berkshire and Wiltshire downs; along the Chiltern escarpment; on the High Cotswolds, and in the deep valleys of the small Cotswold rivers; across the wide river plains of the Trent, the Nene, and the Ouse; over the fens, the dry Brackland, and around the shores of the Wash; along the east coast from Thames to Humber.

'These', recalled Baker, 'were the traditional wintering places, remembered and revisited by dynasties of peregrines, deserted now because there are no descendants, because the ancient eyries are dying, their lineage gone.'[12]

Yet however justified in the case of peregrines, and whatever the visually and ecologically damaging long-term trends of modernising, subsidy-conscious agricultural practice, to leave it on that apocalyptic note would be seriously wrong. Take a couple of moments, one of them broadly feel-good and the other entirely so, from the summer of 1962. 'On Monday the 18th of June, members assembled at 6.30 pm and set off in a cavalcade of private cars (our thanks to the owners) to that haunt of nesting birds in a delightful woodland setting in the Washburn Valley,' recorded the annual report of the Leeds & District Bird Watchers' Club:

Arriving at Lindley Bridge we passed through the farmyard of a friendly farmer who had house martins on his roof and swallows darting in and out of his barns. On our way to the lake we heard the bubbling call of the curlew and a wren with its exploding song. In the fields were lapwing, common partridge, rook and jackdaw, and nearing the lake a heron rose slowly. We were then greeted, but somewhat subdued, by our old friends the whooper swans, late of Harewood Park, a thorn in the side of many members when visiting that area. There were murmurs of disappointment from those who had known the lake area, when it was seen that practically all the cover for nesting birds at this end of the lake had been destroyed by the felling of timber. On the lake were twenty mallard, a few teal, five pairs of tufted duck, coot, a mute swan and the ever-present great crested grebe, the latter without signs of breeding. Up the ghyll redpolls flitted in the treetops and their calls were recorded. Near the stepping stones to the island, amongst the reeds, John Armitage, in dire peril of submerging, unearthed a reed buntings nest with eggs, much to the surprise of the keeper to whom it was shown. Amongst the brambles some members were shown a garden warbler's nest with four young and also a stock dove's nest with two eggs. In a silver birch were nests of chaffinch and wren ... Altogether 32 species were seen and everyone enjoyed a welcome change from town and suburb.

Almost three weeks later, on Saturday, 7 July, the botanist Hilda Murrell, living in Shrewsbury and running her family-owned rose nursery, went to Hereford to be a judge at the Rose Show there:

A perfect summer day [she wrote in her diary], not too hot or too cool, with all the summer flowers blowing in great profusion. Dog Roses arching out from the hedges, creamy masses of Elder blossom, Honeysuckle in lumps, and the later umbelliferous plants threading among them all. I came back by the country route – Mortimer's Cross, Wigmore, Leintwardine, and what a good idea it was. I only met about half a dozen vehicles and the country was wonderful. Stopped and brewed tea, and sat on the hedge-bank on one of the high spots on the Roman Road, about two miles out of Craven Arms. Had hardly moved off again when I saw an owl fly into the hedge. I stopped, and there it was in a tall Elder or thorn just above me, a Little Owl, looking at me very intently with piercing yellow eyes. This was 5.40 pm. It was mouse-brown, with streaks of lighter colour above and the same scheme reversed below.[13]

'The Seasons Round' was a traditional folksong, cataloguing the round of agricultural tasks through a year. The last four of the eight verses give the flavour:

Now seed-time being over, then haying draws near
With our scythe, rake and pitchfork those meadows to clear.
We will cut down their grass, boys, and carry it away.
We will turn it to the green grass and then call it hay.

When haying is over, then harvest draws near.
We will send to our brewer to brew us strong beer,
And in brewing strong beer, boys, we will cut down their corn.
We will take it to the barn, boys, to keep it from harm.

Now harvest being over, bad weather comes on.
We will send for the thresher to thresh out the corn.
His hand-staff he'll handle; his swingel he'll swing.
Till the very next harvest we'll all meet again.

Now since we have brought this so cheerfully round,
We will send for the jolly ploughman to plough up the ground.
See the boy with his whip and the man to his plough.
Here's a health to the jolly ploughman that ploughs up the
    ground.

By 1955, when the Copper family of Rottingdean in Sussex came to record the song, they had added a ninth verse:

Now things they do change as the time passes on.
I'm afraid I'll have occasion to alter my song.
You'll see a boy with a tractor a-going like hell.
Whatever farming is coming to, there's no tongue can tell.[14]

Occasion indeed ... And for many farmers and farmworkers alike, as the second agricultural revolution gathered pace, such seemingly timeless songs were poised to become museum pieces from a vanished way of life.

In addition to the usual suspects – increasing mechanisation, declining manpower (around 20,000 employees leaving the land annually by the early 1960s), increasing size of farms, the need for ever-greater capital, increasing specialisation (as opposed to traditional mixed farming) – another important element in the mix was the historic shift, as many of the great landed estates broke up under fiscal pressure, away from the landlord–tenant system (in 1950 the case with over three-fifths of farming land) and towards greater owner-occupation (by the late 1970s the case with at least two-thirds of farming land). But whether a tenant or an owner-occupier, the farmer trying to make a living on a small farm did not on the whole find it easy. By the early 1960s there were still plenty of them: even though the average farm size was bigger than on the continent, a quarter of Britain's 480,000 farms were of less than fifteen acres; and given that, across the sector as a whole, around 50 per cent of farms employed no labour at all, presumably the majority of those small farms were essentially one-family enterprises. 'It is difficult to see how these farms can remain in existence on any full-time, self-dependent basis,' asserted a 1962 report by the University of Nottingham based on an analysis of almost a hundred low-income East Midlands farms, all of them of less than 150 acres. 'There will', added the report, 'have to be other income of some kind for the farmer and his family.' And indeed the Labour Party's study soon afterwards found that, across England and Wales, around half of farmers were in effect working on the land on only a part-time basis. Generally calling for rationalisation, this report (probably written by Peter Shore, not yet an MP) concluded that 'farmers have no divine right to stay in one occupation'.[15]

Britain's farmworkers certainly enjoyed no divine rights. In 1949 the average agricultural worker earned per hour only 69 per cent of what the average manual worker in manufacturing industries earned; by 1959 that was down to less than 65 per cent; and by 1964 to less than 60 per cent. Moreover, not only were payments in kind (as cited by apologists for low cash earnings) becoming increasingly marginal, but the deeply invidious system of tied cottages, which were often badly run-down, remained firmly in place. As for any modern ideas of training and career progression, another University of Nottingham report, this time in 1963, conclusively showed that, far more often than not, 'to be a farmer's boy' – title of the optimistic, rags-to-riches traditional song – was by the third quarter of the twentieth century to be in a dead-end job, all too likely to lead to the exit door when it came to claiming an adult wage. 'Boys soon become aware of this prospect and cannot be blamed for seeking other employment (frequently non-farm employment) before they are dismissed,' noted the report. 'In addition to the prospect of being pushed out of agriculture, the boy on the small farm rarely has the opportunity to develop particular skills or responsibilities. Even if he strives to acquire these, he has little prospect of using his special knowledge or of being paid a premium for it ...' Inexorably, the overall trend was towards low levels of unionisation (the ever-greater problem for the NUAW, the National Union of Agricultural Workers) and, among farmworkers, a significant degree of social atomisation. 'At the workplace an occupational sub-culture with its own set of draconian norms and values was once reinforced by the comparatively large number of employees, often working in gangs with a horse-and-hand technology which allowed for easy and persistent communication between workmates,' Howard Newby wrote in the 1970s. Whereas, he went on, 'today' (and already even by the early 1960s increasingly applicable) 'the number of employees on each farm has been drastically reduced, work in gangs has virtually disappeared as far as the regular farm labour-force is concerned and the new machine technology not only physically isolates one worker from another but renders communication difficult owing to the increased pace and noise associated with it'. In short: 'Working on the land is now a rather lonely occupation.'[16]

Yet just as 'horizontal' interaction between employees was reducing, so 'vertical' interaction between farmworkers and farmers was almost certainly on the rise. 'The decline in the labour force, the removal of most gang labour, and the tendency for a growing proportion of workers to live on the farm have all resulted in the growth of closer, more personal and informal relationships between farmer and farm worker, extending to consultation about day-to-day farm management and even outside working hours into the domestic sphere,' reckoned Newby, again in the 1970s and again with at least some relevance to a decade earlier. 'Increasingly,' he added, 'relationships have become established on a face-to-face, "gaffer-to-man" basis, with farmer and worker often seeing each other several times a day, sharing break-times (often in the farmhouse kitchen) and even working alongside

each other on the jobs that demand it.' There was also what one
might call the eternal factor. 'Employer and worker respect each other
because they understand each other,' declared the NUAW's less-than-
firebrand General Secretary, Harold Collison, as he sought in 1964 to
explain the 'good' state of farming's labour relations. 'Both are aware
that they have a joint and difficult task – to conform to, but also to
subdue and direct, the forces of nature. They have common enemies –
the weather, disease, pests and the like. All this makes for a unity of
purpose and an understanding …'

But could it *really* be such a harmonious as well as close relationship
when the economic gulf was becoming ever wider – which, across the
sector, despite the struggles of many small farmers, it undoubtedly
was – between master and man? Ronald Blythe, writing about the state
of play by 1967, offered a perspective informed by many interviews in
and around the Suffolk village of 'Akenfield':

> Before the war, farmer and worker shared the slump and were
> plunged into common hardships – 'there worn't no money
> about', and that was that. But since 1956 farm profits have
> increased forty-three per cent – by £113 million in eleven years –
> and evidence of this new wealth can be seen in every village. Old
> farmhouses are beautifully restored and made luxurious with
> fitted carpets and oil-fired central heating, deep-freezes for game
> and fruit, and new furniture. Rovers and Jaguars fill the garages,
> also the son's new sports car. This prosperity is more wondered
> at than resented by the worker, who, if he is middle-aged, might
> remark, 'When I went to work along o' him afore the war, he
> hadn't got two ha'pennies to rub together.'

Wondered at rather than resented? Even though (Blythe again) the
contrast between 'the financial position of the ordinary "working"
farmer' on the one hand, and 'that of the two or three men he employs'
on the other, had become 'as extreme as that which existed between
landowner and labourer before 1914'? A key insight comes from
Newby, who (with fellow sociologist Colin Bell) argued in 1973 that
'as long as the farmer conforms to the worker's image of "the good
farmer" it seems that employer–employee relationships will remain
harmonious, however great the disparities of income and life-style'.

As to what earned that accolade, the two crucial matters were whether the farmer was a 'local' (good) or a 'newcomer' (bad) and whether he was a 'working farmer' (good) or an 'office farmer' (bad), with local working farmers tending in practice not only to 'work as hard if not harder than the worker himself', but to show 'a paternalistic concern for the wider personal affairs of his labour force and the area as a whole'. 'The greater the conformity of the employer to the appropriate image of the "good farmer", the greater is the possibility of the contradictions of the situation being contained and conflict avoided,' concluded Bell and Newby. 'This may inspire sufficient personal loyalty on the part of agricultural workers to inhibit across-the-board praise or condemnation of "bosses" or "farmers" as an undifferentiated group – particularism over-rides universalism.'[17]

The labour-saving mechanisation of Britain's farms meant many things, among them – on the part of farmers almost as much as farmworkers – a changed, more distant relationship with animals, as the animal-to-human ratio rose rapidly. One historian, Jeremy Burchardt, has identified 'a growing tendency within agriculture to regard animals less as individual creatures than as one of a mass', a process 'taken to its extreme in the case of battery poultry', and he is surely right. But what about the relationship with the land itself? 'In the nineteenth century, farmworkers spent much of their time in direct contact with the soil,' notes Burchardt without excessive sentimentality. 'Hoeing and harvesting were still largely carried out by hand, and even ploughing involved actually treading the soil.' Whereas in the twentieth century, especially from the 1940s onwards, 'farmworkers spent an increasing proportion of their time cocooned in the cabs of their tractors, touching plastic, glass and metal rather than earth and vegetation, and hearing the sound of tractor engines and radios rather than of horses' hooves, the wind in the trees and the cries of birds'. Not that the cocooned were necessarily complaining. 'I'm definitely happier than I was years ago and I'm sure most farm-workers are,' a 45-year-old interviewee told Blythe. 'We had depressing jobs which lasted so long. Sugar-beeting was very depressing. You'd start it in September and it would go on till January. It made life seem worthless. Now you just sit on the harvester!' In any case, many of the broad seasonal rhythms remained largely intact. Take arable farming: hedging and ditching (the nadir of the year) in

January and February; seed-time in the spring, involving the often frenetic preparation of seed beds, drilling and rolling; in the early summer, if in East Anglia, sugar-beet hoeing; later in the summer through to September, most of the different phases, depending on the types of crops, of harvesting; and over the rest of the year a mixture of activities (autumn ploughing and muck-spreading; main drilling of winter barley, wheat and beans) as well as the final harvesting (spring beans, sugar beet, main crop potatoes).

Did mechanisation lead to deskilling? Here, according to Burchardt, the picture is mixed: yes, in the sense that old-time skills such as hand-milking, scything or thatching hay ricks were largely lost; no, in the sense that not only were new skills demanded ('applying fertilizers and herbicides at the right time, in the right quantity, and on the right soils and crops, requires considerable expertise'), but the sharp reduction in manpower meant that the tasks facing farmers became ever more various, especially on mixed farms where 'the formerly separate roles of ploughman, stockman, shepherd, hedger and general labourer' now all had to be combined, not to mention the almost daily challenge of trying 'to discriminate effectively between the torrent of competing products which manufacturers have made ever more strenuous attempts to persuade them to buy in the postwar period'. Agricultural education, it is true, was still in the 1960s lagging behind the new functional requirements, but few doubted that that necessary blessing would arrive sooner rather than later. And of course, far from all farmers – especially older farmers running small or relatively small holdings – unreservedly welcomed, or even welcomed at all, technological change and its potential for much greater output. A study in the late 1950s of small farmers in Yorkshire found that their priority was not profit maximisation or long-term expansion, but rather the simple, time-honoured goal of keeping the farm within the family. Another study around the same time came across many older farmers opting for the easier if less profitable life of beef or sheep farming, as opposed to the rigours of milk production. Or in the telling words of a third report about a part of society renowned for its deep-dyed conservatism, 'provided there is enough for maintenance of buildings and equipment, few farmers are much concerned about the rate of interest on their capital'.[18]

Edward Dean (probably not his real name) might have gently – or not so gently – scoffed. In his mid-thirties when in 1958 the sociologist W. M. Williams interviewed him as part of a study of a West Country (probably Devon) small rural community called 'Ashworthy', he owned a large farm where he had always lived and which he had taken over from his father four years earlier. Williams asked him about relations with neighbouring farmers:

The war made a big difference to neighbours. Machinery came in and changed everything. Ask my father how it was in his day … Take threshing. It was a big day round here. Now I combine most of mine and rick the rest. I have four people in for two days and I pay them … I'd rather do that than keep going back [that is, to neighbours' farms] for their threshing. The only big thing left here is the dipping; ten farmers came to that: most of them keep about thirty sheep and it isn't worth fixing up a bath because it costs five or six pound.

If it wasn't for dipping I wouldn't hardly see my neighbours, although I sometimes ride round on a pony … I do my own hay with the baler … These days you only see a few neighbours – those who are friends or who you borrow things from. I borrow O's potato digger and he borrows a disc harrow … I lend him more than I borrow from him … Of course I see a lot of my father and brother-in-law – with they being near-by, us work like a family …

There have been a lot of changes round here … I would visit a new farmer, but most [farmers] wouldn't bother these days. Us have always lived in Ashworthy, so us generally like to meet them. Mind, a lot depends on what they be … If they'm a bit – um – well, if they've studied farming in a book and class theyselves higher than farmers, they don't get mixed in very much … but a happy-go-lucky sort mixes in very well. I think I'm lucky, the new ones are a nice lot.

'Farmers these days can't *afford* the old-fashioned ways,' concluded Dean. 'I prefer to pay older men and such for jobs … If I held a proper threshing I'd be bound to go round all the farms and I can't afford the time …'

It was a different world, almost a different planet, when two or three years later another sociologist, John Nalson, went in search of two unmarried sisters as part of his fieldwork in rural north-east Staffordshire:

'Climb over the wall, to round the hill and down to the stream at the bottom. Over the fence you'll see a hen hut. The path runs from there to the house, they're sure to be in.'

I picked up the grocery box from the niche on the leeward side of the wall and set off across the field. The slope was steep, the grass slippery and the grocery box awkward to carry. I reached the stream, and there over the other side was Alice. At least, that is who the figure in army greatcoat, beret and boots turned out to be. She explained that, as the coalman and the corn merchant could not get down to the house, they left the bags over the wall and she and her sister sledged them down to near the hen house. 'We've got to come to feed 'em and collect the eggs, so we always bring the coal bucket along too. It saves carrying the coal bags over to the house. We carry the corn home, though, so that it doesn't spoil.' Alice led the way along the narrow track, a bucket of eggs in one hand, a bucket of coal in the other.

The house nestled under the hill. In the field below half a dozen cows grazed contentedly on the new spring growth. I reminded myself sharply of those bags of corn; the three-hundred-yard-long path to the hens and the coal; the fifty-inch rainfall and the seven weeks in 1947 when every time the main road half a mile away was cleared of snow the wind blew it back in twenty-foot drifts.

Alice wiped her boots on the sack mat and we went in. She emptied the groceries on to the table – a thick wedge of cheese, a tin of treacle, three large loaves, three two-pound packets of sugar and a pound of tea.

Mary poked the fire and went out into the scullery to fill the kettle from a bucket. Alice explained, 'She's had bilious attacks all her life. She started with St Vitus' Dance when she was at school and she never seemed to get over it.'

A place was cleared on the table for my papers and I started to ask questions. 'No, we don't sell milk, it would be a bit awkward to get it out to the road, so I make a bit of butter and sell it round about. Anyway, *they* wouldn't pass the buildings, and we can't afford to do them up with buying the farm.'

The other sister went out into the scullery again, came back with a bucket of mash and started to mix it. The kettle boiled, she wiped her hands on her sack apron and made the tea.

Alice continued. 'Folk said we were daft to buy this old place, yet what else could we do? It's our home and it's been in the family that long … My great-grandfather came from Manchester and built this house and the buildings, but *they* got it off him like they got a lot more. They tried to get us out a time or two after Father died, but he'd put the tenancy in our name aforehand, so we were all right. There's no houses to rent round here, and if there was what would we do? It's five years afore I get the pension and longer for Mary. We've only done farm work all our life and nobody round here needs an old maid to do their work for them. Not that we haven't had our chances, mind you, but Mother was nearly forty when she had Mary, so by the time we were looking round a bit they were needing looking after and didn't seem to see things our way. Then, of course, Father lived 'til he was eighty and so here we are on the shelf.' Alice excused herself, picked up the bucket and an empty egg basket and set off for the henhouse again.

Mary busied herself washing eggs in a bowl at one corner of the table. I sat at the other, sipped a second cup of tea and looked around. The wallpaper was peeling from one corner of the room where the damp was coming in. I began to understand why the coal fire was so big. The previous day had been a wet one and clothes were drying everywhere. Socks on a string across the mantelshelf, boots at the hearth, skirts, pullovers and shirts hanging on lines suspended from the low ceiling. And this was late spring!

I shuddered to think of the confusion, the all-pervading smell of cows and the cold striking up through the uneven stone flags in the wintertime. Three times a day they would fight their way in the teeth of a gale to feed the hens and fetch the coal; twice a day break the ice on the trough and lead each of the fifteen head of stock individually to drink. Thankfully they would return to milk the cows and thrust their frozen hands into that cosy warmth where the udder meets the hind leg.

'Of course,' reflected their visitor, 'the farm was uneconomic. Of course their man-days of work would not entitle them to governmental assistance. Of course their farm should be amalgamated with the one next door. But, as Alice said, what else could they do? They had to live.'

A mellower – but not entirely mellow – mood was to be found near the Essex–Suffolk border, where Henry Warren a little later in the 1960s evoked a retired farmhand called Tom, living with his wife in an isolated cottage. It looked over the fields to which for so many years he had devoted his working life:

> He reads them like a book (his only book) and the words they spell are ones that he really does understand. He knows the nature of the soil in every field and its subtle variations within that field. For years back he knows the crops each field has carried – and, often, the exact yield, too. He can say the year, for instance, when Further Much Field yielded a record crop of barley; and the year when Calves Pightle was first put under the plough; or, again, the year when the oats in Cozick Croft stood about so long in foul weather that in the end they were not even fit to feed to the pigs. He knows how all the drains run, and where the outlets are. He remembers the prices of corn, year by year, as if the money had been paid into his own pocket.
>
> To us the fields look empty. For days on end, even for weeks, not a man is to be seen in any of them. There would be nothing for anybody to do in them now that machines can achieve in a day or two what gangs of men took weeks to do. So the fields stand empty for most of the time – to our way of seeing. But to Tom they are all peopled with the memories of the men he knew intimately, the men he worked with day after day, and whom a hundred small ties bound into the nearest he knew of fellowship. Of them all, now, only himself remains.

What does Tom think about the new farming methods, the machine usurping the hand, and the fields silent as well as empty? ' "It seems all wrong, somehow," is the most he says; but usually he states no opinion at all.' Instead, keeping his thoughts to himself, he gets on with his garden, until eventually, tiring of it, he fills his pipe and stands gazing out again. Warren's nicely judged pay-off – that fraught but inescapable relationship between the ancient and the modern – comes now:

> On the other side of his hedge, the fields are ripening to harvest – and never a weed showing anywhere. Even he has to admit they never looked better. 'It's this spraying business,' he says, seeming almost to withhold the credit as he gives it, recalling, no doubt, the long hours he spent hoeing between the rows in years gone by and the sturdy crop of weeds that nevertheless showed up in the end.[19]

'Thrush Green had changed little since she came first to it as a young wife,' reflected Winnie Bailey in Miss Read's *Winter in Thrush Green* (1961), the second of her novels set in an Oxfordshire village based on Woodgreen near Witney. It was almost half a century since Winnie had married Dr Bailey. 'True,' she went on, 'there were new houses along the lane to Nidden [another village] and a large housing estate further west, and in Lulling [Witney] itself there were twice as many inhabitants. But the triangular green, surrounded by the comfortable Cotswold stone buildings, had altered very little.' Villages remained a special glory. Take just a few pages, at semi-random, from the 1962 third post-war edition of the AA's *Illustrated Road Book of England and Wales*. Chiddingstone, Kent, population 1,018, 'a very attractive village, with some half-timbered houses and a Perp Church tower'; Chideock, Dorset, 610, 'picturesquely situated among the hills, looking northwards towards Marshwood Vale'; Childswickham, Worcs, 510, 'a most attractive village, with an old Cross'; Chilton, Bucks, 326, 'a picturesque village on high ground providing notable views'; Chilton Foliat, Wilts, 373, 'an attractive village on the River Kennet'; Christow, Devon, 590, 'a delightful Teign Valley village'; Clapham, Yorks, 607, 'an attractive village in a moorland setting'; Clavering, Essex, 831, 'a village of old cottages'; Claypole, Lincs, 672, 'a pleasant village' …

Sadly, a mention only, with no accompanying description, for Rushall, Wilts, 135. Set in the Vale of Pewsey, it was where Mike

Pitcher (born 1942, stepfather a farm labourer) spent most of his childhood. A 'tiny sleepy village' whose population density had barely changed since the fourteenth century, indeed 'everyone seemed to have lived there since time began'; most villagers keeping chickens and a pig at the bottom of the garden; beef, lamb, cheese, milk and butter all coming from local farms; flour milled locally; the family's only toilet a bucket under a wooden seat in a shed; no flushing toilets either in the village school; nearest restaurant eight miles away – it was in the round, reckoned Pitcher half a century later, a 'safe, cocooned, secure, structured, isolated and well-nourished' environment for his formative years. 'Any contact with the law, the church, the civil service and indeed any form of authority was', he added, 'to be avoided if possible. You didn't want people outside your close-knit community knowing anything about your business, and there was a nervousness about dealing with organisations you didn't really understand.'[20] In almost all essentials, it was a world that would have been broadly familiar a century or two earlier; but, like all villages, a world by the early 1960s on the verge of major, irreversible change.

Of course, the pace of that change, some of it already well under way, would vary from village to village, often to do with size and location. And usually, a point not always sufficiently made, the appearance of villages, their historic centres anyway, remained remarkably constant during these post-war decades. 'Most villages in the year 2000,' noted Burchardt early this century, 'looked very similar to how they did in 1940. Most have a core of pre-twentieth-century buildings, including a few which stand out visually because of their size or quality, such as a church, manor house, rectory or large farmhouse. These older buildings have almost invariably been carefully conserved.' Yet in terms of post-war day-to-day village life, the litany of change was soon familiar enough: a serious reduction in the number of shops (in one area of rural Norfolk, north-west of Norwich, down from 227 in 1950 to 140 in 1964); small primary schools being steadily closed (evidence again from Norfolk, where eighty closed between 1951 and 1971, leaving almost half the county's parishes without a school); and pubs likewise shutting their doors for good, though probably more after 1962 than before. Predictably, the overall evidence is of declining levels of social interaction. 'The village is no longer an isolated, self-contained social unit, dependent upon its own people for the provision of its entertainment,' lamented the NUAW's magazine, *Land Worker*, in 1960:

> The young lads seek, and get, motor-cycles which will take them into town any evening they wish to go, with the girls on the pillion. Those who are not so young, and who are tired after a full day's work and overtime, get all the entertainment they want from the television by their own fireside. The Union branch meeting, once a monthly social event, can no longer compete with TV quiz-shows and regular radio features. Contributions, once collected with comparative ease at well-attended meetings, now have to be called for, thus increasing considerably the work of the branch secretary.

Two years later, in the large Berkshire village of Stratfield Mortimer (roughly halfway between Reading and Basingstoke), Ruth Crichton undertook a careful survey of voluntary associations there, including the British Legion, the Men's Club, the Boy Scouts and Girl Guides movements, the Women's Institute, the Young Wives' Club, the Mothers' Union, the cricket club, the bowling club, the dramatic society and so on, before concluding rather pessimistically that 'many struggle along with barely enough members to keep going'. Herself a village resident of seventeen years' standing, she noted that many of these societies 'are disappointed to receive so little support from the new immigrants', while adding tactfully that 'without that support they might well have had to close down'.[21]

What were the residential-cum-occupational trends in villages by this time? The most visible was undoubtedly the continuing decline of what has been called the occupational community, in which (to quote Newby) 'the population of the majority of rural villages were dependent upon agriculture for a living'. Importantly, it was not just farmworkers (above all young farmworkers) who, for a mixture of economic and other reasons, were feeling compelled to leave the village and head to town, but also many of those rural craftsmen servicing the agricultural trades. Take wheelwrights in Hampshire: over forty of them in 1939, but only one by the 1990s. 'Not so long ago,' reflected H. E. Bracey in his 1959 survey of English rural life, 'every village had its team of craftsmen – carpenter, painter, wheelwright, blacksmith, thatcher, saddler – but many rural areas have been almost denuded of these crafts.' Inevitably – and especially in more remote villages, most of all if the part of the country was agriculturally poorer – the consequence could be serious rural depopulation, quickly leading to a vicious circle in the provision of services. 'The dry rot of depopulation has drained away some of the vigour and variety of social life,' lamented one of the English countryside's most sensitive chroniclers, E. W. Martin, in 1965 on the basis of a close study of the parishes around the Devon town of Okehampton. 'It has meant a waste of human material because where institutions are not sensibly organized there is discontent with what is available. The young man will be tempted to look over the brow of the hill in search of better things ... The effects have been that the number of active workers has declined, to be replaced by elderly and retired people. Social life is restricted, institutions suffer and the young are outnumbered by those whose days are far spent.'

Precise figures are hard to come by, but undoubtedly urban retirees were by the 1960s increasingly likely to move to villages, though the real rush probably came somewhat later. 'In the early sixties when people started to build new estates the village began to expand,' recalled in 1995 a woman who had been born in Polegate in Sussex in 1954 and still lived there. 'I remember feeling a bit resentful of the people who moved in. They were mainly people who had retired from London. They were different to the local people I knew.' Bracey in 1959, in one of the less arid passages of his survey, took the long view of this phenomenon:

Two centuries ago well-to-do elderly people used to retire to Bath, Harrogate and Cheltenham. A century later, joined by others less affluent, they journeyed to Brighton. In the twentieth century, Bournemouth, Torquay and other South-coast resorts have become favourite towns for retirement. These fashionable seaside places are clearly too expensive for most of the greatly increased number of persons who now retire on pensions which seldom permit them to continue living in their old style even in town. For many of these people, the logical decision may be to move to a pleasant village where they can live economically, which is within reach of the town where their friends and relatives are still living and to which they can return for short visits.

And he added, not uncontentiously, that it was 'in the national interest' that 'as many retired townspeople as possible should vacate their homes close by urban workplaces, thereby making room for households with children and young people who have more frequent need than elderly people to use centralised social services such as health and education'.[22]

Yet in practice, by the early 1960s, it was neither urban retirees nor second-home owners (even by 1968, barely 100,000 of them, excluding caravan owners) who were starting to compensate for the drift away from the land, but instead the increasing number of those who, whether newcomers or not, were commuting to work (usually by car) from village to town or city. Back in 1921, only 14 per cent (probably an overestimate given the date of the census) of the economically active living in rural areas in England and Wales travelled to jobs in urban areas, whereas by 1966 that proportion was up to at least 37 per cent and set to rise sharply further. Much of southern and Midland England came in the 1950s within the scope of commuting from the countryside, plausibly reckons Burchardt; while a study of West Berkshire shows 'the better-off local businessmen' settling in villages in the course of the 1960s, but the major inflow of 'middle- and upper-middle-income executives and professionals' awaiting the opening of the M4 in 1972.

Overall, a two-way process was clearly at work. 'The urban, middle-class exodus to the countryside would not have occurred without certain culturally induced assumptions about the wholesome authenticity of rural life,' concluded Newby in 1979 – perhaps thinking of writers like H. E. Bates, Miss Read and James Herriot – as he considered 'the urbanization of rural England' over the previous quarter-century or so. 'But, equally,' he went on, 'the newcomers could not have been accommodated without an exodus of the rural working population in the opposite direction, an exodus provoked by the continuous substitution of capital for labour in the system of agricultural production.'[23]

Who ran the show? Traditionally, of course, just one man. 'East Clandon [in Surrey] under squire's aegis was still an almost feudal village,' remembered the journalist Maurice Wiggin about moving there in the early 1950s. 'Squire lived in the great house, Hatchlands, and though he didn't own the entire village he owned so much of it that his word was virtually law.' But already the break-up of the great landed estates meant that the rule of the squire was, in most places, becoming a memory; and Bracey, in part quoting from a study by E. W. Martin, was adamant that the old days, especially when it came to attitudes, were conclusively over:

> Any claim to *automatic* leadership of a rural community by one of the old ruling class would now be ignored or rejected. Occasionally, one meets a woman of the 'manor-house stratum' hovering rather pathetically on the fringe of village society. From time to time she is discovered making tentative attempts to exercise her old authority, 'pathetically trying to hold aloft the tattered flag of local patronage by entertaining carol singers during the Christmas season and making small gifts to a parish which regards her struggles without a great deal of interest'. Her efforts meet with resentment or toleration according to her own personality and the temper of the village people.
>
> This is not to say that the manor-house stratum of rural society has no influence on village activities and welfare – it often has a very great deal – but the relationship has changed very considerably, and direct action by members of the old 'ruling class' can be regarded as interference in village affairs.

To a degree, farmers took up the leadership slack, with research in the mid-1960s revealing that, at 35 per cent, they were far likelier than any other occupational group to be members of rural district councils. Even so, apart from that responsibility, Bracey was probably not far wrong when he pointed out that 'farming is a way of life which engages the attention of the farmer all his working hours' and that, consequently, 'relatively few farmers can be induced to take an active part in village affairs'. What about the squirearchy's traditional helpmates, the clergy? 'In many villages,' noted Bracey without apparent regret, 'the status of the parson as a member of upper-middle-class society is questionable and questioned because of his urban origin and his near-poverty.' In short, there was something of a vacuum – into which, to judge by Crichton's 1962 survey of Stratfield Mortimer, stepped what she called 'men and women of relatively high occupational status', with doctors (still usually male), ex-army officers and their wives to the fore. 'They come', she remarked of the military types, 'largely because they value village life and are prepared to contribute towards it, and if they are immigrants from urban areas they clearly enjoy feeling a bigger fish in a little pond. The pond benefits.'

More generally, the rural invasion by outsiders was still at a very early stage. Even so, the elements were already in place for what would often be a difficult relationship with insiders. 'Newcomers', noted Bracey disapprovingly (though without providing significant empirical evidence), 'fail to acquire a feeling of local loyalty':

> They remain strangers to each other and to older residents too long for a number of reasons, most of which are related to their different, usually un-rural, experience which gives them a sense of insecurity in their new surroundings. Villagers are not usually very quick to see this or to do anything to break it down; they themselves are influenced by various factors – shyness, resentment etc etc. As a result, old residents and newcomers live separate lives.

Newcomers' stereotyped expectations about the life more simple, insiders scapegoating newcomers, conflict over issues of housing and the environment – Newby and others would write illuminatingly of these problems and much else, but in relation more to the 1970s than to the 1960s. Yet in any decade the great healer was almost certainly time. 'Commuters are almost as well integrated as those who work locally,' recorded Crichton about the results of her detailed 1962 'social integration' questionnaire for her Berkshire village's residents (an impressive 98 per cent compliance rate). 'It is', she concluded, 'length of residence and not commuting that counts most ... Provided the commuter can enjoy stability of employment, the chances are that when he has lived in the village at least six years, he will be as well integrated as the local worker.'²⁴

The village under the most heavy-duty scrutiny in the 1960s, from a team of anthropologists and others, was the small, pretty village of Elmdon in north-west Essex, where from 1962 onwards the locals found themselves becoming the rural case-exhibit equivalent of Bethnal Green for urban sociologists in the 1950s. In her eventual history of the village, covering 1861 to 1964, Jean Robin imagined the village's main landowner of the 1860s, the Rev. Robert Wilkes, returning in the year that Harold Wilson came to power:

> As he descended the steep path from the church [with a little-changed interior] to the old vicarage where he had been born, he would have been surprised by the absence of movement in the scene. There would be no horses striking sparks from the flints in the rough road as they went down the hill to be shod at the Brands' forge or pulled carts and wagons into the yards at Hill or Church Farms; no village women visiting the two grocers' and drapers' shops below Charles Monk's beer-house; no smell of freshly baked bread from Susannah Bowman's premises; and no children playing up and down the road. Instead, he would see that the bakery and shops had been turned into private houses, and it might be many minutes before he was startled by a passing car.

Robin then provided a series of comparisons between the states of play in 1861 and 1964: population down from 525 to 321; the proportion of older people (sixty and above) up from 10 per cent to 25 per cent; proportion of residents born outside the parish up from 27 per cent to 59 per cent; by 1964 only one in twenty marriages having both partners born inside the parish, but almost half of them including at least one partner born in the parish; proportion of male employees who were farmworkers down from two-thirds to one-third; and one professional family (the vicar) in 1861 rising to thirteen in 1964.

Continuity and change was, inevitably, Robin's big theme. On the one hand, 'as an Elmdon farmer said in the early 1960s, if you passed a man whose name you did not know and said, "Good morning, Mr Hammond", you had a 50 per cent chance of being right'; on the other hand, the residents in 1964 included a widow from Chile and the wife plus two children of a businessman in Baghdad. Overall, in her concluding remarks, Robin emphasised continuity at least as much as change, noting that 'even as late as 1964' more than half the population was 'linked with the village through birth, upbringing, marriage or other kin connection'. But in terms of social integration, what about Crichton's six-years rule? 'I was struck in the first few days by remarks made at a visit with a couple of students to a woman who had lived forty-four years in Elmdon and had acted as midwife to the village,' recalled the distinguished Cambridge anthropologist Audrey Richards (who with Edmund Leach had really got the project moving). 'She was pushed aside by her sister-in-law who said "Don't ask *her*. She knows nothing about the families. She is a stranger here." In the same week [probably in August 1962] a butcher, a stranger from Ely with seven years' residence, said bitterly "Don't ask *me*! You'd have to have been here since Hereward-the-Wake to belong." '[25]

The complementary narrative of traditional village life in decline and of insiders and outsiders in a state of unproductive mutual suspicion was an easy enough – and not necessarily mistaken – narrative to plug into. Such broadly was Geoffrey Moorhouse's take when in about 1963 he visited seemingly prosperous and undeniably chocolate-box Painswick, nestled in the heart of the Cotswolds and regularly voted Gloucestershire's best-kept village. 'Appearances', he noted, 'are everything in Painswick, and there is not an inch of woodwork that goes without its regular lick of paint, not a yard of ground that is not ruthlessly deprived of its weeds, scarcely anything to offend the casually roving eye. All is limestoned, mossy tranquillity.' Yet in truth, he went on, almost all had changed. Well within living memory, it had still been 'an agrarian community, when the inhabitants of Pitchcombe, a mile or so down the hill, were regarded as foreigners, and when every Painswick man gloried in his nickname – Brandy Bridgeman, Mangle Smith, Toff Ireland, and the like'; whereas now 'the men of Painswick take themselves off to the ball-bearing works in Stroud or the thatcheries of Gloucester', and 'you will have to take a fair step outside the parish if you wish to find anything as quaint as a blacksmith, though the village offers a choice of three shops selling electrical equipment'. Appreciably less than half the inhabitants, moreover, were now Painswick born and bred, as they and the well-off newcomers conducted 'a wary relationship' with points of contact, outside shops and church, 'few and far between'. For 'the gentleman' (largely incomers) it was whiskies and sodas at the Falcon; for 'the Painswick folk' (often working-class) it was a pint of beer or cider at the 'not half so smart' Royal Oak or Golden Hart. 'For a nostalgic whiff of that cosy England which we sell with our tourist brochures,' he fully accepted, 'the connoisseur can do no better than to visit Painswick.' Even so:

Let him inhale deeply and he will catch the more tantalizing airs
of change and decay and exploitation. He can then collect his
souvenirs at random – a stick of Painswick rock, say, or a notice on
the doorway of the Brockley (Painswick) Investment Company
Ltd, or even a fragment of conversation from a Foreign Office
mother towing her small daughter along Friday Street. 'We're
going to see our new house afterwards,' she was saying, 'and all
the things they've been doing to it. Come along lambkin!' An
echo from the past.

'But a past', concluded Moorhouse bitterly enough, 'which the ghosts
of Brandy and Mangle and Toff, if they had been cruising within
earshot at that moment, would not have recognized as their own.'

All no doubt true, yet such was not the only reality of village life
in the early 1960s. Crichton's 1962 survey of Stratfield Mortimer
suggested notably high overall satisfaction ratings: of 139 respondents
asked whether they liked living there, 48.9 per cent liked it 'very much',
31.0 per cent liked it, and 18.7 per cent 'quite liked it' – compared to a
paltry 1.4 per cent who disliked it and 0 per cent who disliked it very
much. Even if 'quite liked' is filed under the negatives, that still left
four-fifths of respondents distinctly on the positive side. What would
have improved the living experience? More police (particularly to deal
with gangs of youths from the recently built council houses), better
street lighting, better paving, better bus services, the building of bus
shelters, more shops (especially a hairdresser and a draper) – the wish
list was predictably prosaic. More atmospheric responses came after
Crichton had persuaded the schoolmaster teaching 10- and 11-year-
olds to get them to write a composition about their likes and dislikes
in relation to living in the village, including any ideas for making
things better. On the whole, but only on the whole, an urban child
born in 1951 or 1952 might have envied them:

At Mortimer there is streams to fish in and you can go for walkes
over the coman. They orta have cottages in sted of councile
houses it would look more country like. I like Mortimer because
of the birds and flowers in the country side.

I like livinng in Mortimer because of the fresh air. When I was
in London I could see the duest on the window seel of houses

and the air was smokey. There are lots of pleasent views instead of rows and rows of coronation streets like there are in Reading and London.

Living in Mortimer is very pleasant, but I am against the building of Council Houses for the men who work at the AWRE [the Atomic Weapons Research Establishment at Aldermaston]. I myself would rather live in the country because of the fresh air, fields, ponds, woods, lanes, and nice little cottages, but all those will go if they build these large rows of Council Houses.

The thing what I dislike Mortimer is its to dull, because theres no cinema or theartre which you could go to ... and theres not a swimming pool ... I would improve mortimer by building a cinema and amusement arcade and outdoor swimming pool and big shops and more good houses and not council houses.

The thing I don't like about mortimer is the teddy boys and the bulies because they hit you wen you are playing in the wood.

I do not dislike anything about Mortimer. The people of Mortimer are nice. In towns there are not many trees to climb but in Mortimer there are good trees to climb. I like the stream that runs through Mortimer. I like the first wooden bridge where you catch minows ... I like the waterfall that you can cross. If someone asked me where I would rather live I would say nowhere but Mortimer.[26]

For cathedral cities, market towns and suchlike – urban centres for the surrounding rural population, but not themselves great urban conurbations – the early 1960s were still on the whole the eve of the great disruption, before urban redevelopment did its worst (and very occasionally best) between roughly the mid-1960s and early 1970s. Take Northampton and Tamworth, twin subjects of a heartfelt chapter ('The Destruction of Towns') in *Goodbye, Britain?*, Tony Aldous's passionate, well-informed lament of 1975. 'It had some notable buildings, but many more townscape and architectural delights not noted in the guidebooks and perhaps rather down-at-heel, though appreciated by the more discerning townsfolk,' he wrote in the past tense of Northampton. There, although in fact the tale of destruction had begun in 1962 itself with the demolition in the Market Square of the seventeenth-century Peacock Inn (to make way for a supermarket), the most tragic single loss was the demolition ten years later of the nearby late nineteenth-century Emporium Arcade, complete with a brick clock-tower and Art Nouveau tiled façade. 'Its façade was not everyone's idea of beauty, but it had in seventy years become part of the square's character for almost everyone who lived there,' reflected Aldous. 'It had a distinctive personality, was a key point of reference visually ... Northampton's memory, and sense of identity and direction, have faded badly because of that demolition.' As for the market town of Tamworth in Staffordshire, it still had in the early 1960s, before the bulldozers got to work, 'a compact and fine-grained townscape' – a townscape which included not far short of a hundred listed buildings, of which little more than half would survive the next decade. Aldous was particularly indignant about the fate of Church Street's five gabled shops, 'the epitome of medieval Tamworth', all demolished in 1968. 'One dated back to the 1400s and contained a nearly complete medieval hall and solar – a rarity which the town, and indeed the nation, should have cherished. Another had Tudor windows looking out on the street – again an irreplaceable feature of the street scene which should have been cherished ...'

Unlike many state-of-the-nation investigators, Moorhouse was not oblivious of market towns as he travelled around in search of material for what became his 1964 Penguin Special on *The Other England*. In East Anglia he worried that 'the markets, and particularly the cattle markets, have over the past few years become more and more concentrated in the biggest towns – Norwich, Lynn, Bury, Cambridge – and the justification for places like Stowmarket, Diss, Eye, and Downham Market in their traditional form has been rapidly disappearing'; in England's highest market town – Alston, some 900 feet up in the Pennines – he worried how long the thirteen-mile, single-track South Tyne branch line, running from Haltwhistle in Northumberland to Alston in Cumberland, was going to survive; and in Shrewsbury he wondered how the plans afoot ('a swimming bath of international standard with a restaurant so that diners can see the swimmers underwater, riverside illuminations, ten-pin bowling alleys, roller skating in The Quarry, and better boating on the Severn') were going to be compatible with remaining the finest Tudor town in England. 'The traffic still goes thundering around the half-timbered buildings as it has done in increasing and unchecked volume since the war,' he wrote of the town where I was at that time at boarding school though very seldom allowed into it. 'The open spaces which have been the proper counterpoise to the packed conglomeration of Tudor streets have steadily yielded to bus stations and parking lots; Murivance and Shoplatch, Wyle Cop and Dogpole, and all the other tempting alleys which have given Shrewsbury its composure in the past are today becoming hard-pressed relics which may yet, in the new temper of the town, have to struggle for survival.'[27]

Where did power lie in these sort of places? The short answer, based on Margaret Stacey's study of Banbury (published in 1960) and E. W. Martin's study of Okehampton (published in 1965), is the Conservative-supporting middle class, dominant not only in formal local politics but also in all sorts of voluntary associations, including churches, chambers of commerce, rotary clubs and sports clubs. 'When the middle class do come across a member who is a Labour supporter, they are surprised and shocked,' noted Stacey. 'They avoid social relations with the recalcitrant ... In practice in Banbury this means that while Liberals and Conservatives of similar status will join common associations, Labour is isolated because there is neither parity of status nor of outlook.' Martin quoted one of Okehampton's few Labour councillors: 'For more than fifty years this borough has been dominated by a Tory clique ... Of course there's a party-political battle going on. Anyone who says this isn't so lives in a fool's paradise and had better get elected to a council so that he can see the scheming and jockeying that goes on. This is a friendly town and I wouldn't go on record as saying anything else.' While an experienced journalist, who had lived in the town for several years, had this to say:

Any sort of controversy is frowned on by officials and councillors who have grown to be past-masters in the art of 'passing the buck'. When anything really important or controversial has to be discussed, this is done in committee and I'm asked to withdraw. The 'hush-hush' attitude is maintained deliberately. The real work is done behind the scenes and by telephone. A few people really run things and keep as much as they can out of the public eye. That's how councillors want it ...

At its worst, this was the world of *Swizzlewick*, David Turner's coruscating if crude comedy-drama TV series in 1964 about a corrupt local council in a fictional Midlands town. Mayor Augustus Bent, Harry Jolly, Ken Wiley – the names of the leading councillors spoke for themselves. The wrath of *The Times* rapidly descended. 'The salient fact about local government is a growing and courageous acceptance of responsibilities and challenges long neglected,' declared a stern editorial, insisting that the programme was fundamentally unrealistic. And the paper ended: 'It is part of the old Swizzlewick joke, now being given a new run, that councillors are often contractors on the make. But too many tunes have been played on that old fiddle.' Very soon, *Swizzlewick* was no more.

By altogether more benign contrast, it was Sudbury ('an attractive town on the River Stour, with old houses and inns, including Gainsborough's birthplace', in the words of the AA gazetteer) which inspired perhaps the most evocative description around this time of the long human and social continuities at work in old market towns. 'Neighbourly, I think that is the word that best describes Sudbury, at any rate on market-day,' wrote Henry Warren, probably in the mid-1960s:

After all, the people who then gather there [especially in Market Hill, with its closely packed stalls 'of fruit and flowers, plastic gadgets and groceries, fish and crockery, eiderdowns and frocks'] are neighbours, even if they have come in from villages far afield and at some distance from one another. They all speak with the same accent and use the same age-old Suffolk expressions; they have friends and relatives scattered about the district; they are familiar with the same crops, the same husbandry, even the same architecture; they take their news from the same local papers. And so Thursday is the day when they can foregather here, meet one another, and catch up with news and gossip. Indeed, to judge by the way they impede traffic on the pavements, and bump into one another in and out of shops, and stay talking just where they bump, it often seems as if the gossip is more important than the shopping. Well, perhaps it is ...

The secret of Sudbury's neighbourly atmosphere is that it is a country town with no pretensions to be anything else. The voices in its streets are country voices, the speech is country speech, and the matters discussed are, for the most part, country matters.

As for the forces of modernity, Warren seemed reasonably relaxed. 'Developments there certainly will have to be, in the future, just as there have been developments in the past. Change is all.' And he cited the old weavers' cottages tucked away in the narrow back streets, remnants of the old local wool trade: 'For the most part these have been pulled down, but a row or two of them still remain (though probably not for long) with their big windows on the first floor where the looms were situated, mere picturesque survivals that can have only antique value in the Sudbury of today.'

Warren would probably not have convinced John Betjeman, who during the summer of 1962 made a series of West Country television films, including one on Chippenham and Crewkerne. 'Local tradesmen still sometimes think heavy traffic brings business,' he observed regretfully during the Somerset segment. 'It doesn't. It takes it away to larger places and makes the old streets smelly, noisy, and dangerous and unfit to shop in.' But it was in Wiltshire's Chippenham that he really let himself go:

Modern motor traffic is no friend to an old town ... There's the town bridge over the Avon as it was till four years ago. Modern traffic takes its toll. And here it is today. [*Shot of drably functional new bridge*] Do you really think it's an improvement? There's a fine Georgian house [*old print shown*] which once stood in the high street. Modern traffic takes its toll. And there's the site today. [*Shot of shiny glass façade of Woolworths*] ... Modern traffic hates the pedestrian. It stinks. It shouts. It kills. I wonder what it's going to do to that bit of Tudor Chippenham in the high street. I hardly need to ask. Modern traffic is driving even the borough council out of these Georgian store houses it occupies in the middle of the town. That's going ... Modern traffic is draining Chippenham dry. This is the death of what once was River Street. The old houses are being destroyed to make a car park ... I'm not a mad preservationist, but I hate to see the heart of an old town left to go to ruin ...[28]

As Betjeman walked along Market Place, did he glance at the auction offices of Tilley & Culverwell? And if he had been there on 18 July, might he have wondered sympathetically about the human story behind the comprehensive sale of everything to do with Horwood Farm, Ansty? Possibly; yet over the years, he came ever more to identify farmers as the undisputed villains of the despoliation and – as he saw it – ruination of the English countryside. But in July 1962 itself that government-encouraged theft of our natural heritage was a story only just starting to unfold.

4

No Jam Roll? Give Over!

Main event at Lord's on Thursday, 19 July was not the second day of Gentlemen versus Players, but the announcement of which of the three amateur cricketers would captain England in Australia. The popular press that morning was confident the job would go to David Sheppard – who apparently had reassured MCC that, for all his well-known anti-apartheid views, he would not make a public stink about Australia's whites-only immigration policy – but in the event it was Ted Dexter who got the nod. 'Doubts here revolved around his independent spirit, which manifests itself, at times, in a rather high-handed manner,' noted *The Times*'s John Woodcock, otherwise positive about the appointee. Up at the Cambridgeshire High School for Boys ('the County'), 16-year-old Syd Barrett was caned for 'absences', just before leaving school for good; the Lord Chief Justice, Lord Parker, told judges at a Mansion House banquet that, in relation to the operation of the 1957 Homicide Act (in effect, hanging for premeditated murders, a prison sentence for non-premeditated), 'many of us are coming to the conclusion that we have got ourselves into a hopeless muddle'; and in the Commons the new Home Secretary, Henry Brooke, was obstinacy personified over the Carmen Bryan case ('No, I am not prepared to look at it again'), provoking some uproar on opposition benches before later on agreeing to postpone her imminent deportation. John Osborne's *Plays for England* double bill was unveiled that evening at the Royal Court. 'Sometimes intriguing, occasionally stimulating, but more often irritating or boring,' reckoned Anthony Heap; among the paid critics, Gerard Fay found that the suburban-set, Miller-directed *Under*

Plain Cover 'neither hangs together nor hits its target', including as it did 'long passages about knickers hard to put up with'; Roger Gellert thought the opening play, *The Blood of the Bambergs*, 'a tediously padded-out skit on a royal wedding', not helped by 'interminable, uninspired send-ups of Dimbleby, cabinet ministers and civil servants'; and Harold Hobson reflected on how it 'leaves one with the impression (which one has always had about Mr Osborne) that in his secret being, unknown to himself, he regards royal personages, professional military men, and the upper classes generally as having just about ten times as much sense, ability to handle a crisis, and survival capacity as Labour leaders, clergymen and the average voter'. The real-life aristos were not in Sloane Square, but in Park Lane, where 24-year-old Lord Londonderry was entertaining 300 friends at the magnificent, double-fronted Londonderry House, London's last surviving great town house, before it came under first the auctioneer's hammer and then the wrecking ball. 'It was a wonderful, gay night,' said young Lady Londonderry after the strains of Benny Goodman had apparently played out an era.[1]

Next day, the *FT*'s economics correspondent, George Cyriax, examined spare capacity in the economy and concluded there was enough to justify Macmillan's new, less cautious Chancellor, Reginald Maudling, initiating 'a small stimulus'; Macmillan himself went to lunch at the Baltic Exchange and addressed a thousand or so cheerful brokers and clerks, before going on to inspect the new Chelsea Barracks, housed in two 13-storey concrete tower blocks; Brooke ordered Bryan's release from Holloway Prison pending a Commons debate on her case; latest figures showed 300 cinemas as having closed in the year ending March 1962, with audiences down 12 per cent as television exercised an ever-tighter grip on leisure time; the world's first passenger-carrying hovercraft service ('not quite as comfortable as a private car, but better than a double-decker bus', pronounced one passenger, 'marvellous' kept repeating another) went into operation across the Dee estuary from Wallasey to Rhyl; and Birmingham's latest development scheme (four new shopping precincts and a fourteen-storey tower block rising above Corporation Street) was announced, with the developers (Jack Cotton's Raventop outfit) promising that 'the design will open the shopping to light and air on every side, creating larger areas of open space than ever before existed in the city centre'. At Lord's that morning, the newly crowned Dexter came out to bat for the Gentlemen, with a photograph revealing five of the professionals in shot (including the Players' captain, Fred Trueman) applauding him but four choosing to keep their hands studiously apart.[2] The match itself finished as a draw – late-afternoon rain preventing a likely win for the Players – and thirteen cricketers and two umpires left the field of play not knowing that this most socially piquant of fixtures, first contested at Lord's in 1806, would never be seen on the ground again.

Saturday the 21st was the end of the Haines family holiday at Homelea Camp (Ione buying the *Express* for her father, but it 'didn't contain sufficient cricket news', so Pamela got him the *Telegraph*); that morning's big cricket news was a fulminating Fred Trueman being sent home after reporting late for Yorkshire's match at Taunton, accounts differing as to cause of lateness; that evening, more than 300 railway enthusiasts were aboard for the last passenger train to run on the branch line from Wellington (Salop) to Much Wenlock via Coalbrookdale, its front carrying an inverted spray of roses and a notice saying, 'The Beeching Special (he's broke)'; the maverick record producer Joe Meek spent the weekend putting the finishing touches to the version by the Tornados of his very recently composed instrumental number still known as 'The Theme of Telstar', due for release in August; Penelope Gilliatt in the *Observer* gave a scathing review to the new film *Some People* starring Kenneth More, 'a fictionalised propaganda piece for the Duke of Edinburgh Award Scheme' with such a 'soggy, priggish script' and a tone which 'so exactly reproduces the beefiness of a clergyman on *Sunday Break*' that 'it is no wonder it has nothing to do with art'; Lord Cromer on the 23rd assured Sir George Bolton that the Bank of England was 'sympathetic' to his proposal to establish in London a long-term, dollar-denominated capital market and would 'give it what practical support we can'; the Vickers hovercraft ran aground that day on a sandbank on its return trip from Rhyl to Wallasey, with Ken Dodd among those left stranded; a Commons debate that evening ended with Brooke reluctantly cancelling the deportation order ('I warn people that they are not to think that if they commit an offence and are recommended for deportation they can then count on escaping deportation because of the case of Miss Bryan'); 'Saw TELSTAR

Europe-to-U.S. and U.S.-to-Europe programmes', recorded that night
14-year-old Roger Darlington, living in Manchester, after an evening
starting with 'Go, Europe, Go' from the American end and a more
restrained 'Hello, North America' from Richard Dimbleby at this end
against the backdrop of pictures of Big Ben and a London policeman;
Tuesday began with the *Daily Herald*'s new regular TV critic, Dennis
Potter, mulling over *Coronation Street* ('strange that in this slick, neon-
lit age, we should find solace in the gossipy vindictiveness of old ladies
in hair nets'), followed by the truly right-field news that the manager
of the MCC's tour of Australia was to be the Duke of Norfolk, an
announcement which had the *Daily Telegraph*'s E. W. Swanton
looking forward unreservedly to the Earl Marshal's 'brave adventure';
Wednesday evening featured the latest *Bucknell's House*, as the D-I-Y
guru Barry Bucknell continued converting a London terraced house
into two separate dwellings, earning the highest possible praise ('He
is one of "us"') from a viewer who was a traffic marshal; the Court
of Appeal on Thursday the 26th rejected the habeas corpus claim of
Robert Soblen, the 61-year-old Soviet spy who had fled the US while
on bail and, having got to Britain in early July in a sick state, was
seeking asylum; Macmillan that afternoon successfully came through
a no-confidence debate, which included a maiden speech by one of
his backbenchers, John Biffen, championing the government's new
incomes policy; competing attractions that evening were the Beatles
at Southport's theatre-like Cambridge Hall (only Joe Brown and the
Bruvvers above them on the bill) and on BBC TV *The Good Old
Days* (as usual from City Varieties, Leeds, a typically high RI of 72,
and the ventriloquist Ray Alan and 'Lord Charles' the most popular
act); on Friday, *The Times*'s art critic, reviewing the 'Four Young
Artists' exhibition at the ICA gallery in Dover Street, hailed David
Hockney as 'a fantasist with an entrancingly original imagination in
which quaintness and caricature are combined', while warning that
though 'the balance is perfectly held, pretentiousness and whimsicality
seem to yawn on either side'; that evening on *It's My Opinion* (a
kind of early version of *Question Time*, with in fact a 23-year-old
David Dimbleby in the chair), Patricia de Trafford visibly stumped
Labour's Anthony Wedgwood Benn with the question, 'If you're not
going to have profits, what are you going to invest with?'; Saturday

the 28th featured an epic traffic jam on the Exeter bypass ('you can still walk from one end of the by-pass to the other on the roofs of queuing vehicles', reported the AA after ten hours); Richard Hoggart next day made his debut as the *Observer*'s temporary TV critic, calling *Coronation Street* 'a complicated and shifting combination of virtuosity, glossy production, good insights and exact dialogue all mixed together with banal situations and stereotyped dialogue'; and Macmillan spent the day at Chequers with senior party colleagues and advisers.

Inevitably not present was Selwyn Lloyd, abruptly ejected from No. 11 a fortnight earlier – although, while trying to find a flat in London, he had left his black Labrador, Sambo, in the temporary care of the staff at Chequers. 'As Macmillan sat on the terrace that balmy July evening, chatting expansively about the middle way ahead, other members of the entourage gradually became aware of the inquisitive presence of Sambo, walking along the line of the assembled company, vainly looking for his master,' relates the political biographer D. R. Thorpe about the moment the group photograph was about to be taken. 'The dog eventually settled in front of Macmillan, gazing mournfully up at him. Those who were present never forgot the frisson that went through the gathering, nor the studied disregard with which Macmillan ignored the animal, knowing better than most what memories its presence evoked.'[3]

Something else was going on during these summer days and nights. The most obvious, attention-attracting symptom was Sir Oswald Mosley, who on 22 July, three weeks after Colin Jordan's Nazi rally, held his own London rally. 'Serious fighting this afternoon with Mosley's gangsters in Trafalgar Square; a large crowd of 8,000 people, 300 police, 50 arrests,' noted Hugh Selbourne, a leading Manchester doctor. 'Psychopaths, preaching hatred to the neurotically unstable masses, should be taken into custody and given ECT to rehabilitate them.' A week later, Mosley and his anti-Semitic, anti-black Union Movement supporters were marching through the back streets of east Manchester ('Why is Racial Incitement not banned by law?' wondered Selbourne), protected by 250 policemen and, in the words of one report, 'surrounded by hundreds of bawling, jeering, jostling, and fighting detractors'. Two days later, the 31st, it was the turn, more than a quarter of a century after the Battle of Cable Street, of east

London – specifically, Dalston's Ridley Road – resulting in fifty-four arrests, including that of Mosley's 22-year-old son Max, who had joined in the scuffle around his father that saw Sir Oswald knocked down and kicked. Next morning, the Oxford student was cleared at Old Street Court of using threatening behaviour, but altogether more important were the after-effects of his father's latest reappearance on the British scene.

'RASH OF MOSLEY SIGNS IN CLAPHAM', invariably of forked lightning inside a circle, reported the *South London Press* on 10 August, detailing recent 'cowardly attacks' in the area on the property of 'a number of coloured people'; also on the 10th, members of the London County Council were recalled from their holidays to discuss race hate, with one of them, Ashley Bramall, reading aloud an essay by a fifteen-year-old Brixton schoolboy:

In the year 1962 Brixton all black and very few white people about. Blacks live together as many as four families to one room, taking white men's jobs and living on vice as well as the National Assistance.

Big marches with banners saying 'Chuck all wogs out', and shouting 'Keep Britain White', causing trouble and fights leading to the slaughter of all wogs and wog-lovers.

In the end Britain is all white and not a mixed, smelly, dirty race.

The meeting ended with the LCC unanimously deciding to ask the government to make incitement to violence by racial hatred a criminal offence. But of course racial hatred took other forms as well, and about this time one black man, Oliver Jackman, returned to England and found it – after eight years of significantly higher immigration numbers – much less tolerant than the country where he had lived between 1949 and 1954:

The unpleasant truth [he reflected in September] is that people like myself cannot long live in, or be tolerant about, a country where more than once taxi drivers have made a face when I flagged them in broad daylight and where I have once had to call a policeman to stop one for me at night. (And this is *commerce*!)

Where the most insensitive, undemanding coloured man can report a whole new gamut of hostile pressures: glances of distaste in public places that make one look round to see what rule one is unwittingly breaking: is one's hair too long, one's dress or voice too loud, what has one done to make the wonderful English policeman impatient and unfriendly in giving a simple direction? Why does a black face now close up an English face as tight as a bank at midnight?

'And more and more of us are realising', he concluded, 'that there is one answer to all the questions: we are here.'⁴

Some of the highest concentrations of non-white immigrant numbers were in the West Midlands. 'There are areas of Birmingham where a virtual breakdown of our accepted standards has taken place,' declared on 20 July a report from a local Conservative Political Centre study group. 'It cannot be right or in the interest of the country that this state of affairs should continue.' About a week later, there started in the Worcestershire town of Dudley, traditional centre of the iron industry, a sequence of four consecutive nights of race riots and disturbances, including one night when 150 to 200 white men, 'armed with sticks, stones, chair legs, coshes, and bottles', marched into the black quarter in North Street and, added the town's Deputy Chief Constable subsequently giving evidence to magistrates, behaved 'like a pack of ravening wolves after their prey'. 'I have been here for eight years and made white friends,' a West Indian woman told *The Times*'s indefatigable Midland Correspondent. 'In fact, a white neighbour has offered to protect me if I need it this week. I cannot understand why this has suddenly started here. It makes you feel sick inside.' Why indeed the troubles, especially given that the town's non-white population, divided roughly equally between West Indians and Pakistanis, was only about 1,000 in a borough of 65,000? 'Of about 40 people whom I asked for their views on the situation, a number were convinced the coloureds must be running prostitutes to be able to afford houses and cars in spite of police certainty to the contrary,' noted one visiting journalist. 'Some were aggrieved that West Indians should still be in jobs when some whites were on short time. Others recalled with resentment occasions when they had had to queue on equal terms with coloured people in applying for jobs.'

Resentment too in Smethwick, 'a Black Country industrial town', noted the AA's gazetteer, where 'James Watt's first engine was set up at the Soho foundry'. There the seat belonged to Labour's rather patrician spokesman on home affairs, Patrick Gordon Walker, but an ambitious, energetic young Conservative councillor, Peter Griffiths, had his eyes on it. 'We do not want another Varna Road in Smethwick,' he wrote in the local paper (the *Smethwick Telephone*) on 20 July, referring to the road in Birmingham notorious for its prostitutes; on 2 August he warned that a single incident could spark off race riots in Smethwick similar to those in Dudley; next day he reflected in the *Telephone*, 'How easy to support uncontrolled immigration when one lives in a garden suburb', a dig at Gordon Walker living in Hampstead Garden Suburb; and on the 12th his forum was a national paper. 'I feel that we should keep the white/coloured ratio in true proportion,' he asserted in the *People*. 'We want to see whites in these roads where coloured people are living so that they can set an example to the coloureds, and live free from racial troubles.'[5] Griffiths and Smethwick: two names with plenty of charged mileage still left in them.

August began with the 500th *Twenty Questions* on the radio ('Anona Winn, Joy Adamson, Jack Train, Richard Dimbleby ask all the questions and Kenneth Horne knows some of the answers'), Ken and Val getting hitched on *Coronation Street* (most of the women crying through the service, Emily Nugent depressed afterwards that she's been a bridesmaid but never a bride), and a senior scientist at the Microbiological Research Establishment at Porton Down dying that night from pneumonic plague, causing a major flap. Next day, Thursday the 2nd, Brooke stated that he could do nothing for the Soviet spy Soblen; on the 3rd, Northampton's local paper announced with satisfaction that work was to start immediately on the next two stages of the M1 extension; and on the 4th, 'Right, Said Fred', the humorous but faintly macabre tale of three movers and a piano as related by Bernard Cribbins, reached its highest position (10th) in the charts. That Saturday was also the annual church fete at Loders Court in Dorset, courtesy of the village's new squire, the Hon. Alexander Hood, following the recent death of Sir Edward Le Breton. On a rare day of glorious sunshine, and with 'band blaring, stalls doing a roaring trade and sideshows up to the neck in all the fun of the fair', the Rev. Oliver Willmott was able to itemise in his next parish notes gross takings in excess of £255:

Gate 16-9-9 [that is, £16 9s 9d]; Teas 28-12-4; Donations 18-14-11; Cakes 19-11-10; New Stall 20-4-4; Ices 6-10-0; Flowers 5-11-0; China 6-17-4; Jumble 8-2-6; Books 1-0-0; Photos 1-2-6; Toys 2-18-6; Produce 9-12-6; Bottles 23-14-0; Dottery [nearby village, part of the parish] stall 21-10-0; Skittles 6-9-9; Roulette 19-13-4; Fishing 5-15-9; Hidden Treasure 2-10-6; Ping-pong 19-11; Chinese Laundry 2-5-6; Rifle Range 1-3-0; Colour Slides [as exhibited by Miss Punshon, the district nurse] 2-2-6; Darts 2-0-0; Pennies-in-bath 11-5; Pony Rides 1-19-0; Fortunes 3-1-0; Hairstyling 7-0; Budgerigars 5-3-3; Port 5-2-6; Chocolates 3-8-6; Bath Set 2-6-0.

With expenses (including £9 for St Swithun's Band and £10 4s for prizes) amounting to barely £26, the gratifying outcome was a record balance of £228 16s 8d to help maintain the church's fabric. 'We are not unmindful of all the work and giving done cheerfully by our present residents,' gratefully reflected Willmott. 'They are written in the Vicar's Book of Life.'⁶

Richard Hoggart was on pop duty next day in his second *Observer* stint – *Juke Box Jury* 'showing ever-increasing signs of strain and tiredness'; *Needle Match* still trying 'to have everything: a panel (British and American), a matey chairman, a visiting celebrity singer as well as the dance routines'; the broadcasters continuing to 'under-estimate their audience' – but it was a Sunday more notable for Nelson Mandela being recaptured and news coming through that a troubled Hollywood spirit had set herself free, though only the latter event having an immediate global impact. 'Poor little Marilyn Monroe,' reflected Nella Last in Barrow. 'I wonder if she suddenly felt she had reached the end of the road. If I was asked to choose a "top ten" pitiful figures, she would be in them – I mean of "today". Her "wistful" appeal I should think equalled her "sex" appeal … She would have made a darling tired Mum for the two little babies she didn't have.' Then, after two sunny days, came the rain, causing the biggest August Bank Holiday wash-out for years. Record entries (233 in the singles, 140 in the pairs) at Bexhill-on-Sea for the bowls tournament, and the

Mayor duly bowled the first two woods under dark clouds overhead, before torrential rain in the afternoon led to the loss of more than four hours' play and matches being decided on the toss of a coin. That evening, while Selbourne as usual watched *Panorama* ('some parts of Marilyn Monroe's films were shown, and Dame Sybil Thorndike said a few words about her'), for Last it was her own regular Monday line-up to make the time pass pleasantly enough: 'The Archers, All Our Yesterdays, Coronation St & Bonanza, & then bed.'[7]

Over the rest of the week, a poll in the *Express* revealed that Alf Ramsey (whose Ipswich Town had recently been First Division champions) was narrowly the readers' choice to succeed Walter Winterbottom as manager of the England football team; Philip Larkin, staying in his mother's house in Loughborough, told a friend how he had 'foolishly' taken her 'on a *bus excursion* into the *Peak District* wch didn't end till nearly *10* – God, I must *never* do such a *mad* thing again: it was boring, irritating *hell*'; a British couple now living in America cut short by a month their holiday to see old friends in and around Colne in Lancashire because, Mr and Mrs William Hounslow told a reporter at Manchester Airport, 'whenever we suggested an evening out it seemed people were either about to watch "Coronation Street" or were too busy discussing it to do anything else'; Last reckoned *No Hiding Place* 'tonight with its "delinquents" not as entertaining but, I suppose, really a slice of life today'; the Bishop of Bath and Wells pronounced 'Splendid, splendid' after three laps of go-karting at Castle Combe; and Sir Laurence Olivier was appointed as the first director of the National Theatre, to be based temporarily at the Old Vic pending a new permanent home, hopefully in the not-too-distant future, on the South Bank.[8]

Among the weeklies, the *New Statesman* noted in an editorial that 'gradually the full facts of the great thalidomide scandal are becoming known' (by this time some 5,000 deformed babies in West Germany, compared to about 600 in Britain), profiled the rising young Conservative politician Peter Walker ('in all the years of Tory affluence there has never been a personal advertisement for the Opportunity State to rival him'), and had Francis Williams in his Fleet Street column calling it 'a sad reflection' on 'what much of the public really wants' that the *Daily Mail* under William Hardcastle's editorship was moving in a more liberal direction but failing to pick up circulation. But the stand-out article (based on a talk for the BBC's European Service) was in the *Listener*, where Malcolm Bradbury, 29-year-old English lecturer at the University of Birmingham, contemplated 'Literary Culture in England Today':

> The literary intelligence as a cultural force, as a way of knowing, is not, I think, as central as once it was. Society seems to seek a new way of knowing. Sir Charles Snow thinks science can provide it; my own view is that we are moving away in England from the traditional liberal culture, centred on literature, to a new and less liberal and more descriptive kind of culture based not on science, which is specialist, but on sociology. Society is what, in our moral fragmentation and our mass social circumstances, we now have in common. Sociology is one of the most pervasive of subjects within the university, and one of the most popular. Sociology is practised by the mass media. It is even practised by the novel, which now tends to be descriptive and provincial, not concerned to chart the international modern mind but simply to show social progress, often from the point of view of the under-privileged. The kind of writer who is committed to an ideal of civilization seems to give way to the anti-cultural writer, the writer who, in fact, sees no use for art.

'In our new epistemology,' concluded the future author of *The History Man* in a rather gloomy early take on the seemingly irresistible rise of sociology, 'we know not by judging but by describing, and there is nothing we are not entitled to know. In a general loss of shared values, culture thus becomes a way of coping with the world by defining it in detail.'[9]

The holiday season was now, whatever the vagaries of the weather, moving into full swing. Anthony Heap and his son Frainy set off on Saturday the 11th for the newly opened Butlin's holiday camp in Minehead; a Giles cartoon in the *Sunday Express* showed rain pouring down as Grandma and co. trudged away grumbling from a seaside boarding house; and Selbourne in Manchester noted on Monday that it was the 'beginning of Wakes holiday', with 'most people absent at Arnfields', the Audenshaw engineering works where he was visiting doctor. Still comfortably in pole position among British seaside resorts, Blackpool featured all through August an impressive roster of familiar names: Thora Hird at the Grand Theatre, Ken Dodd at the Opera House, Arthur Haynes in a record-breaking season at the Winter Gardens, Harry Worth and Bert Weedon among Bernard Delfont's Show of Stars at the North Pier pavilion, Sooty and Sweep in the South Pier's Rainbow Theatre – the list was almost endless. Blackpool, of course, was not necessarily typical, and Keighley's Gladys Hague, on holiday in Fleetwood the previous month with her sister, 'noticed many shops and cafés closed' and 'a general air of depression'. 'In conversation with some Cleethorpes people,' she added, 'we learnt how quiet it was there, that weather had been very poor and that the resort only came alive on Sundays. Partly the result I should say of so many people with their own cars.' Even so, to judge by the setpiece account by the writer Richard West of the scene around mid-August in Morecambe (nicknamed 'Bradford-on-Sea'), the traditional British seaside holiday still had life in it:

> On the beach you can hear snatches of hymn from a Salvation Army group with a squeeze-box; whippets run rings round the Shetland ponies; someone has decked the towers of a sandcastle with Commonwealth flags. Father may dirty his brilliantly-shined shoes with a spot of cricket or catch. Mother tucks herself up in a deck-chair in a cocoon of rugs, sweaters and plastic macs …
>
> In spite of its roulette and a Chinese restaurant, Morecambe remains utterly old-fashioned English. In a week of the high season you would be most unlikely to find a foreign car licence or hear a foreign language. The town is so stuck with its English conception of pleasure that, although the illuminations this year were gayer than ever, pub opening time on Saturday night has actually been reduced by half an hour. And Morecambe demands the traditional food: 'No jam roll?' I heard a diner say, 'Give over! There must be.'

Hundreds of miles away, in Newquay and other places on the north Cornwall coast, a new seaside culture, little noticed at the time, was under way: the start of British surfing, after four young Australian lifeguards had brought with them from Sydney the first fibreglass surfboard seen in the country.

Yet perhaps the most emblematic holiday experience this summer belonged to the 13-year-old future historian Robert Colls, who at the end of July, once school had broken up, set off from South Shields to a Boys' Brigade camp at Humshaugh in Northumberland. 'We went in the back of a lorry up to Gateshead, over the Tyne bridge, through Newcastle, and out west,' he would recall almost half a century later. 'Passing the folks along the road, we waved and shouted. There were no seats, though someone had neatly folded coal sacks for our benefit.' His account ends with the backward-looking meditativeness of age and the future-facing exhilaration of youth. 'The same place is never the same place twice. The past looms up on every corner, but not the same for you as for me. On my first journey out, in July 1962, where there had once been trams and bustling streets, the people of Scotswood Road in Newcastle's west end [at the sharp end of the city's transformation under T. Dan Smith] saw only demolition, dirt, high-rise blocks and the back end of a coal wagon. On that wagon looking forward and waving, however, I saw only New York skyscrapers, the coming summer, and the road to indescribable happiness.'[10]

The PM began his summer break on the Glorious Twelfth, leaving by train for Lord Swinton's grouse-laden Yorkshire estate and expressing hopes of 'fair game'; the papers that Sunday featured Hoggart's penultimate TV column (Benny Hill 'a fugal comedian in both the musical and the psychological senses' whose 'scripts can't always take the strain' as he 'moves them into the insecurely grotesque'), models in a *Sunday Times* fashion item posing contentedly against the ironwork of the condemned Coal Exchange, and Peter Griffiths quoted in the left-leaning *Reynolds News* ('My purpose is to bring about better integration between the coloured and white communities') as well as the *People*; Larkin next day had his regular *Archers* fix ('I wonder if they are working up to making Dawn Kingsley an unmarried mother?'); following the government's easing in early June of hire-purchase restrictions, Great Universal Stores reported continuing buoyant summer sales of 'white goods' such as refrigerators and washing machines; Fife Council warned tenants of much stronger action against those failing to keep their gardens in proper order ('tenants knew when the annual visitation of gardens was to be made and had the gardens in fairly good shape for that, but the following month the gardens would again be covered in weeds'); and Jacqueline du Pré, still seventeen, made on the Tuesday her Proms debut at a packed-out Albert Hall. Calling her 'the first of the postwar generation of soloists to emerge from prodigyhood', *The Times*'s critic put in broader generational context her performance of Elgar's cello concerto:

> Miss du Pré is a remarkable interpreter and cellist, but her attitude to Elgar's concerto was that of a thinking adult and not of an intuitively musical child. It is her generation, and not her youth, that makes some episodes in this old man's retrospective concerto sound unconvincing – they are no longer meaningful to our world – and the rest of it free from all the unappetizing self-indulgence that can be the failing of the piece.

A debut too, on Wednesday the 15th, for the British Motor Corporation's Morris 1100, forerunner of the Austin 1100 Countryman which one evening on the outskirts of Torquay would receive a 'damn good thrashing' from Basil Fawlty; while on the news-stands by this time was the August issue of *Queen* magazine, whose associate editor, Robin Douglas-Home, dropped into his column a seemingly random reference to how a 'chauffeur-driven Zil drew up at her *front* door' just as 'out of the *back* door into a chauffeur-driven Humber' slipped someone else. Those relatively few in the know knew that the man in the Zil was a Soviet naval attaché, the man in the Humber was the Secretary of State for War, and that the 'her' being visited was a young model called Christine Keeler.[11] A year or more after the start of the story by a swimming pool at Cliveden, this particular shooting game was at last on.

––––

'No one who lived in Lancashire, in Yorkshire, and in the North-East during the late fifties and early sixties could fail to be aware that these areas were gradually falling behind the national averages in many ways – in tolerable housing conditions, in mortality, in investment, and, above all, in employment,' asserted Geoffrey Moorhouse (born in Bolton, educated at Bury Grammar School) in 1964. 'But until the late summer of 1962', he went on, 'there was precious little sign that the whole country recognized this situation. As far as the Government was concerned it seemed that it was being allowed to drift along on the assumption that something would eventually turn up to put things to rights. The article in the *Guardian* was some kind of turning point.'

The article he referred to appeared on 15 August, was by George Taylor (chief education officer for Leeds) and had the headline 'The gulf between North and South'. Soberly, he set out what he saw as the big and undeniable national picture, though with special reference to inequality of educational opportunity:

The nine county boroughs in England with the highest standard mortality rate (i.e. the crude death rate corrected for the age structure of the populations) are in the industrial North; the 10 county boroughs with the lowest mortality rate are south of a line drawn from the Severn to the Thames. Whatever the reasons may be for this difference in longevity, they are unlikely to affect the level of intelligence of the children in these areas, but they will affect their environment and consequently their educational progress. Overcrowding, poor living conditions, and polluted atmosphere – all contributory causes of the high death rate – will, among children, lead to frequent absences from school and a lack of vitality in school; the high death rate (which includes not only death from illness but from accidents in foundry, mill, and mine) leaves a number of families with only one parent – a well-known reason for children terminating their school life as soon as it is legally possible to do so; a high death rate implies a high sickness rate (whether due to illness or accident) among parents, another factor discouraging extended education among children.

'The northern child', reckoned Taylor on the basis of considerable professional experience, 'will receive his education in an old, insanitary building planned on lines wholly inappropriate for contemporary teaching, his teachers will be too few in number, probably inexperienced, possibly unqualified, and constantly changing'; and, he concluded, unless the industrial north began to receive substantial financial support, 'it will not take a generation to complete the establishment of two nations, or, in contemporary language, two cultures, divided by a line from the Humber to the Wirral'. According to Moorhouse, it was this article which triggered, over the next two years, a sustained national debate in the press and on TV and radio. 'The idea that over the past few years two Englands have taken shape, one in the North the other in the South, unequal socially and economically, has become our major domestic preoccupation.'

The coal industry in decline, the cotton industry in decline, the steel industry in decline, docks in decline, unemployment two to three times the level of southern England, population drifting southwards – little wonder that many city councils in the north were by now resting hopes on large-scale urban redevelopment, including the most up-to-date retail centres, as a key way to help break the downward cycle. Understandably in this context, local boosterism often ran rife, typified by the case of Liverpool. 'Brilliantly conceived' was the *Liverpool Echo*'s view in September 1962 of the projected new shopping centre, St John's Precinct – part of the comprehensive redevelopment scheme presented that month by the city's visionary planning consultant, Graeme Shankland, at the heart of which was a forty-acre pedestrian precinct accompanied by a 320-foot tower block above the Central Station concourse. 'Altogether these plans are unique, there is nothing like this anywhere in this country, nothing even in Europe, outside Venice,' declared Alderman H. Macdonald Steward, chair of the Development and Planning Committee, acclaiming their 'astonishing architectural ingenuity'. As for the *Liverpool Weekly News*, civic pride was unconfined. 'This, then, is the city centre of the future,' it trumpeted. 'With far-reaching developments such as this, the whole world can see how this lusty growing city is casting off its long-held reputation as a city of slums and is pinning its faith in all that is best in this revolutionary space age.'[12]

If that was one possible route – though, in the event, deeply flawed – to a northern renaissance, then popular culture represented another. By summer 1962 the cinema's British New Wave, majoring on emphatically non-southern social realism, was an established fact: *Room at the Top* (1959), *Saturday Night and Sunday Morning* (1960), *A Taste of Honey* (1961), *A Kind of Loving* (April 1962) already in the bag; *The Loneliness of the Long Distance Runner* due for release in September; and *This Sporting Life* and *Billy Liar* both in progress, due for release in 1963. But would the phenomenon, giving the north an extended and richly treated moment in the cultural sun it had arguably never quite had before, last? And if not, would Granada's twice-weekly offering of *Coronation Street*, simultaneously intriguing and repelling middle-class viewers, be enough to take up the slack? Or were the new northern voices, cutting through the national consciousness, going to come from somewhere completely different? Questions, questions – and probably not being asked during these actual real-time weeks and months of 1962.

'Had a lovely day in London,' recorded Judy Haines in Chingford on Thursday, 16 August after taking her daughters and Danielle (Pam's French penfriend who had been staying with them) up to town:

> Bus to Piccadilly (had to change in Bakers Arms!). We had coffee at Lyons in Lower Regent Street. Through St James's Park to Admiralty (across Horse Guards' Parade), we saw the Changing of the Guard. Danielle also snapped the lake, and musicians marching from Buckingham Palace. We walked to Hyde Park Corner where we lunched in Lyons. After lunch we went to Kensington High St shops, where an elderly assistant failed to sell me a pink coat.
>
> Danielle bought her presents of chocolates. I bought a box of 'Ballerina' chocs for her parents and Danielle an Everly Bros record. I also treated girls to combs with gold lettering 'DANIELLE', 'IONE' and 'PAM'.
>
> There is a boy's and girl's Exhibition at Olympia but we hadn't time or energy. Visited gardens on roof of Derry & Toms, paying 1/- each – for charity.

No charity for poor Pete Best, the Beatles drummer whom Brian Epstein, sitting behind his desk in his Liverpool office, summarily sacked that morning. 'It was vicious and back-handed,' recalled Best a quarter of a century later, 'and I felt like putting a stone round my neck and jumping off the Pier Head.' Over on the east coast, Alan Ayckbourn's production of *The Caretaker* played in the evening to a packed house at the Library Theatre, Scarborough, with high praise from the local paper's drama critic about the contribution of Pinter, among others, to 'ending the hitherto undisputed sway of middle-class idiom':

> The three characters, the old tramp and the two brothers who almost take him in to look after their flat, are completely real, credible human beings. And yet their relationship, their situation itself, has all the mystery and depth of a poetical dimension. This is perhaps the quality of the play which points into the future. For the future may well belong to a new type of drama which will be realistic and poetic at the same time. Stanley Page, excellent as the tramp in Studio Theatre's in-the-round production, shows that, although he wants to 'communicate', wants to get on with people, he does not, like many of us, really want to get involved with them.

A less challenging watch was to be found on BBC TV, as *Dr Finlay's Casebook*, set in interwar rural Scotland, made its debut. 'Compared with the shiny surface of Dr Kildare's world,' thought Dennis Potter, 'this was a neat little study in social history,' while an RI of 73 boded well for the rest of the series.[13]

Next day the *Bideford and North Devon Gazette* announced that David Owen, a 24-year-old doctor at St Thomas' Hospital in London, had been chosen as prospective Labour candidate for Torrington; the PM, still in pursuit of grouse, moved on to the Duke of Devonshire's estate at Bolton Abbey; William Burroughs in Paris told a friend that, 'principally motivated by all expenses paid and prospect of seeing twenty-five Cuban writers who are scheduled to appear', he was on his way 'to a writer's conference in Edinburgh'; Roger Darlington, staying with his grandmother near Dudley, after lunch went with her into Wolverhampton and 'bought a box of gramophone record needles (each play 20) – price 2/3 – and my first balsa-wood aircraft kit, a Keil Kraft Sedan'; news that English Electric would be closing its Luton factory (following the government's recent abandonment of the Blue Water surface-to-surface guided missile) prompted the secretary of the local trades council to pronounce that 'this is the end of Luton as a boom town'; Beethoven's Eroica Symphony on the Third Programme was, noted Selbourne, 'suddenly interrupted by a Pop-Singer'; and Alan Plater's second TV play, *A Smashing Day* featuring John Thaw, caused one critic to hail it as 'the voice of *Coronation Street* with the spirit of Chekhov'. Earlier that evening it was the turn again of *It's My Opinion*, with (according to one appreciative viewer, an architect) a 'nicely balanced' panel of 'a wit [Michael Flanders], a beauty [Nemone Lethbridge, in fact one of Britain's first female barristers] and a solid citizen [Lord Mancroft]'. By a small majority, the general opinion among viewers was that the chairman 'coped very well' and indeed, added several, 'was improving week by week in his control of the proceedings'. Others, however, wondered whether he was 'sufficiently mature' to be 'elevated' to this sort of programme. 'David Dimbleby', commented a sceptical viewer, 'is too young to handle this as yet. The questions, at least one anyhow, about Thalidomide, were hardly for his years and experience.'[14]

The new football season began on Saturday, with Bobby Moore, Geoff Hurst and Martin Peters all playing in West Ham's 3–1 defeat at Villa Park. 'I have only one complaint about football – it is about the number of "moaners" in the game,' wrote Sheffield Wednesday's homegrown star Tony Kay, a 25-year-old wing-half on the fringes of the England team, in *Charles Buchan's Soccer Gift Book, 1962–1963*. 'By "moaners" I mean those players who are never satisfied with their lot and are always wanting something more. Usually, they are the types who take all they can from professional Soccer and put nothing back. I can't understand their attitude.' As for his own future: 'I intend to stay at the top as long as I can. It took me a long time to get there.' That afternoon in West Sussex, entries for the Rustington Flower Show were up from 206 to 543, but that was small beer compared to Port Sunlight's seventeenth annual Flower Show, where the day culminated, once all the exhibits had been cleared from Hulme Hall, in an evening performance by the Beatles, now for the first time with Ringo on drums. 'I am told that this Common Market will make good French wine prohibitively expensive here,' was Evelyn Waugh's grumble on Sunday to Nancy Mitford; the Third Programme featured Sylvia Plath's *Three Women*, a set of soliloquies from a maternity ward, prompting the response from one (male) critic that 'although they were read [Jill Balcon one of the performers] in the kind of actressy manner which does nothing for any poetry, it seems unlikely that, even in print, they would amount to much'; and Hoggart signed off as a TV critic, taking particular aim at ITV's *No Hiding Place*:

This edition had the usual technical efficiency; it was easily watched. But it was full of automatic scriptwriting, built around its 'natural' breaks, riddled with rock-bottom character clichés (a poet was a silly dodderer in a velvet jacket; a psychiatrist was a whinnying polysyllabic screwball by the side of the granitic Superintendent).

I don't believe these kinds of faults are more than a little excused by the pressures of weekly production. They more often come from an unconscious decision that, since 'they' seem to be willing to sit quietly through almost any story which has suspense, there's not much point in thinking freshly.

'Perhaps I may make a final wish on behalf of both channels,' he concluded. 'It is that they try harder to shake off their most pervasive common fault – mindless cosiness.'[15]

'I have braved the outside world with a new hair style – at last,' noted Judy Haines on Tuesday the 21st, the same day that Sir Winston Churchill left the Middlesex Hospital, his broken thigh healed, after almost two months. 'A French roll,' she added. 'John thinks he will get used to it.' Next day, the new issue of the *Architects' Journal* included 'Astragal' appraising Jane Jacobs's *The Death and Life of Great American Cities*, causing waves since its American publication in 1961 and now on its way to British bookshops. 'So readable and persuasive,' he reckoned, 'it could quite likely be the death of low-density planning and zoning by use.' And he went on:

As you probably know by now, it is a hymn of praise to crowded, multi-use streets, with their interlocked patterns of neighbourliness, community spirit and trade, none of which ever seem to survive urban renewal. Friends in Swiss Cottage and St John's Wood tell me that community break-up is happening up there at the moment – clean new redevelopment is not only breaking up the social patterns of mews-living, but it is also turfing out the small personal-service shops (on which they, like Mrs Jacobs, place a high value) because they cannot hope to pay the new rents. So the area is being denuded of ironmongers, radio-TV repairmen, little cafés, even quality grocers, and other tradesmen whom the supermarket cannot replace.

No complaints that Wednesday, though, from West Worthing's 13-year-old Diana Griffith. 'We all went to London, arr. 11 am. Had lunch in the Chicken Inn (Baker St.). Fantab. After lunch (3 pm!) walked down Oxford Street. Luverly. Got shoes in Dolcis. Fab!' Judy and the girls escorted Danielle to Folkestone to catch the ferry home, with Danielle's last words to them from the jetty, 'My boomerang won't come back!', a nod to Charlie Drake's novelty hit of the previous autumn. The Beatles were filmed by Granada TV playing a lunchtime gig at the Cavern, where a man shouted out, 'We want Pete!'; Everton's first home match of the season (a 3–1 win over Manchester Utd) had the boys in blue running out for the first time to Johnny Keating's 'Theme from Z-Cars'; and Anthony Heap took an evening stroll. 'The square garden, with its elaborate new café, fountains, flower-beds and rockeries, has been redesigned, trimmed up and altered almost out of recognition during the last three or four years,' he noted about the revamped Russell Square. 'It all looks, in fact, as new and spruce as the recently built and opened President Hotel on the east side of the square between the stately turn of the century piles of The Russell and The Imperial. But I liked the old square better. It wasn't so darned tourist conscious.'[16]

Thursday saw the unveiling by an ICI subsidiary, Plant Protection Ltd, of the paraquat weedkiller given the appealingly neutral-sounding trade name of 'Gramoxone'. 'There are', declared a spokesman, 'millions of acres of poor permanent pasture which either cannot be ploughed or where ploughing is difficult. "Gramoxone" can be used at the rate of one gallon per acre to kill the existing sward. New and improved strains of grass can then be sown …' Paraquat rapidly became one of the most commonly used herbicides; but over time a link would be discovered between it and Parkinson's disease, leading to its being banned in the EU from 2007. Nothing about it in next day's *New Statesman*, but instead Malcolm Muggeridge's seasoned appraisal of the satire boom, above all the 'delightfully and offensively rude to one and all' *Private Eye*, almost a year old. Even so, he could not help but regret that the magazine lacked 'a sense of purpose' and was far from Swiftian: 'To *Private Eye*, authority is a schoolmaster, who, when his back is turned, can be pelted with paper darts and mocked with mimicry and funny faces. Such insubordination can easily be laughed off; boys will be boys.' Nella Last probably went to her grave oblivious of the very existence of Soho's finest. 'I see in our local Mail tonight', she recorded that Friday, 'a big garage in town has started giving "Green [Shield] Stamps" – 10 stamps given for a gallon of petrol or oil. Servicing from 50 stamps up to car radios from 1,500 stamps. Quite a new idea for Barrow ...'[17]

This was also the week of the Writers' Conference, running from the 20th to the 24th as part of the Edinburgh Festival and organised by the publisher John Calder and George Orwell's widow Sonia.[18] There were plenty of no-shows (Greene, Huxley, Sartre, Duras, Robbe-Grillet among them), but plenty of notable in-person appearances too: Henry Miller, Norman Mailer, Muriel Spark, Mary McCarthy, Rebecca West, Lawrence Durrell, Angus Wilson, Hugh MacDiarmid, Edwin Morgan, L. P. Hartley, Alexander Trocchi, Stephen Spender, Malcolm Muggeridge, Colin MacInnes, plus of course Burroughs. Monday was lively enough – McCarthy calling the French novel 'simply a form of dressmaking'; Spark rebutting Durrell's claim that literature should change people ('I think that for a novelist to try and change anybody, for anyone to try and change anybody, is horrible'); West declaring that 'it wouldn't matter if most of the critics now writing had been strangled at birth'; Wilson dismissing the English novel as 'essentially middle-class, a novel on the defensive, conservative, attempting to protect the English way of life, the English country way of life, against town life and against cosmopolitanism'; Burroughs describing to some audience incredulity his 'cut up' and 'fold in' method of writing *The Naked Lunch* – but the real sparks came on Tuesday, as two Scottish writers of different generations tried their hardest to take each other down. Trocchi claimed that all his own writing was inspired by sodomy; MacDiarmid called him 'a cosmopolitan scum', adding that people like him and Burroughs were 'vermin who should never have been invited to the conference'; and even the announcement by Mailer of the arrival of a baby daughter in New York failed to lighten the tone. Next day, after Hartley had expressed a preference for the term 'dedication' to 'commitment', MacDiarmid declared that he himself was 'the only fully committed writer present'; later in the session, following a flood of personal confessions, West wearily remarked that what was needed was a separate, non-literary conference, 'at which people could thrash out whether they were homosexuals, or heterosexual, or whatever'; on

Days (and Nights) of 1962

Harold Macmillan takes the Bromley Express

Above: first 'Bingo Special' train from London to Brighton, with members of the Top Rank Social Club from the Odeon, Hackney Road, on board

Right: Blackpool

Opposite: Great Windmill Street, Soho

Previous: Bangor City go one-up against Napoli

Punch Unit, Data Processing Centre, Shell Centre, Waterloo

Liverpool

Above: Pity Me, County Durham

Below: Number Two Court, Dickenson Street, Oldham

Above: Whetley Lane Secondary School, Bradford

Below: Devon

Waterloo Station

Temporary residents at a Salvation Army Home, Manchester

Above: Eastbourne

Below: Blackpool

Seventh-day Adventist Church, Holloway Road, London

Above: Grimsby dockers cycling to work

Below: The Potteries (Stoke-on-Trent)

Glasgow

London Pavilion, Piccadilly Circus

Thursday a debate on censorship had Mailer accusing Burroughs and Henry Miller of undermining the young ('sexual literature, you see, does weaken warlike potential because it tends to drain it'); and Spender applied a full stop on Friday by noting with patrician finality that 'everything that Mr Trocchi has said has been said in 1905'. 'Moral striptease artists only too ready to disrobe to their jock-straps and beyond,' was Muggeridge's verdict after it was all over. 'It was rather a relief to get in a sleeper and go away. I spent the week-end near Leeds, at a school for Yorkshire colliers, organised by the National Union of Mineworkers. Compared with the Writers, the colliers seemed almost fabulously attractive, articulate and amusing.'

That weekend, on Sunday the 26th, at a 'national protest meeting' against the Common Market at the Albert Hall, the ultra-patriotic Lord Sandwich, in a barely disguised anti-Semitic trope, inveighed against the 'merchants of the City of London' whose origins were in Hamburg and Frankfurt, adding that 'by their roots shall ye know them'. Next day, the Council of Industrial Design's annual report declared that 'unless modern British design can be recognised not only as modern but also as British, foreign buyers will naturally turn for their modern purchases to those countries [typically Sweden, Germany and Italy] that have established a recognisable national character in their work'; Madge Martin and her husband visited the nearly completed Guildford Cathedral ('entirely beautiful – clear, light, serene, uncluttered soaring lines – so unlike the restlessness of Coventry Cathedral'); and *The Parksider*, the programme for Hunslet's rugby league match at home to Bramley, invoked from Hoggart's old stamping ground the long reach of local collective memory, the time-tested right way of doing things:

Writing immediately after the game versus Hull K.R. [Kingston Rovers] we can well understand your feelings of disappointment as they coincide with ours. A lead of ten points should be sufficient to ensure victory but to see it frittered away is to put it very mildly, extremely galling. For what reason is it that the position has been reversed, when for years we could be relied upon to exert pressure in the last quarter of a game?

Memories are not dimmed in the passing years of the great 1907/8 team, the Four-Cup team, who hardly ever failed to grind their opponents into the ground during the last twenty minutes. It has been an unwritten law ever since, that on winning the toss we play uphill first and then in the second half call the tune.[19]

Nostalgia for the past or welcoming change: the dialectic was eternal but perhaps developing a peculiar sharpness in the Britain of the early 1960s. During the rest of this particular week, episode three of *Dr Finlay's Casebook* received another high RI of 72 ('the whole production really caught the atmosphere of the period') and Patrick Gordon Walker sought to neutralise Griffiths by publicly insisting that 'this is a British country with British standards of behaviour', that in fact 'the British must come first'; at the same time, 'Adventures in Eating' was the title of a *Guardian* analysis of changing daily habits prompted by the spread of packaged foods, supermarkets and refrigeration ('one of the major producers has introduced complete main course meals, Dinners-for-one, in compartmented foil dishes'), and yet more ambitious plans were announced for Birmingham's city centre ('the £4 million entertainments centre will include 100 shops, a department store, a small specialist cinema, a dance-hall, offices, several public-houses, a building housing an ice-rink and a ten-pin bowling centre, and two car parks, one for 1,000 cars'). It was a dialectic that Dennis Potter over the coming years would explore and work through, but at this stage he was firmly in favour of change and the modern, with television potentially a force for good on their behalf. 'In the abuse we need to throw back at the little grey-faced monster squatting in our living rooms,' he reflected on Friday the 31st, 'we sometimes fail to notice the growth of the medium into something which attracts and holds creative writers and talented performers'; and he added that the 'new men' in the BBC and ITV, making 'splendidly worthwhile' programmes, 'do not yet get enough credit for what could yet turn out to be the most significant cultural revolution of our times'.[20]

The September issue of *Town* magazine (prop. M. Heseltine) featured David Hockney ('I wish I could dye the whole of Bond Street blond, every man, woman and child') and also a hitherto unknown but fiercely ambitious 14-year-old 'mod' called Mark Feld (later Marc Bolan), who quite apart from boasting 'I've got 10 suits, eight sports jackets, 15 pairs of slacks, about 20 jumpers, three leather jackets, two

suede jackets, five or six pairs of shoes and 30 exceptionally good ties',
also explained candidly ('They're for the rich') why he supported the
Conservatives; the more humdrum *Birkenhead News and Advertiser*
reported on Saturday the 1st the impending closure of Wright's Biscuits
Ltd in Stanley Road, with a largely female workforce and known
locally as the 'Happy Factory'; and members of the geography section
of the British Association, accompanied by journalists, enjoyed – or
anyway experienced – a vivid field trip:

'Here', said the group's leader as the day tour of the industrial
geography of the Lancashire coalfields stopped in a smoke-
grimed Wigan backstreet by a railway yard, 'is one of the most
desolate pieces of land you could find.' Eagerly the geographers
climbed out of the coach. They marched briskly over an iron
railway bridge, along an unmade-up track between shunting
trains burping black smoke, and stood on rusty tracks to gaze
at a 'flash' of oily water flanked by mounds of rubble and slag.
     Their leader, Mr H. B. Rodgers, a lecturer in geography at
Manchester University, talked about subsidence and spoil-heaps.
He mentioned 'the ravaged landscape of South Wigan, where
the noble masses of the Wigan Alps tower over man-made lakes
thinly coated with coal-dust'. The two-score of geographers
nodded in glum agreement as he waved a hand to show the vast
scale of the land dereliction problem. Wigan's smoke-smeared
skyline loomed in the distance. 'What an awful place,' said one
man calmly.

Monday saw the start of the Farnborough Air Show, boosted by the
FT's assurance that the British aircraft industry was 'far from dying
and there is no reason to assume that it will not be as strongly in
evidence a decade or more ahead as it is today'; Jacqueline du Pré's
performance of Brahms at the Edinburgh Festival went down poorly
with the critic Desmond Shawe-Taylor ('disappointingly forced ...
this brilliant child needs to watch the quality of her tone ... she also
needs some sort of bandeau for her mop of fair hair, which swings
constantly to and fro with the distracting abandon of a Betjeman
tennis girl'); and Anita West appeared as usual on *Blue Peter*. It
proved to be her swansong: in the middle of divorce proceedings, she

decided it was inappropriate to continue as a presenter of a children's programme, giving way to the above-reproach Valerie Singleton.[21]

For Arnold Wesker early this month, the big question was whether his series of trade union arts festivals planned for the autumn, under the banner of Centre 42 with himself as director, would prove rather more successful at bringing improving culture to the masses than the at best semi-flop of his Wellingborough foray the previous autumn. A television programme on Monday the 3rd, when Wesker and a colleague explained what they were intending to offer shortly at the first of the festivals (Northamptonshire's Wellingborough again the chosen venue), failed to convince at least one viewer. 'I must say the whole business still makes no sense to me,' noted the always perceptive critic P. N. Furbank. 'The problem surely is that there is an inherited and increasing working-class hostility towards high culture because of its middle-class associations – it is one of the most deeply implanted and wasteful of our social patterns – and the very thing likely to drive it even deeper is to proffer some hole-and-corner alternative for the real thing, like propagandist drama and folk-singing in pubs.' That same day, getting close-up to the working class and presumably taking notes furiously, the sociologist Brian Jackson was visiting Hillhouse and Birkby Bowling Green, a flourishing bowling club in Huddersfield with nearly 600 members:

> By and by an old man came in wearing a black tie. 'How's the wife then?' 'Oh, she died on Wednesday, five minutes to twelve.' He explained how he hadn't seen her at the last, because his son-in-law had been late on his train and they hadn't managed to get him to hospital in time. There was a short silence. 'Ah well it's a pity to say it, but it's a release for both sides int it,' said one of the other men. The widower said, 'She hadn't eaten anything for nearly a week. We'd only have just seen her, I mean she couldn't have known us or anything, it would just be to say we'd seen her like.' Somebody else said, 'Aye they can't last long at that job can they, when they don't eat.' There was a silence from the men around, broken occasionally by the one word, 'Aye,' spoken in different tones of sympathy. Carrying the weight of meaning. The conversation immediately tracked off on to something else. But came back at intervals to the bereavement.

'Nobody playing too heavily on it,' reflected Jackson, 'and yet there was the sense all the time that the widower was being specially treated. That he was among friends.'[22]

Next day, thousands lined Glasgow's soaked streets to see the last of the city's trams, while that evening the Beatles – including Ringo, and with George sporting a black eye given to him by a fan of Pete Best – were in the Abbey Road studios to record 'How Do You Do It' (intended A-side of their first single) and 'Love Me Do' (intended B-side). On Wednesday the 5th, Liverpool City Council unanimously called on the government to take emergency measures to combat rising unemployment on Merseyside; the Ministry of Transport, following the palpable failure of the recently introduced panda-crossings experiment, provoked yet more indignation by proposing that three London boroughs (Ealing, Paddington and Tottenham) make it, on an experimental basis, an offence to cross the road except at pedestrian crossings; and in the European Cup Winners' Cup, little Bangor City took on mighty AC Napoli in a first-leg encounter at the Welsh club's ground with wooden boards in a tiny grandstand and a roofless Wesleyan chapel behind one goal. It proved the proverbial night to remember: two goals for the home side, none for the visitors, an exuberant pitch invasion, and all over bar the return leg in three weeks' time.[23]

It had been quite an epic for Bangor City to win that 1961/2 Welsh Cup in the first place. Mold Alexandra, Llay Welfare, Bethesda Athletic, Brymbo Steelworks, Brecon Corinthians, Ebbw Vale, Ton Pentre, Abergavenny Thursdays, Caersws Amateurs, Merthyr Tydfil, Barry Town, Haverfordwest County – these were among the teams that had fallen by the wayside, even before more familiar names like Newport County and Swansea Town were knocked out. Wrexham were Bangor's eventual opponents in the two-legged final: at Wrexham's Racecourse Ground, 3–0 to the hosts; at Bangor only 2–0 to the hosts; and yet, by a quirk of that season's rules, it had been decreed that overall aggregates would not count if each side won once, and so accordingly a play-off was arranged at Rhyl. There, Bangor prevailed 3–1, and Europe awaited.

Traditional industrial Wales – the world of Brymbo Steelworks, of Ebbw Vale ('an industrial town, with collieries, steel and tinplate

works, and brickworks', in the AA's words), of Ton Pentre, of Merthyr
Tydfil ('a coal-mining town', though also 'with many factories for
light industries') – was in some trouble, though on the whole not yet
decisive trouble, by the early 1960s. The crux at this stage was coal.
'From the valleys that spread northwards from Pontypridd like dark
fingers has come stupendous wealth, a wealth of coal and above all a
wealth of people,' proudly ran the commentary (by the novelist Gwyn
Thomas) for a promotional film of the 1960 South Wales miners' gala
in Cardiff:

> The men and women of the mining villages show the capital
> some part of their traditions and their pride. Banners, bands,
> gaiety, and besides the brass bands, the colourful character bands
> are an interesting echo of the gazooka bands of the 1926 period.
> A day of explosive joy.
>
> History marches here, these are men asking for security and
> peace. The names of their lodges are a fanfare of heroic conflict
> for the achievement of a saner social set-up, for greater happiness
> and peace: Mardy, Newlands, Penallta, Penrhiwceiber, Tower,
> Duffryn Rhondda, Cambrian, they're all here.
>
> We enter Sophia Gardens. This would have been a place
> denied to us in the long ago but now it is part of our inheritance,
> and we are prepared for a day in which gaiety and thought will
> compete for equal place in the long years of endurance, the long
> years of conflict. These men have listened, thought, planned,
> worked. Their hands have been hands that sustained a nation.
> Strong creative hands on which a community can always rely …

Yet in truth the coal-mining industry in Wales was by this time, as
in several other parts of Britain, perilously placed, given the larger
context of rapidly growing consumption of alternative fuels, especially
oil. Between 1957 and 1965, coal production in Wales fell from over
23 million tons to about 17 million tons, and manpower from some
105,000 to some 67,000. 'With banners furled we go back to our valleys,
to work, to remember the laughter of the day and to think about
the future,' concluded Thomas's commentary. Realistically, it was
unlikely to be a rosy future in those legendary mining communities
of the valleys.

By contrast, the other key Welsh industry, steel, was for the moment looking healthy enough in the early autumn of 1962. The steelworks at Port Talbot, now eleven years old, had 18,000 employees and was Europe's largest integrated steelworks; the Queen was due on 25 October to open Llanwern steelworks near Newport, set to employ 3,500; and Shotton, Cardiff and Ebbw Vale also hosted major plants. Moreover, for redundant or anxious or ill-paid coal miners, there was a reasonable range of alternative (and in many ways more attractive) blue-collar employment, including Morris Motors at Llanelli, BP at Llandarcy, British Nylon Spinners at Pontypool, Metal Box at Neath and Hoovers at Merthyr Tydfil. But was there enough diversification? 'Those with decent wages and decent jobs were never entirely confident of keeping them, especially if they were old enough to remember the austerity of the 1930s,' notes Martin Johnes in his magisterial survey of the creation of modern Wales. 'They were right to worry. With over a quarter of the workforce still employed in metal and mining, the Welsh economy was still fragile.'[24]

As for rural Wales by around this time, some trends were inevitably much the same as for rural England, including mechanisation, depopulation and larger farming units. There were many pockets of real poverty, perhaps especially in mid-Wales, where over a third of homes had no hot-water tap, hill farmers struggled, economic prospects generally were poor, and a county like Radnor was steadily losing many of its economically active inhabitants. Serious deficiencies in public transport did not help, with a September 1962 report from the council for Wales and Monmouthshire (the largely ineffectual body that had been set up by the Attlee government soon after the war) concluding not only that such deficiencies (both road and rail) 'have tended to reinforce the factors which cause depopulation', but also that, in relation to the increasingly widespread ownership and use of private cars, 'it is a fallacy to suppose that every rural dweller can be equipped with his own means of transport'. Why, asked the report, was transport treated differently from other public services? 'In the case of the latter, it is recognised that the rural population should not be denied the everyday amenities of modern life notwithstanding that they cannot be economically provided; the provision and maintenance of public transport services, on the other hand, has come to depend more and more on considerations of accountancy.'

Such issues of temporal amelioration mattered little to R. S. Thomas, poet-priest of the Church in Wales – so different from rural Wales's overwhelmingly Nonconformist, non-Anglican traditions – who in 'The Welsh Hill Country', his most famous poem, addressed from a farmer's perspective that most despised of creatures, the romantic (probably English) tourist:

Too far for you to see
The fluke and the foot-rot and the fat maggot
Gnawing the skin from the small bones,
The sheep are grazing at Bwlch-y-Fedwen,
Arranged romantically in the usual manner
On a bleak background of bald stone.

Too far for you to see
The moss and the mould on the cold chimneys,
The nettles growing through the cracked doors,
The houses stand empty at Nant-yr-Eira,
There are holes in the roofs that are thatched with sunlight,
And the fields are reverting to the bare moor.

Too far, too far to see
The set of his eyes and the slow phthisis
Wasting his frame under the ripped coat,
There's a man still farming at Ty'n-y-Fawnog,
Contributing grimly to the accepted pattern,
The embryo music dead in his throat.

That had been written during Thomas's rectorship at Manon in rural Montgomeryshire; between 1954 and 1967 he had the living of Eglwysfach in northern Cardiganshire; and though his poetic preoccupations would become increasingly religious he had definitely come by the 1960s 'to represent to the English-speaking world', in the words of an obituary, 'the voice of a vanishing culture and way of life in a manner inevitably denied to those of his countrymen who wrote solely in Welsh'.[25]

What about 'Welshness' itself? Here, our most intimate source for these years is Isabel Emmett's 1958–62 study of the parish of 'Llan' (in fact Llanfrothen) in Merionethshire in North Wales – comprising four villages, predominantly Welsh-speaking, and in her words 'firmly embedded in the most Welsh part of Wales'. Of the 241 adults in the parish, 131 had the surnames Jones or Williams or Evans or Griffiths or Owen; and in some suggestive passages Emmett sought to get to the heart of what she saw as a distinctively Welsh world-view shared by all but a relatively few of those 241:

> Llan people see the people of their community in terms of places and see farms and cottages with families attached, and both people and places are always seen embedded in and embroidered by the history of Llan's past fifty-odd years. This history is not one of important events: the two world wars left the lives of most Llan people unmarked. It is a history of scandal and jokes, a gossip history, whose power on people and beauty for people it is hard to express. Part of the power derives from the fact that everyone is familiar with that past; anyone can describe it ...
>
> Much of the life was like country life anywhere. But the chapel was woven through it all in a way that gave it distinction. Moreover, that which makes country life meaningful is the talk; and the talk was in Welsh and so the whole life was peculiarly Welsh. The very bleakness of the life made the talk rich and Llan people learnt everything from that talk. They learnt the unique culture in which they lived. Quarrymen talked philosophy; relatives talked kinship; farmers talked economics; everybody talked religion and scandal. So people learnt to think of their community past and present, in the light of their system of values, which are not only 'country' values, but also emphatically 'Welsh' values. The whole of that past life was strongly imbued with the essence of Welshness ...
>
> The Welsh value system is a relatively coherent mixture of chapel and all which the chapel is against, but which is Welsh. Those who go regularly to chapel and those who do not, tell the same stories, admire the same characters and do not feel part of the 'respectable' or 'disreputable' group so much as they feel part of the Welsh-speaking community of North Wales.
>
> The frequent presence of English visitors and the constant presence of the anglicized landlords and English people with top

jobs, make Llan people very aware of their Welshness, and what permits the presence of apparently contradictory elements in their value system is the fact that all elements in it are Welsh. In the presence of the enemy, Welshness is the primary value; deacon and drunkard are friends, old schisms become unimportant.

In other words, it was, insisted Emmett, a value system in which not only was the distinction between chapel and non-chapel people relatively unimportant, but so too was social class, or at least among the Welsh-speakers. As for their actual views of England and the English:

> A stereotype of the English, as representatives of the abstraction 'ruling England', is at the root of many of the attitudes generally held in North Wales, and is, therefore, impervious to quick adjustment. Adjustment is not demanded by many of the English people who are seen regularly in Llan, since for most people they fit the stereotype. The lack of class divisions in Welsh society itself is due partly to the anglicization of the upper strata of Welsh society and partly to the fact that the rulers of Wales have long been English corporations and English-speaking individuals. The English take the place of the upper, upper-middle or ruling class, and nationalism is the dress in which class antagonisms are expressed. The stereotype which Llan people have of English people as snobbish, rich and lacking in understanding, was formed in pre-war days when most of the English they saw were powerful and rich. This type of English person [including the owners of the parish's two main estates] still has enough power over the lives of the Llan people and the people of North Wales generally to reinforce the stereotype.

'It would', added Emmett, 'take great changes to upset radically the stereotype Llan people have of the English and of "England" as an abstraction because upon it depend so many of their attitudes; in it are included so many of their antagonisms and conflicts; and around it have grown up so many of their modes of behaviour.' Emmett herself was English (albeit married to a native of Llanfrothen who had lived there most of his life), so it was perhaps with a slightly self-conscious nod that she finished her chapter on 'Welsh and English' with the reflection that 'the stereotype can confront English people seen as modest, charming and unassuming and survive the contact unscathed'.

The larger situation was of course more complicated, for in effect there were by the 1960s what George Thomas (miner's son from Tonypandy and future Speaker of the House of Commons) would describe as 'two separate populations in Wales: the vast majority in the English-speaking areas, and the small Welsh-speaking minority, who are widely scattered over the rural areas'. The number of Welsh speakers, moreover, was in serious decline: from 909,261 in 1931 to 656,002 in 1961, with by that stage only 13 per cent of three- and four-year-olds speaking Welsh, compared to 37 per cent of those aged over sixty-five – a contrast that was the surest sign of a seemingly dying language. Among the prime causes were the various forces of modernity (above all omnipresent, English-language-dominated media) and economically driven dispersal from Welsh-speaking industrial valleys as well as Welsh-speaking rural communities. It is also clear, from the work of Johnes and others, that in post-war Wales most people combined *some* sense of being Welsh with *some* sense of being British – and that when it came to choosing between the two identities, for example over what type of TV programmes to watch, the latter often trumped the former. 'A cottonwool fuzz at the back of the mind' is the apposite title of Johnes's relevant chapter, words taken from one of the narrators of Alun Richards's 1973 novel *Home to an Empty House*:

Somehow I always associated Welshness with quarrelling committees, with things going wrong, little political men with vested interests and families of unemployable nephews screwing money and jobs out of the State for their own special, personal causes. And the Language that nobody spoke much in the towns, unless it was to get on in the BBC or Education. Of course, I remembered the more emotive things, hymns at football matches, those great spasms of emotion that swept across the terraces of the football grounds, waves of feeling and piping tenor voices, patterns of song as intricate as a folk weave, but meaningless in terms of my present. Welshness was like a cottonwool fuzz at the back of the mind because Wales was always round the corner where I lived. Men remembered it beerily when the pubs were

closed, or at specially contrived festivals – somebody's pocket
and kudos again. We had come to be the St David's Day Welsh
and nothing changed in our lives ever.

Richards himself (born 1929) came from Pontypridd, the market and
mining town at the foot of the Rhondda valleys; and *his* Wales was
firmly the outward-looking, non-Welsh-speaking, predominantly
urban South Wales. That, he enjoyed saying, was the Wales which
bred – whether boxers or rugby players, whether politicians or
intellectuals – 'champions of the world, not bloody Machynlleth'.[26]

Wales in general remained solidly Labour territory: even in
Macmillan's landslide 1959 election victory, over 56 per cent of
voters there backed Gaitskell's party. 'A way of life, passed on from
one generation to the next', is how one historian (Andrew Walling)
has characterised voting Labour in post-war industrial Wales, but in
local government there were inevitably negative aspects to one-party
rule. 'The councillors have been unopposed for about forty years and
mostly ignore any applications for membership to the Labour Party
to ensure that they will remain unopposed,' an angry Jill Craigie wrote
in 1960 about Ebbw Vale Borough Council shortly after her husband
Michael Foot had won Aneurin Bevan's old Parliamentary seat; or in
the subsequent scathing words of Alun Richards about the problem
more broadly in Labour Wales, 'unchallenged political power creates
grubby nests where cosy improprieties fester'.[27]

What about nationalism? The sober truth, albeit unpalatable to
some, was that during most of the twentieth century – and arguably
all of it – the overall Welsh attitude to home rule was hostile or, at
most, lukewarm. Even after the considerable storm provoked by
the decision in 1956 to flood Tryweryn Valley in order to build a
reservoir to supply water to Liverpool, the nationalist party, Plaid
Cymru, secured barely 5 per cent of votes in Wales in 1959 and still
awaited its first MP. But in 1962 three moments were pointers to a
potentially less subordinate future: in February a much discussed
radio lecture by one of Plaid Cymru's founders, Saunders Lewis, who
warned that without 'determination, will power, struggle, sacrifice
and effort' – if necessary involving 'revolutionary methods' – the
Welsh language was doomed; in August, at a Plaid Cymru summer
school at Pontarddulais in South Wales, the passing of a motion to

start what became the Welsh Language Society; and in September (the 22nd) two Plaid Cymru members attempting – of their own accord, but with the prior knowledge of their instinctively reluctant party leader, Gwynfor Evans – to sabotage an electricity transformer on the construction site of the Tryweryn dam. In years to come, an obituary of Evans (born 1912) would reflect on 'his characteristic emphasis on tradition, communal values, the culture of ordinary people and the value of the individual, particularly in the small, rural, Welsh-speaking areas, which were at the heart of his nationalism'; also in the years to come, but across the aisle, an obituary of his old adversary George Thomas (born 1909) would reflect on how he was 'the archetypal middle-of-the-road Welsh MP of his generation, formed by the fortifying curriculum of the valley, the pit, the chapel, the temperance movement, the Co-op, the trade union and the Labour Party'. But in both cases, whether it was the rise of more militant nationalism or Wales's Labour MPs increasingly coming from a very different background, the days were starting to look numbered for their own particular deep-rooted political culture.

In 1962 itself, and far removed from the political arena, Wales had its own sporting folk hero in the making. On 18 August, as the newly constituted Beatles played at Port Sunlight just the other side of the border, a capacity crowd of 4,500 at the County Pavilion, Newtown, rose as one to roar their approval after Howard Winstone, the frail-looking 23-year-old British featherweight champion, had seen off Durham's rugged and experienced George Bowes. 'One wonders what more one can expect from this brilliant young man from Merthyr,' speculated the Welsh boxing and rugby writer Terry Godwin. 'Clearly he has not yet been extended, and where, apart from world champion Davey Moore and perhaps a few others, is there anyone with the speed and destructive enough punch to bring an end to his unbeaten run?' Winstone's trainer was the former pugilist Eddie Thomas – hugely capable, hugely warm, also from Merthyr Tydfil, where nearby he had acquired a small open-cast mine with his earnings from the ring – and together they were poised to take on the world, for style as well as championship belts. 'For pure unadulterated craft, Winstone obviously has no equal in Europe,' reckoned Godwin; and at the end of the bout, the 'game' and 'durable' Bowes 'nodded full approval when referee Billy Jones raised the Welshman's arm'.[28]

5

Brothers and Friends

On 6 September, the day after a truly notable Welsh sporting triumph in Bangor, a still unknown novelist was home again in north London after a Roman holiday. 'The grey shock of England and the English,' recorded John Fowles. 'It seems most like a colossal lack of style, an almost total inability to design life, to express life through the way one lives one's daily life. The British sit like a fat pasty-faced bespectacled girl at the European party.' And he added, with an almost bemused incredulity: 'The 1962 British seems really to still believe Britain is best. Cleaner, nicer, honester, more civilized.' On the political front that Thursday, the PM promoted his nephew the Duke of Devonshire ('a tall, gay, quite witty duke who talks fast and irreverently', noted Sampson in *Anatomy*) to the newly created post of Minister of State at the Commonwealth Relations Office, while at Blackpool the tone of the TUC's transport debate was one of bitterness and frustration. 'A hell of a lot of people are going to have to walk,' predicted the National Union of Railwaymen's General Secretary, Sid Greene, about the consequences of Dr Beeching having, under government orders, such a profit-driven approach to Britain's railway system; 'over the last ten years the objective of an integrated transport system has steadily receded', lamented W. H. Peacey, an employee at Swindon's historic railway workshop; and J. L. Simons, of the Associated Society of Locomotive Engineers and Firemen, envisaged in a few years' time people being able to travel to the moon but no longer by train from Worsley to Bolton or from Kidderminster to Tenbury Wells. The evening featured the start of Frankie Howerd's improbable comeback – that of an apparently washed-up variety comedian reinventing himself at Soho's The Establishment club, co-owned by Peter Cook and at the very cutting edge of the satirical-cum-fashionable. 'I hope you haven't got the wrong impression, ladies and gentlemen, if you've come along here tonight expecting Lenny Bruce [the outspoken American comedian who had occupied the previous residency], I'm sorry, I'm no Lenny Bruce,' he explained disarmingly before going on to land (in his biographer's phrase) 'a thumping uppercut':

> And if you've come here expecting a lot of crudeness, and a lot of vulgarity, I'm sorry, but you won't get it from me, so you might just as well piss off now! Admittedly, this is the home of satire, Peter Cook has made it very clear, he's said, 'You must be *satirical*, you must have a go, *knock*, you must be *bitter*, they must leave here *angry* – otherwise they aren't satisfied! Knock the establishment!' So I said, 'Look, I've done nothing else since I've been here!' He said, '*No!* Not *this* place – the people, the Establishment, the faceless ones!' It was a battle of wits from now on. So I said, '*Whom* had you in mind?' So he said, 'The Government. Macmillan. The Establishment. The civil service.' I said, 'Make them *angry*? But these are your *audience*. These are the people who come here. You don't want to make them angry. They think it's all rather sweet! They enjoy it! It's water off a duck's back!' After all, the whole place is only a snob's *Workers' Playtime*, let's face it. Instead of making jokes about the foreman we make jokes about Harold Macmillan – it's the same thing.

The performance was a triumph, so too the month-long residency. 'Mr Howerd, his face hanging in huge petulant folds, a convulsive blend of Oscar Wilde and one of the more endearing Roman Emperors, is visually superb,' observed one favourable critic among many, 'even when he is merely dithering his way towards the next gag.'[1]

September for cricket enthusiasts meant as ever the Scarborough festival, where the Gentlemen on Saturday the 8th did their bit with a free-scoring 328 against the Players (Trueman once again captain), before viewers across the country tuned in to the return of *The Billy Cotton Band Show*. 'The majority were clearly in no way disappointed,' noted the BBC's report, reflecting with satisfaction on a show 'brimming over with lively good humour and homely fun'. Even so, individual ratings varied considerably: 71 per cent 'enjoyed very much' the contribution from Russ Conway ('a grand pianist and a *lovely* man', according to one viewer); but only 54 per cent felt the same for Billy Cotton himself (some irritation with his 'larking about' and 'gate crashing' each solo act), 51 per cent for the Shadows and 49 per cent for Cliff Richard, while for Alan Breeze and Kathie Kay it was just 38 and 33 per cent respectively, with both said to be 'past their best'. On Monday a new timetable came into operation for British Railways' Western Region (slow trains from Oxford to Worcester still stopping at Adlestrop) and Val Singleton slipped into the vacant seat at *Blue Peter*; next day, *Needle Match* came to a merciful end, so too (all things considered) did the Gentlemen versus Players fixture (a win for the latter, just as the rain came down), and Robert Soblen in his prison cell committed suicide by overdosing on barbiturates. For one troubled West Midlands MP, it was the day of an important meeting with his party leader. 'Saw Gaitskell,' recorded Patrick Gordon Walker. 'Explained to him difficulties in my constituency owing to colour and that I might lose the seat. He agreed that we should go all out to stop overcrowding. We would favour immediate introduction of Registration of multi-occupational houses and Government support for places like Smethwick.'[2]

A good day for the long arm of the law on Wednesday the 12th: John Vassall, a clerk at the Admiralty and son of a part-time curate at St James's, Piccadilly, arrested on justifiable suspicion of being a Soviet spy; the new Solicitor-General, Sir Peter Rawlinson, insisting publicly that though 'many people believe that the death penalty should be abolished', nevertheless 'there are more, I believe, equally intelligent and sincere people who believe that the penalty must be retained'; and a five-year sentence for Larroque the abortionist ('You have traded on girls in their distress for substantial sums of money'), after he had asked that thirty-five similar cases be taken into consideration. In Southport the annual conference of the Association of Public Health Inspectors agreed that the national clean-air programme was achieving good results in London ('people are of their own free will turning from the wasteful, smoke-producing, open coal fire'), but less so elsewhere, especially in some predominantly coal-mining areas. One of those areas was probably

Fife, where the miner, trade unionist and New Left activist Lawrence Daly issued this day a circular letter to members and supporters of the Fife Socialist League that had a twofold purpose: partly to urge them to get behind the Labour Party and 'push like hell', including for a Labour victory at the next general election; and partly to argue that the time had come to disband the League, in the context of it having been 'more or less inactive' over the past twelve months. '*Interest has practically disappeared*,' regretfully noted one of the most eloquent and charismatic men of his generation. 'This, I think, is mainly due to the general political apathy …'[3]

Was there apathy too at Wellingborough? 'If we do not succeed, a vast army of highly powered commercial enterprises are going to sweep into the leisure hours of future generations and create a cultural mediocrity,' proclaimed the 1962 mission statement for Centre 42. The disastrous result would be 'a nation emotionally and intellectually immature, capable of enjoying nothing, creating nothing and effecting nothing'. The warning could hardly have been more solemn: 'This is not an idle prophecy; it is a fact in the making. Bingo is only the beginning.' This second week of September saw at the East Midlands town, best known for manufacturing footwear, the first of this autumn's trade-union-sponsored festivals, as Centre 42 sought to bring to the contemporary working class the right sort of authentic and non-commercial traditional working-class culture. An exhibition ('Bread and Roses Too') opened by Billie Whitelaw, two versions (one set to classical music, the other to jazz) of a Wesker-scripted episode from Nottingham's history about the rigged trial of a Luddite, the under-rehearsed premiere of *Enter Solly Gold* by the East End playwright Bernard Kops, a poetry and jazz evening featuring Christopher Logue, a prize for 'the best-dressed lady, not the most expensively dressed' – such were among the attractions, but seemingly to an underwhelming reception. 'It was like presenting an obstinate child with a plate of spinach,' reported the *Sunday Times*'s Susan Cooper. 'Doesn't appeal, see,' a boy with a Tony Curtis haircut told her in a local café. 'Not that kind of stuff. We get all we want. Cinemas, dancing twice a week … there's six caffs, twelve pubs. Anything else you want, you go to Northampton, only ten mile.' But perhaps the last word went to another genuinely authentic working-class voice. Why, wondered Shelagh Delaney soon afterwards in another Sunday paper, was it that 'some people seem to think that 100 years ago, everybody was speaking poetry in pubs?'[4]

The robustly pragmatic Phyllis Willmott, also authentically working-class in her origins, would have been firmly on Delaney's side of the argument. 'A publication for the intelligent layman to keep him informed on social policies etc,' she noted on the 13th in the context of having an article accepted 'by this new mag. coming out in October and called "New Society"'. And, referring to the magazine publisher's son Timothy Raison (head of the Youth Service Development Council), she added, 'the editor is apparently one of the bright boys of the Bow Group – that's probably not going to be too far right for us right-side left!' Judy Haines in Chingford went shopping that Thursday ('exasperating wait in Sainsbury's for two chops, which turned out to be not so good as Faulkner's'); at the Proms, this one in the series of William Glock's Thursday Invitation Concerts (or Irritation Concerts, as the musical old guard called them) included the latest work by Peter Maxwell Davies; and it was probably this Thursday evening, at the Glasgow Folk Club in Paisley, that the 18-year-old Scottish guitarist Bert Jansch was captured on tape for the first time. On Friday, just as 'Telstar' entered the Top Twenty, Joe Orton and Kenneth Halliwell were released from prison after doing time for stealing and defacing books from Islington Public Library; on the TV front, around 330,000 homes were now able to enjoy Wales's own channel (Teledu Cymru), but the almost infinitely larger viewing figures were for *Dixon of Dock Green*, returning on Saturday evening (straight after a vintage *Juke Box Jury* of Dion, Fenella Fielding, Rupert Davies and Jane Asher) for its ninth series. 'This programme', warmly welcomed a bank manager, 'is like a pair of old slippers – one can relax in the utterly familiar comfortable cosiness. Dixon is a slice of life seen through rose-coloured glasses – and why not? I'm glad he's back.' Or as a secretary put it about the acting: 'Everyone is so completely natural, especially the regulars, that it is difficult to imagine they are anyone else.'[5]

Next day, while the Bishop of Woolwich, John Robinson, preached a sermon at Canterbury Cathedral appealing for reform of 'our utterly medieval treatment of homosexuals', calling it 'unworthy of a civilised, let alone of a Christian, country', the *Sunday Times*'s colour magazine majored on 'The New Age of Leisure', including a discussion between

Liverpool playwright Alun Owen and psychologist James Hemming. 'Why', asked Owen, 'are the people that I come from, the working-class people, so utterly indifferent to live theatre? Why?' 'Class,' bluntly answered Hemming. 'A matter of identification. You either say that "this is for me" or "this is not for me".' And a third participant in the discussion, the sociologist Hannah Gavron, agreed that, even though rates of social mobility were broadly the same as in the States, 'we still feel we're a class-bound society'. Elsewhere in the magazine, 'Cooking with Robert Carrier' highlighted the joys of fondue, especially Swiss cheese fondue for ' "do-it-yourself" parties': 'equip each guest with a long fork, cubes of crusty French bread, a glass of dry white wine (I like a Sylvaner or a Niersteiner) and a napkin'. Monday lunchtime had a topical discussion programme *Table Talk* on BBC TV, with Brian Redhead and Elizabeth Jane Howard among those grappling with the Common Market, thalidomide babies and chemicals in tinned foods; in the small hours of Tuesday, the well-known working-class Glaswegian bandleader Tommy Watt left Ronnie Scott's jazz club in Soho only to find himself being arrested for possession of Indian hemp; later that day, lamenting to J. B. Priestley how the Leavisites had 'a stranglehold on the schools as well as the universities (and the high brow press)', C. S. Lewis described F. R. Leavis himself as 'a perfectly sincere, disinterested, fearless, ruthless fanatic'; and in the evening Richard Cawston's TV documentary *The Schools* included one of the most haunting of all clips from the era.

'I hardly think that failed is the right word, Mrs Kitchen,' the not unkindly headmaster says to Janet's mother after she has expressed regret about Janet having failed her eleven-plus. 'You see what happened was that Janet took a test so we could find out which school suited her best. She would have failed the test if she had been selected for the wrong school, and so if she has been selected for the right school, she has really passed the test.' This cheers Janet herself up, but the mother's expression remains palpably unconvinced. The programme also had some eighty-five teachers talking in an open forum. 'The onslaught on the eleven-plus examination had few dissentient voices,' noted a reviewer. 'And almost everyone approved the idea of comprehensive schools.' Did parents share that progressive perspective? Quite possibly not, to judge by the previous month's Labour Party report on attitudes to secondary education, revealing that only 10 per cent of

Labour voters and 11 per cent of Conservative voters were critical of
the eleven-plus. Arguably, though, much of that absence of criticism
was due less to a settled, thought-out position on the issue than to
sheer fatalism – a passivity strongly encouraged by many of the
schools themselves. Such was the view of Brian Jackson, director of
the Advisory Centre for Education (ACE), who in the summer issue
of its magazine *Where?* had described his recent experience of walking
past a primary school in suburban north London:

> The school announced itself to the district with a large official
> notice board ...
>
> PARENTS ARE NOT ALLOWED BEYOND THIS POINT
>
> UNLESS THEY HAVE AN INTERVIEW
>
> WITH THE HEAD TEACHER
>
> How absurd. 'Parents are not allowed ...' I know this school
> isn't typical (though I could take you to many others), but its
> clumsy 'Trespassers will be Prosecuted' attitude is symptomatic
> of a basic flaw in our whole system of schools and colleges. We
> need, very badly, to *humanize* our education system.

ACE's founder was Michael Young, who in *Where?*'s autumn issue
argued for a general expansion of university education, including
taking the 'step, not as far as I know suggested before', to 'establish
an "open university"'; and later in the article he declared that 'a new
centre is needed – a National Extension College – to act as the nucleus
of an "open university"'. 'The National College', added Young,
'would work with the BBC and ITV to secure programmes for its
students.'[6] One of the decade's defining achievements, the Open
University, was under way.

The second post-war royal commission on the press reported on
the 19th and was scathing in its depiction of the production side of the
national newspaper industry, still based in and around Fleet Street, as
being in a state of unmistakable malaise: overmanning of the order of
34 per cent; demarcation often excessive, even 'grotesque', preventing
'the development of new processes'; casual non-craft labour not only
rife, but 'paid at premium rates'; and a whole, byzantine plethora of
'house extras negotiated to meet special conditions', many of them
'based on reasons sometimes anachronistic and often fictitious'.

Exhibiting the purest of wishful thinking, the commission (chaired by Lord Shawcross) called for 'unity on the part of employers' (that is, to counter the existing divide-and-rule strategy of the print unions) and 'a more constructive spirit on both sides'. Also this Wednesday, John Bloom's Rolls Razor entered a new phase of its already remarkable growth with the announcement of a trading agreement with Pressed Steel, enabling greatly increased production of its combined washing machines and spin dryers, sold directly and (to the discomfort of AEI's Hotpoint division) ultra-competitively priced; the Middle School Debating Society at Roundhay High School in Leeds considered whether 'the age of marriage without parental consent should be lowered to 18' (motion defeated); Z Cars, returning to the screens, began its classic period with an episode ('On Watch – Newtown') written by John Hopkins which included a future Monkee, Manchester's David Jones, as the boy footballer; and Sheila Hancock, starring in the first night of Charles Dyer's comedy Rattle of a Simple Man at the Garrick, was acclaimed by the still-unknown Tom Stoppard (trying his hand as theatre critic for the trendy, newly established magazine Scene) as among 'the new clutch of toughened individualists now ousting the tradition of sweet young things who once conquered all with a wistful lift of a false eyelash'. Next day, Larkin 'cackled' (he told Monica Jones) when he 'read of Marples wanting to test cars when they were ONE year old – shows what shoddy rotten swindles they are'; and the Banbury Guardian printed diverse views on the town's redevelopment plans, including fifty new shops in the centre, forty old-established shops in and around the market place to be demolished, four new car parks, a ring road around the town centre and considerable pedestrianisation.

'You could save all the expense of knocking the shops down and building new ones simply by giving the present buildings a face-lift,' reckoned Mr R. L. Webb, manager of a tailor's shop due to meet the bulldozers. 'The existing shops are perfectly all right – there's nothing wrong with them structurally, and most of them have the advantage of living accommodation above them. All they need is to be re-fronted.' At a nearby showroom, two sales reps disagreed with each other. 'Keep these places of character – I've spent a number of years travelling, and seen many different places,' declared Mr E. Barzey, a native of Liverpool. 'Among the little market towns, I think Banbury takes a lot of beating. I'd like to see it kept the way it is.' 'Nonsense,' countered his colleague Mr F. A. Harvey. 'For years we've been knocking down historical buildings and nobody has bothered about it. Why start worrying now? I'd like to see a new shop for us here – new and big and attractive, so that customers will want to come into it.' Representing local shoppers, and perhaps in effect speaking for many of them, was Mrs A. Parker of Westcote Manor Farm, Edgehill. 'I'm looking forward to the day when you can shop in comfort,' she told the paper. 'I want to see new shops, wider streets – and lots of parking space. I come into Banbury every week to go shopping, and I think the parking situation is terrible. Not only is it difficult to park, but driving through narrow congested streets is dangerous. I'd like to see the new plans extended to Parson's Street. It's the worst of the lot.'[7]

Two fires in a week at Pakistani cafés in Bradford's Lumb Lane – situated in the 'coloured quarter', home to up to 10,000 non-whites – prompted a local committee to meet that Thursday to discuss ways of avoiding racial strife in the city. Comprising half a dozen Pakistanis and Indians, plus one Jamaican, it suggested the appointment of a full-time PRO. 'A public relations officer will help us to get closer to the English community,' argued Mr Mirza Beg, a refugee from Kashmir now living in Bolton Road. 'We want to be treated as brothers and friends. If there is race hatred, both our communities should try to tackle it. If we do anything wrong we should be helped to rectify it, not criticised.'

Across Britain as a whole at this time, the overwhelming majority of non-white residents were of West Indian, Indian or Pakistani origin. Precise figures are impossible, but a reasonable computation is that the population from those three areas of the 'New Commonwealth' amounted to some 630,000 – or, put another way, around 1.2 per cent of the total UK population. Some of those 630,000 residents (especially of course children) had been born in the UK, but the great majority were immigrants.[8] A selective roll call suggests something of their human range and the diverse talents they had brought with them.

Tassaduk Ahmed (who had come from East Pakistan in 1952) would shortly establish in Soho the Ganges restaurant, one of London's first to feature a tandoori oven; Rudy Narayan (Guyana, 1953) was training to become an activist, take-no-prisoners barrister;

Frank Crichlow (Trinidad, 1953) was proprietor of the El Rio Café in Notting Hill's Westbourne Park Road, decorated with fishing nets liberated from Southend-on-Sea and, in his own words, a 'school or university' for hustlers; Errol Brown (Jamaica, 1953), future Hot Chocolate main man, was working as a junior clerk at the Treasury; Wilbert Augustus Campbell (Jamaica, 1954) had experienced close up the Notting Hill riots (a white mob petrol-bombing his house, shouting 'Burn the niggers, kill the niggers!') and would, as Count Suckle, become the sound-system king of black London; Ivan Weekes (Barbados, 1955) was living in one of Peter Rachman's Notting Hill properties and would become a pioneer black magistrate; Carmel Jones (Jamaica, 1955), having been turned away by an Anglican vicar soon after arrival, was on his way to becoming a stalwart of the Pentecostal Church; Joyce Estelle Trotman (Guyana, 1955) was teaching at a boys' comprehensive in Bermondsey and listening to her class singing 'I'm dreaming of a white Christmas just like before the niggers came'; Hargurchet Singh Bhabra (Bombay, 1956) was only seven, already precocious, and would write one of the great first novels (*Gestures*, 1986); Charlie Phillips (Jamaica, 1956), living in Notting Hill, had recently left school and acquired his first camera (a Kodak Brownie), poised to become a key photographer of the black British experience; Anwar Pervez (Rawalpindi, 1956) had spent five years (seven days a week, double shifts) working on the buses in Bradford and was now planning to open in Earl's Court a specialist store, Kashmir, selling masala and halal meat to west London's Muslim community – first step of a phenomenal retail-cum-wholesale (Bestway) career; Norwell Roberts (Anguilla, 1956), dropped on his head by sixth formers at a secondary modern in Bromley so that they could see the colour of his blood, was now working as a laboratory technician at the University of London, and would become the Met's first black officer; Sybil Phoenix (Guyana, 1956), currently working in the fashion industry, would become famous in south London for helping young black women, for her youth and community centre the Moonshot Club and for seeking to heal wounds after the infamous Deptford Fire of 1981; Arthur France (St Kitts & Nevis, 1957), living in Leeds's Chapeltown, was an energetic educationist who would soon co-found the city's West Indian Carnival; Herman Ouseley (Guyana, 1957), at school in south London, would become chief executive of Lambeth

Council and later try to kick racism out of British football; Lincoln Cole (Jamaica, 1957), living in Nottingham ('there were teddy boys with bicycles – from six o'clock you couldn't go out, because they would kick you left, right and centre'), would work for over twenty years as a coal miner at the county's 'pit of nations' colliery at Gedling and father a future England footballer, Andy; Joan Armatrading (St Kitts, 1958) was living in Birmingham, forbidden by her carpenter father (who as a young man had played in a band) from touching his guitar; Raj Bagri (Bombay, 1958) was establishing himself as a metal trader and would become the longest-serving chairman of the London Metal Exchange; Caryl Phillips (St Kitts, 1958), future author of *The Final Passage* about his family's emigration to England when he was four months old, was growing up on a white working-class council estate in Leeds; Jocelyn Barrow (Trinidad, 1959), teaching English in Hackney and increasingly dismayed by the gulf between well-resourced schools for mainly middle-class white children and poorly resourced schools for mainly working-class black children, would soon become General Secretary and co-founder of the influential Campaign Against Racial Discrimination; Alex Pascall (Grenada, 1959), future host of British broadcasting's first black show (*Black Londoners*, on BBC Radio London), was working as a ticket collector for London Underground; Heather Rabbatts (Jamaica, 1959), the future first non-white (and first female) board member of the Football Association, was being bullied at her primary school in London; Eddy Grant (Guyana, 1960), future founder of the Equals, was living in Kentish Town and learning to read and write music at Acland Burghley, one of London's pioneer wave of comprehensive schools; Laurel Aitken (Jamaica, 1960), future 'Godfather of Ska' and 'Boss Skinhead', was setting a musical style that 'would spawn', noted a 2005 obituary, 'a uniquely British style of rocksteady and reggae before cross-fertilising with punk'; Leonard Woodley (Trinidad, 1960), a pupil in the Inner Temple, would be the first black barrister to become a QC; Salman Rushdie (Bombay, 1960) was in his third year at Dr Arnold's old shop, Rugby School, and being given 'a difficult time' because 'I wasn't English-white', a situation not helped by being 'lousy at games'; Wilfred Wood (Barbados, 1961) had just been ordained, was now doing his first curacy (St Stephen's Church, Shepherd's Bush) and as Bishop of Croydon would be the Church of England's first black bishop; Darcus Howe (Trinidad, 1961), in addition to studying law by day in the Middle Temple and clubbing at night (money permitting) at Roaring Twenties, was being attacked by teddy boys at the Swiss Cottage Odeon for refusing to stand for the National Anthem; and Mustapha Matura (Trinidad, 1962, just before Trinidad gained independence that August) was writing plays in his head as he worked as a hospital porter (a 'theatre job') at the National Temperance Hospital.⁹

To seek employment? To join relations? To study? For any other reason? Such was the multiple-choice question given to a sample survey of West Indian migrants in 1961. Almost without exception, they answered 'to seek employment'. Very often in practice, the jobs that those and other non-white immigrants secured were the lowest-paid jobs available; and very often, too, they were the jobs that Britain's white working class had no appetite for doing. Such was almost certainly the case in the unmodernised Black Country factory where in 1961 an observer for the Institute of Race Relations spent six weeks, watching the workforce (75 per cent of them from Asia and the Caribbean) in action. Knocking out and quenching castings, electrode cleaning, scrap crushing, loading and unloading pitch – all these were unskilled, physically demanding jobs that the white workers successfully sought to avoid. 'The highest job done by any coloured worker', related the manager, 'is fork-lift truck operator.' Elsewhere, an understandably jaundiced perspective belonged to Enid Rodie. Arriving from Guyana in 1961, she lived in Fulham, working first at Sunbright laundry in Wandsworth and then 'at Lemco, which is London Electrical Print':

I was [she recalled many years later] a printer, printing condensers, printing the voltage on condensers. It was a big coal and electric company, printing the condensers for everything – planes, televisions, whatever.

I worked mainly among white people, and I show you, when I went to London Electricals they got a long line. When she [the gaffer] come out to choose, she choose all the white ones. They get a job. Don't matter how old they are, they get a job first, then the blacks, Indians, whoever. She choose the youngest out of the set and then the rest she say, 'Well, try again.' You understand the reason for that? Try again because every week they have to take on people because these white people that she take on … the white people do not keep the job because the job is very dirty. The paint do not come out of your nails, right. You doing something, spill it, messin' up all your clothes … you understand? But it's a dirty job. They don't stick it, young white girls that go there and ting for work. They don't stick it.

'So yes,' she concluded. 'They don't stick the job, so the people that working and keeping the factory going is the blacks because you got the children at home, you got your parents back home, you got to send money, some people borrow the money to come, you know, so you gotta work, you gotta send more money, you gotta buy stuff for your children.'[10]

There seems little doubt that, in the workplace, white prejudice was stronger against West Indians than against Asians. 'Whenever I have to put off staff,' one manager of a non-unionised engineering works had half-guiltily justified himself back in the mid-1950s, 'I sack the coloured ones first. I must. There would be a riot if I did anything else. The trouble is that whenever you dismiss West Indians they make such a fuss. They say you have done it because of colour prejudice, and that makes you feel a rotter.' Nor did it necessarily help the position of West Indian workers if a company was unionised, given the considerable degree of ambivalence felt by many trade union officials, especially at a local level, towards lofty aspirations of universal working-class brotherhood and non-discrimination. And in any case, irrespective of unionisation, the fact remained that by the early 1960s – until race-relations legislation in 1965 – blacks facing employment discrimination had no legal redress.

Ultimately, of course, the problem was societal. 'I think a woman might object if they were served by a coloured girl in corsetry,' one retailer baldly explained at around this time. The experience of the distinctively spelled Francis Williams, soon after she left Jamaica in 1961 and settled in Leeds, speaks eloquent and entrenched volumes:

I heard about this job in the Leeds Infirmary kitchen, I went out and got the job. That's where I started my catering, because one day I went in and the kitchen superintendent asked me, 'Would

you like to be a chef?' I said, 'Of course, that will help me out a
bit.' So, he put me in a room working with these white men and
one white woman. I was glad and not glad. The white chefs were
calling me all sorts of names. They were calling me a monkey,
they were calling me a baboon and all sorts of names. The white
lady chef, her name was Amy, she said to me, 'Francis, don't take
notice of those idiots.' I didn't, I ignored them. But many times,
I went down to the toilets and I cried, and I said, 'Father, I'm just
asking you to give me courage.' I prayed and I cried.

'Damned if they worked and damned if they didn't' is how one
historian, Marcus Collins, neatly sums up the plight of West Indian
men, still at this stage the bulk of the West Indian immigrant
workforce. 'They were made deskilled and then considered unskilled.
They were accused of sloth and warned against ambition.' Or as he
quotes one exasperated teenager asking his white friends at a youth
club: 'How can we be taking all the jobs, and at the same time be living
on National Assistance?' 'But', comments Collins, 'so wide was the
gap between white and West Indian perceptions of the matter that he
could expect no sensible answer.'[11]
    A particularly detailed study of West Indian immigrants in the
workplace was made by Sheila Patterson, doing fieldwork in the
borough of Croydon, home to many manufacturing as well as service
firms. One of the largest was Telelux (not its real name), employing
over 3,000 people to produce a large range of valves and tubes. In 1960
she listened to views, mainly from white managers, about the roughly
250–300 West Indians working there, many on shift work (well paid
but unpopular with younger local men):

> I think that as a general rule the rate of learning is slower with
> the West Indians. Their manual dexterity often seems lower and
> their eyesight poorer. They're usually slow starters and more
> patience is needed to train them. (*Supervisor in training unit*)

> The first coloured charge-hand here would have to be
> exceptionally good. One must consider the general labour
> situation. It's hard enough to get local labour now. You don't
> want people to start saying: 'If you go to work at Telelux you'll
> have a black man bossing you.' I think that when they start

appointing black policemen in London, that will be the time for promoting them here. *(Manager)*

West Indian women often take longer to train than local girls, but they are just as good in the long run. *(Supervisor)*

Almost all the white workers have been here four or five years. The West Indians have about two years' service each. They brought one another in and they're fairly stable. There is a feeling of shift community but the coloured men tend to keep apart and don't talk much. In the canteen they sit in groups or join with coloureds in other sections. They join the union but they don't join the clubs much. As for their working ability, they look slow but they get the work done. They tend to be colour-conscious and abrupt in their manner, which puts some people against them. *(Foreman)*

Some shop stewards are a bit 'anti' so they're not used on trouble involving colour. But in this section we don't have much of that – there was no demand for coloured men to go first when we had some redundancy during the credit squeeze. The main spot of bother I remember was with a West Indian hot-gospelling type who tried to convert the others during the tea-breaks. *(Section leader)*

I don't like to see coloured men with white women – though I must admit that here it's the white women who are after them, and the coloured men don't reciprocate. Some are educated but a lot are not far from savages. *(Foreman)*

They don't behave like you or me. On the buses they sit separately but talk loudly across other people. They've all got a chip on the shoulder. One of the old hands said he was never against coloured people until he had to work next to them. But they've got a lot of go. Look how they buy houses and cars on the H.P. If I had that much energy I'd own two houses by now. But I think it would have been best to build up industry in Jamaica and let them stay there. *(Charge-hand)*

We've tried up to ten West Indians since the section was set up. Most of them were lazy and useless but the three we've got now are all right and have been here a fair time. There's been no trouble except in one case, eighteen months ago, when a coloured girl was sent to Coventry for doing the rate when the shop-steward was fighting it. That blew over and they seem to fit in all right though they are a little aloof. *(Section leader)*

I'm not in love with them but I take them. But one must consider our own permanent people. West Indian workers seem to be either the highly intelligent type who want to go to night school so take day jobs or else the labouring type. Only one of those we have now is of high grade. It's really an embarrassment to offer him a low-paid job – he'd be better off in the lab. The others are slow, whereas the job needs quickness and dexterity. It's also hot and there have been complaints about sweat and smell from the other men. I put two together on testing in a closed booth and I must say I myself didn't like going in there. The other difficulty is that they're cliquish and always attributing a ticking-off to their colour, so that special caution is needed. *(Section leader)*

Disappointingly, Patterson barely seems to have questioned – perhaps was not allowed to – either fellow workers at the same job level or the West Indians themselves. Almost the only exception, and perhaps not very representative, was a West Indian charge-hand who had been working there since 1954 and had shown interest in her enquiry. 'He proved to be from Guyana,' she noted, 'and was a personable, intelligent, athletic young man who came to the interview room not in the customary white overalls but in an elegant tie and well-cut tropical-weight suit':

I've many friends here [he told her] and it's not the first time I've been a pioneer. I was a shop-steward and convener before and I'm proud of it. Some outside the unit and some of the foremen objected but I take a philosophic view and put it down to ignorance. The only one I've ever had trouble from is the West Indian in my unit. He says I'm trying to be a white man. Of course it's a matter of upbringing. My mother and father are of mixed blood and we're more class- and colour-conscious in B.G. [British Guyana] than they are in Jamaica. In fact I wouldn't associate with many of the West Indians who are here, just as

I wouldn't associate with a lot of the English workers. That's why many of us don't join the clubs. We don't like being patronized or forced into them to mix with just anyone.

'His superficial nonchalance', reckoned Patterson, 'seemed to cover a certain submerged prickliness over colour and class.' Unmarried, her informant had not yet made a final decision about whether to stay permanently in Britain or to return home. 'I find England a bit stiff,' he told her. 'The best time I had since I left home was in Paris. I met an English friend there and we had a marvellous international party with some American girls and others who tagged on. Class and colour didn't seem to matter there.'[12]

For Asian immigrants, on the whole more recent arrivals than West Indian immigrants, two places were already by 1962 starting to become emblematic: Bradford and Southall. Textile mills in West Yorkshire had been sending recruitment officers to the Punjab since the early 1950s; but if that was a decisive 'pull' factor, from an immigrant perspective, the key 'push' factor came in 1961, as the towns and villages of the Mirpur district of Pakistan were flooded to make a reservoir, leaving over 100,000 people homeless – just as British textile and engineering companies, including a fair number based in and around Bradford, were in search of cheap labour; and many of the newly displaced spent their compensation money on the fare to Britain. By the 1970s, it was estimated that nearly 70 per cent of Bradford's Asian migrants came from Mirpur, most of them from just a handful of Mirpuri villages. Almost from the start, it was seemingly a win–win situation for all concerned. 'Mirpuris could be relied on', notes Clair Wills in her superb immigrant history (*Lovers and Strangers*) of post-war Britain, 'to find relatives and friends to fill any vacancies, without the mill having to advertise; they could instruct their co-workers on the job, obviating the need for periods of training too.' And she quotes one manager of a Bradford mill recalling the benefits of immigrant night-shift workers:

English people I should say didn't want to work at night due to the unsocial hours aspect of it, but we then had a large immigrant population coming in who were quite happy to work at night. The case that I put was that if we trained one or two as a nucleus, were confident that they knew the job, we could then bring in numbers gradually and we could use them to train their own countrymen. That worked very well and we started to run at night in 1961, and we explained the move to Pakistani and Indian labour to the rest of the workforce to pre-empt any difficulties in that direction by saying that it was essential for survival for us to run three shifts, that they would be on from nine o'clock at night to eight o'clock in the morning, but the practical aspects of the situation were they would scarcely ever see them but they were an essential part of the firm for their survival, and by explaining it to small groups of people we got this point of view across ...

Accordingly, he added, 'we never had the slightest resistance to them coming in'.

Some 200 miles south, 'urban mythology had it', notes Robert Winder in his ever-timely survey (*Bloody Foreigners*) of immigration to Britain across the centuries, 'that hapless Indians who asked to be taken to Piccadilly or Oxford Street were dumped in Southall and told that Buckingham Palace was just up the road. The area became the capital of Asia-in-Britain: the Methodist church became a Sikh *gurdwara* in 1958; a social club was transformed into a Hindu temple.' As usual, job opportunities were the magnet, whether in Southall itself or in such nearby, quasi-industrial places as Hayes, Greenford, Perivale (where the 15-year-old Janet Bull, later Street-Porter, was plotting her escape), Feltham, West Drayton, Uxbridge, Slough, Hounslow and Brentford, with vacancies usually available at firms like Rockware Glass, Lyons Maid, Dura Tube Wire, Chibnall Bakery, Injection Moulding, Wynuna Corset, Combined Optical Industries, Perivale Gutterman, Artid Plastics, Crown Cork, Booth's Gin, Mother's Pride, Chix, Investacast and Meaden Plastics, not to mention the rapidly expanding London Airport (as Heathrow was still called). 'In the main,' reckons a local study looking back on Southall's growth during the 1950s and into the 1960s as a great Asian centre, 'the work that was available was all of a type – defined not by craft or skill but as the work white people would no longer do. It entailed long, irregular hours, shift work, dirty, hot or damp conditions, monotonous tasks, lower-than-average wages, strict discipline, lack of promotion and little or no job security.' As in Bradford, 'with Asian labour on the shifts that local white workers would not do, management found the means to get the most out of its machinery, running it 24 hours a day'; and inevitably, 'Asian workers also often found themselves in types of job or parts of a process which cut them off and marked them out from white workers.'

Probably the dominant employer at this stage was Woolf's, a family firm making rubber accessories (mainly for the motor industry) and by 1960 employing some 40 per cent of Southall's Sikhs, the great majority of them in an unskilled capacity. 'The use of carbon black and sulphur made the work extremely unpleasant,' records the local study. 'Wages were low, conditions bad and work hard. A 60-hour week was considered normal, and large amounts of overtime had to be worked to bring home a living wage – some would work a seven-day week, of 75 hours. Bribery of foremen, to get a job or to keep it and to get overtime, was rife. The management was militantly anti-union ...' But it was not all factory work, for the Sikhs increasingly in the course of the 1960s began to open their own shops, including grocers and butchers as well as the proverbial Asian corner shops. Some were still more ambitious. 'We're long past the stage of street-peddling; now we're manufacturing garments,' declared an Indian leader in Southall. 'It's no longer the question of being able to eat Indian food or buy Indian clothes; nowadays you can hire a car, buy a house or raise a loan through one of us.'[13] That proud observation was almost certainly later in the decade than 1962, but early, unmistakable signs of a fully self-contained, self-supporting eco-system were already apparent.

Whether for Asian or West Indian immigrants, the housing they lived in was more often than not on a spectrum between poor and appalling. Britain's still limited overall housing capacity, a varying mixture of prejudice and financial opportunism on the part of landlords and estate agents, indifferent local authorities, the immigrants' own financial constraints – the causes were by this time well understood by those with a willingness to use their eyes and ears. Based on the 1961 census, a report on 'Commonwealth Immigrants in the Conurbations' – that is, on the households of non-white immigrants in the major cities – provided some hard data: nearly half sharing a dwelling with some other household; a quarter sharing accommodation without the exclusive use of a cooking stove or sink; average number of persons per room of 1.01 against 0.69 for the conurbations as a whole; and evidence of serious overcrowding among West Indian households in London and the West Midlands, where in almost half of those households the number of persons per room exceeded 1.5 (over double the overall conurbations average). The 1965 report of the Milner Holland Committee on housing in London, largely based on evidence from the early 1960s, reached a sombre, unarguable conclusion: 'Although coloured immigrants are in great demand in London for manning many of its services, they are one of the groups who have the greatest difficulty in securing satisfactory housing accommodation.'[14]

In September 1962 the term 'Rachmanism' had not yet been coined and Peter Rachman himself – the Polish Jew whose mini property empire centred upon west London, above all Notting Hill – was still alive. His speciality was turfing out white tenants and, via so-called 'black henchmen', replacing them with West Indians who filled his crumbling Victorian houses to the rafters. 'These middle men used to charge us exorbitant rents, not per room, but I used to pay for a space in a room,' recalled Ivan Weekes, who had become a tenant in one of Rachman's Notting Hill houses soon after arriving from Barbados in 1955. 'There were three of us living in a room at the time when we paid a guinea each, twenty-one shillings in those days, for one room. So it was three guineas for a room, and I had a bed in one corner and the other chaps had a double bed in the other corner.' Even so, Weekes's retrospective take was far from bitter:

> But we were grateful for that. We were grateful for it. Even though it was paying over the top, we were grateful, because you can't stay in the smog and the fog, in those days, on the streets ...
>
> While Rachman was bad, he was the only person that would provide housing for us. You can take that whatever way you want to take it. But it was through him that we got somewhere to stay. So, you pay your money and you take your choice really. And then there were an argument that Peter Rachman himself was fairly reasonable with his charges, but the middle men would bump the charges up by 300 per cent, make a killing for themselves, pay Rachman perhaps a third of that, that's what he charged them for the places. So the middle men really made a killing ...

We didn't know the score, we didn't know what the values were in this country, many of us had just come here a matter of weeks. And in the West Indies, in the Caribbean, one of the most important things about life there is that however poor you are, you had to have somewhere to live. So, somewhere to live, us coming here, was absolutely crucial. And we knew we were being charged an awful lot, but you had to pit that against walking the streets and probably getting hit up for all sorts of reasons. But many of us soon got wise, in a matter of months, we soon got wise as to the ride that were taking of us ...

'But', he added about the great majority who didn't dare risk putting their heads above the parapet and trying their luck with the local rent tribunal service, 'everybody didn't, most people just were passive and decided, well, take an easy life.'

Other non-white immigrants, other housing recollections, the latter mainly negative. 'What got me was the rooms that people live in, just one little room; that really got me,' remembered Agnes DeAbreu about arriving in 1958 as an 18-year-old from St Vincent:

I thought you'd have a bigger area. They said you rent a room, but you couldn't imagine these small little rooms: a little wardrobe, two chairs, a little bed – and the beds were horrible.

My brother Peter was here before me. He took me and I shared a room with a friend from St Vincent and it was a little bed and it was horrible, with those old-fashioned springs. Cooking facilities and washing facilities were shared. It was difficult, a source of tension and arguments. And you could always hear other people in the house ...

We moved with my brother and his friends to another place in Stamford Hill and had a big room, but no heating. We had a paraffin heater, and that's another thing I used to hate. You used to have to put it outside the door for the smell ...

That same year Jessica Huntley, future founder of publishers Bogle-L'Ouverture for Caribbean and African writers, came from Guyana to join her husband. Their stamping ground was also north London:

I remember, once I went to look for a house or a flat, and I went in Haringey, and it was a Greek woman who owned this flat. And it was a very nice flat. And I paid down my deposit. And when I went back to take my suitcase a woman was there, a white woman was there, and she was telling her, 'Don't give the nigger this flat, it's too good for them.' And, of course, we had an altercation ...

Then we lived in another place where the landlord took the fuse out of the lights, so that when you came in and it's winter, the place is dark, you know, you've got to walk up some narrow stairs. Those days there wasn't electric heaters, these were paraffin heaters, we lived on paraffin heaters. We had a paraffin heater in the centre of the house, and you had a kettle on there, so in the mornings, when you woke up, you could do your business, you know. And the thing about it, they didn't want you to live in the place, the houses were so dowdy. I remember the skirting board was dark brown, and they had some hideous wallpaper. And smoky, you know, very, very smoke-filled the houses were, that we lived in, anyway ... Oh, we lived in a lot of places ...

'People were very, very mobile,' added her husband Eric. 'We lived in Waltham, in Haringey, Hornsey, Finsbury Park area, and, most probably, in about a couple of years, we must have changed ten times. Fortunately, there was accommodation available, so that you were able to leave one flat or one room and go to another. You would see that advertisement, that board at Finsbury Park [a large board outside the tube station] was really a historic place for black people.' The pay-off to his reminiscence has a sad inevitability: 'And you would telephone for a flat or a room, mostly, and the person would say, "Yes, it's vacant, come and get it." And then you'd get there, it was so obvious that when you got there, as soon as she saw your face it's gone.'

Or take the city of dreaming spires. There by the early 1960s, especially in east Oxford and the Jericho area of west Oxford, a rapidly increasing number of Pakistani immigrants was settling. Two decades later, Alison Shaw listened to their experiences, including that of 'Amjad', who had come to England to work on a building site:

I came straight to Oxford because I had a cousin here who arranged my accommodation. We lived in a two-bedroomed house. There were seventeen of us living there [and likewise working on building sites], including myself, my cousin Yunis from our village, and also Anwar from a village near ours. The rest were strangers to me. It was terrible living there. We slept two or three men to a bed and each bedroom had two or three double beds in it. People also slept on the stairs and even outside, in the garden, like we do in Pakistan in the hot season. The British Government should not have called us over here for work without telling us how to live and providing some facilities. I was all right because I had been in the army and had learned some of the English ways, but the others did not even know how to use English bathrooms or toilets.

Hardly a comfortable way of life; but as Shaw explains, living with other Pakistanis in multi-occupation lodging houses, as opposed to renting one's own room, had its logic:

A man who worked as many as 75 hours a week as a labourer, by taking all possible overtime, would have little time, energy or opportunity to do anything other than work; often the houses in which the men lived were no more than dormitories. Men working on night shifts would share beds with men on day shifts and further reduce their rent. In the early 1960s, a man could in this way earn between £12 and £18 a week, spend £2 per week on lodging and food, and save the rest. By keeping expenses to a minimum, some men were able to save as much as £500 in one year ... Indeed, saving itself became a source of status among migrants. A man who saved large sums of money for the benefit of kin at home gained considerable status among the relatives and friends with whom he was living in Britain; on the other hand, if the worker saved less than £25 a year, he would be ashamed to admit this to others. There was therefore also a moral pressure from relatives and fellow-villagers which tended to ensure that migrants continued to live frugally, save and remit money home.

To have done otherwise, she concludes, would have involved 'a loss of face'.[15]

What about family life among non-white immigrants? Any generalisations – for example about how mothers of young children often had to manage without the support from extended family customary for white working-class mothers, or about how Asian men, working what Wills calls 'unbelievably long hours', in effect sacrificed family life for higher wages – have to be set against the key contextual fact that, until the admittedly spectacular rush of migration during the year and a half before the restrictive Commonwealth Immigrants Act took effect on 1 July 1962, the great majority of those non-white immigrants (especially Asian immigrants) were single males not intending to settle permanently. Put another way, the subject of immigrant family life would become a much richer one for sociologists and future historians in the years ahead than it was in the early 1960s. Even so, we have already by this stage enough oral testimony to suggest that Marcus Collins is probably right when he argues in relation to West Indian men and family life that, contrary to some white assumptions about what he terms 'an endemic anti-familialism among West Indian men', in practice it was only a relatively 'dissolute' minority who refused to accept and embrace core family responsibilities. The 'pinnacle of morality', according to Wallace Collins in *Jamaican Migrant* (1965), was how the average Jamaican man regarded the family, placing his wife and children 'above his head like a guiding star'; and the same intimate witness, who had migrated from Jamaica in the mid-1950s, despaired that 'the English could not fathom the motivation of the Jamaican male'.

That said, Collins himself did not want to be accused of exaggerating Victorian values, for he also accepted that more migrant Jamaican men than he would have wished were 'polygamous to say the least', that 'in fact they are "wild", for their monumental faith in their virility would incite them to move any mountain just to raise a skirt and claim its contents'. Not entirely dissimilarly, doing her research in the 1980s about Oxford's Pakistanis, Shaw noted that 'while few men in the community today, especially those who hold positions of authority in the mosque or the welfare associations, would admit that they themselves had English girlfriends or visited prostitutes or went drinking during their bachelor years in Britain, accounts of migrants' activities at that time and the rumour and gossip prevalent in the community today suggests that in fact these activities were fairly widespread'. Indeed, 'several men spoke about the prostitutes who used to visit particular multi-occupation houses'.[16]

As for other forms of socialising, Colin Grant points out in his rich oral history of the Windrush generation that so alien to West Indians was traditional British pub culture (quite apart from the often frosty reception there) that the customary place for Friday- or Saturday-night get-togethers was the front room, frequently accompanied by rum and Coke as well as music from the cherished pride-of-place Blue Spot radiogram. Socialising also took place at church: usually either at those of the Seventh Day Adventists (the only established white church which had shown any warmth towards the black newcomers), or at their own Pentecostal churches. 'The church was St John's,' recalls the disc jockey and film-maker Don Letts, whose parents had come over from Jamaica two years before his birth in 1956:

After service they'd gather in the hall which was at the back of the church and it was kind of a way to ease their pain after having to put up with a lot of shit over the week; and it was obviously a way for them to stay in touch with each other, and also get news from back home. It was much more of a community thing, much more of a social affair than people letting their hair down and partying till four in the morning; my parents weren't that way inclined. They would have played early R&B, Fats Domino – Jamaicans love Fats Domino – early crooners, Brooke Benton, Perry Como, Nat King Cole and some of the emerging reggae sounds, but back then it wasn't even reggae – it was ska and Bluebeat. They might even drop a bit of country and western, because one thing about my parents' generation, I don't know what it is, but the old Jamaicans love a bit of country and western, Jim Reeves.

That generation's culinary tastes, however, were not those of Nashville. 'My parents, hardcore Jamaicans,' also remembers Letts. 'Chicken, rice and peas, ackee, salt fish, plantain, dumpling, sweet potato, yam, callaloo, the works.' In order to procure which:

> Every Saturday we went to the market, you didn't have a choice. Rain, cold and fucking freezing wearing short trousers, not wanting to go. You'd have to go with your mum and dad to Brixton market and it was very much an Afro-Caribbean thing back then – not this trendy thing it is now [2019] – totally Jamaican food. The main bit was Granville Arcade, which is now the food village or whatever, but that was just packed with every representative from every Caribbean island.

If Brixton market was not yet multicultural, nor were the 300 or so curry houses by now in existence, mainly owned and run by East Pakistani (Bangladeshi) Muslims and mainly serving an Asian clientele. Indeed, 'in the early 1960s', notes Wills about the host country, 'curry was still pretty much a dirty word'. '"Indians stink of curry" was', she adds, 'a common complaint of neighbours in all the areas where Asians settled, and it crops up continually in the sociological studies of immigrant areas in the 1960s.' And she quotes a Sylheti immigrant who in 1962 opened a café on Whitechapel's Commercial Road: 'We had to sell egg and chips and other things to start with. The customers took a long time before they started trying curry – even then we would have to add milk to it to make it mild for them. At first they would always have chips with their curry, never rice. Once I had a man who wanted to fight me because he found a bay-leaf in his curry. I had to explain we added bay-leaf to give it flavouring.'[17]

Before 'integration' became the hopeful buzzword from the mid-1960s, the term most commonly invoked for the desirable process in those of Britain's cities and towns with significant numbers of non-white immigrants was 'assimilation'. It had, of course, a fundamental flaw. 'Assimilation did nothing to promote race relations or racial harmony because, while black migrants were told by the state that they were British and not a society apart, racism and discrimination kept them on the margins of British society and excluded them from utilizing their citizenship rights,' reflects one historian, Michael Dawswell, in a challenging essay on 'The Pigmentocracy of Citizenship'. 'The process of assimilation', he goes on, 'imposed a set of values that many black migrants openly reacted against by asserting their own culture, traditions, history and lifestyle.' Moreover, for those newcomers positively wanting to be assimilated into British society as smoothly and harmoniously as possible, the sympathetic and well-informed contemporary sociologist Michael Banton pointed out in 1959 the very considerable barriers put up by all the 'unstated assumptions', 'wordless understandings', 'unspoken codes' and 'unannounced rights and obligations' which, taken as a whole, comprised 'the unspoken language' of day-to-day British social life.[18]

Given all of which, the ready assumption might be that most of these members of the Windrush generation planned, as soon as they could, to return home. Perhaps they did, but in practice many – perhaps the majority – stayed. 'Well, as time went by, I get closer and closer to England because I started looking for family, because I started courting, and then getting married, married at Wandsworth,' recalled Oswald (Columbus) Dennison, who had come over on the *Windrush* itself. Or take Connie Mark, who in 1954, with a three-month-old baby, flew from Jamaica to join her (first) husband and fellow Jamaican Stanley Goodrich, a fast bowler playing on a professional basis in Durham. 'I came with a suitcase of clothes hoping to go back in a year,' she explained. 'Well, what it is, you're on a contract, and while you're under contract they keep renewing it and renewing it and renewing it, and then by the time you're here certain years, you think, well, you want to go back but you haven't got the amount of money for the fare, that if you go back, what are you going to do? And it just goes on and on and on.' Another non-returnee, Ben Bousquet from St Lucia in 1957, neatly summed things up, like Dennison and Mark speaking several decades after arriving: 'What went wrong is there's such a thing called time where people change, where the home which you left may not be the home which you could go back to, where the system itself changes, where you yourself change, where you start to have the children and those children begin to have children of their own. So, and that's change. That's what happened.'

Yet, like Chekhov's sisters and going to Moscow, the dream could stubbornly persist. A final voice belongs to an unidentified Jamaican talking in the mid-1960s:

If I dream tonight, you can bet your life it will be about Jamaica. I think so often about going back that the idea of returning has become as inevitable as death. Soon it will be ten years

since I came to Bristol. I was eighteen when I left Jamaica and
I remember boasting to some of my friends that I would be back
before I reached twenty-five. My plan was to get a job and study
electrical engineering by correspondence course and evening
school. I was unemployed six months. When I eventually got a
job as a porter, all ambition was knocked out of me. Instead of
correspondence course I did my football coupon. All I wanted
was to get a better job. So far I have had nine jobs and none is
ever better than the first. I don't mind much about that promise
of returning in six or seven years because all the chaps to whom
I made that promise are all over here. Some doing well at that.
When I think of Jamaica, I sometimes feel as if I never had been
young. The years in England are missing years. I cannot give
an account of them. When I meet a man from back home who
has just come up, we talk and I discover that Jamaica too has
changed. My mother died since I was over here and the house
in which I was born has been pulled down and the graves of my
family have been trampled flat. Yet I still want to go back home.
I know that I will not be going back, but we never admit it to
each other. We have four children and we have a couple of rooms
in a friend's house. Seven years ago we had planned to buy our
own house, then the babies started coming. My wife has not been
able to work since. Yet the last thing we would admit is that we
will not be going home. Of course, it is not impossible. I have
not given up doing the pools. Who knows? Next week might be
my week for the treble chance ...[19]

Since October 1961 the government had been in negotiations about
joining the Common Market (as the European Economic Community
was still often quaintly called). For Macmillan, the motive was
overwhelmingly one of foreign policy: in essence, that this would enable
Britain to forge as close a relationship with Europe as it already had
with America and thereby to be the indispensable link between Europe
and America – crucial, as he had put it in a December 1960 paper on
'The Grand Design', if 'the great forces of the Free World' were going
to come together 'economically, politically and militarily in a coherent
effort to withstand the Communist tide all over the world'. Where did

the Commonwealth fit in? Perhaps inevitably, not very well; and when the Commonwealth prime ministers assembled in London for their conference in September 1962, the mood was one of hostility (as much as anything on economic grounds) to Britain's new foreign policy venture, shading at times into resignation. 'Macmillan is hellbent for Europe,' Jamaica's PM, Sir Alexander Bustamante, publicly declared on the 12th, but there was little he or others could do about it apart from trying to mobilise British public opinion. Macmillan himself delivered a TV address to the nation on the evening of Thursday the 20th, around the time of the meeting in Bradford provoked by Pakistani cafés being set on fire. Here, tellingly, he put the emphasis much less on the grand geopolitical design, much more on Europe coming together (including Britain) as a symbol of progress and modernity. 'A lot of people look backward, but the real test you must bring to this question is – are we going to look forward?' he urged. And his broadcast, delivered from the drawing room of Admiralty House, ended: 'Many of us, especially those who are young in heart or in years, are impatient of the old disputes; intolerant of obsolete conceptions; anxious that our country should take its part, and if possible a leading part, in all these new and hopeful movements.'

Gaitskell replied for Labour the following evening. Whereas most of the Conservative Party was broadly behind Macmillan's initiative, much of the Labour Party was instinctively hostile to, or anyway suspicious of, 'Europe'. Gaitskell's own thinking on the issue had evolved steadily in the course of the year, finally reaching towards the end of summer an overall negative position. 'He had', reflects his fullest biographer (Philip Williams), 'many reasons: his deteriorating relations with the spokesmen of the Six [that is, the pioneer members of the European Economic Community], his shock at the terms, his exposure to the Commonwealth reactions to them, his angry resentment at the government's conduct and at the pressure of the media in favour of entry.' Now, in his TV broadcast, he highlighted the potential grave economic damage to Commonwealth countries as a result of Britain being compelled to abandon its existing trading system; complained that 'the Six' had offered only 'promises, vague assurances and nothing more'; and warned that if Britain by joining the Common Market found that it was actually entering a European federation, then that would mean 'the end of Britain as an independent nation', as it became instead 'just a province of Europe'. Altogether it was a broadcast which, the Liberal leader Jo Grimond sardonically but not unreasonably noted next day, 'showed a proper suspicion of all foreigners and a considerable distrust of all change'.[20]

It is unlikely that at this stage public opinion, taken as a whole, was unduly stirred. 'What a bore the Common Market has become!' recorded Anthony Heap some days later. 'Personally I've no strong feelings in the matter one way or t'other, and neither, I fancy, have the vast majority of people in this country.' Mollie Panter-Downes, writing her *New Yorker* letter at around the time of the broadcasts, sought to gauge the state of play:

> The young, by and large, appear to be in favor, with an instinctive feeling for the big new moment in history and the wider chance, and so are the businessmen, eager to get going in the great new market, plus a majority slice – one could perhaps risk guessing – of educated, thoughtful opinion. The various anti-Market meetings that have been held in different parts of the country have drawn many retired service people, maybe disturbed by the thought of a still further dwindling of the British influence that they helped, in their time, to impose around the world. The farmers are against, and so, on the whole, would seem to be the average man in the pub, though the trade unions, at their conference the other day, decisively voted down a proposal rejecting the Common Market.

She added that 'the public-opinion polls go on reporting a steadily increasing rumble of doubts – one of those strange subterranean movements that sometimes travel across the country, and not always in the direction indicated by the experts'. Those experts were given plenty of space in the press, which, apart from the Beaverbrook papers (*Daily Express*, *Sunday Express*, *Evening Standard*) and the Communist-supporting *Daily Worker*, was, according to Panter-Downes, 'solidly united in backing the government' in its pro-Market stance. For all her many merits, she was almost certainly not a keen *Guardian* reader; and the day after his broadcast, Macmillan relieved himself of some of his anxieties over the Europe issue by observing in his diary that 'the *Manchester Guardian* [as it was no longer called] still hedges – it represents the kind of attitude which Lord John Russell spent his life in promoting – always willing to wound and afraid to strike – and always essentially priggish and slightly dishonest'.

Over half a century later, post-Brexit, this moment in the ultimately tragicomic story of Britain and Europe feels simultaneously a very long time ago and the day before yesterday. Three more or less contemporary assessments, all of them by instinctively pro-Europeans who undoubtedly would have voted Remain in 2016, are worth a moment's pause – the first by the Oxford economist Uwe Kitzinger (in fact still alive in 2016), who as a naturalised Briton had been between 1951 and 1956 the first British economist at the Council of Europe in Strasbourg:

> As freedom of movement clashes with xenophobia [he wrote in 1961], so the problem of supranationalism touches the deeper suspicions against the outside world. In defence, Britain has long abandoned independence; in economics, a country as heavily dependent on the rest of the world can only ever be master of its own fate to a very limited degree; but the formal merger of decision-making procedures, the absence of a formal veto ... go against the grain even of many who on most other grounds would like to see Britain join the Community.

One intellectually super-confident Labour politician was more directly clued in – albeit less sympathetically – to the abiding forces of conservative isolationism. 'We cling to every outmoded scrap of national sovereignty, play the obsolete role of an imperial power, and fail to adjust to the new, dynamic Europe,' wrote Anthony Crosland not long afterwards. 'The cause is partly our oppressive, traditional pattern of class relations, partly the psychological difficulty of adapting from great power to second-rate international status, partly the complacent ignorance bred by an insular tradition.' For Isaiah Berlin, writing to a fellow philosopher in September 1962 itself (the 14th), Macmillan and his espousal of Europe represented in effect a throw of the dice for the only cause – the survival of Western liberal, pluralist civilisation – truly worth fighting for:

> He is an actor and no doubt much of what he says is purely 'political', but I think with regard to the Common Market, even

if it is purely subjective, he feels the emotions of Peel before the Corn Laws, or [Woodrow] Wilson and the League [of Nations]. He knows that he may split the Party and may be defeated, and that the whole thing may be reduced to a fearful shambles; but he has a philosophy of history, he is not a shallow empiricist, despite the moustache, the tastes, the Clubs, the slightly false grand manner. I think fundamentally that he is a pessimist and thinks that the barbarians will win in the end. But he thinks that he can build dams against this and hold out for quite a time and the Common Market is one of these.[21]

Gaitskell may have looked backwards in his broadcast (fearing 'the end of a thousand years of history'), but otherwise the 21st was a day of the new, or anyway the forward-looking. At the Liberal Party's conference at Llandudno, Ludovic Kennedy (prospective candidate for Aylesbury) put his faith in planning ('a concept that every Conservative automatically shies away from, while the Labour Party's way of dealing with the problem is wholesale nationalisation') in order to eliminate poverty, bring Britain up to date and replace ugliness, chaos, stagnation and decay with beauty, order, movement and growth; *University Challenge*, chaired by Bamber Gascoigne, made its debut, though only on Granada (at a far from peak-time 10.45 p.m.) and not yet with the 'College Boy' theme tune, but instead Duke Ellington's 'Ting-A-Ling'; a flat, factual, unadorned sentence in the *NME* announced that 'a Liverpool group, the Beatles, have recorded "Love Me Do" for Parlophone, which is set for October 5 release'; and the Ford Cortina was launched. Its name a nod to the glamorous ski-resort venue of the 1956 Winter Olympics, it would never in truth be the world's most thrilling or fashionable car, but did offer, at low cost, the four cardinal qualities of space, comfort, simplicity and easy-to-service reliability. Soon, with 1,200 rolling off production lines daily at Dagenham, accounting for half the Ford cars produced there, it was set to be middle England's car of the next decade and a half. 'The Cortina', recalled Jonathan Glancey in 1988 (six years after the last of almost 4.3 million had been made), 'was *the* car for fitters and clerks, the newly motorised sales reps and minor civil servants.' That Friday in September also saw one other new thing: the release of Tony Richardson's *The Loneliness of the Long Distance Runner*, which was based on Alan Sillitoe's short story, starred Tom Courtenay and was the latest contender in the British New Wave. 'A British film nowadays, if it is to be taken seriously,' began the *Guardian*'s anonymous, only semi-enthusiastic review, 'must set its scene among the more or less rebellious young people of the industrial North or Midlands; it must be tough, realistic, iconoclastic (possibly nihilistic too) and thoroughly "working class".' The problem, however, was that, for all the film's technical prowess, 'the fashion, being no longer new, is losing the fine edge of its distinction and is beginning to turn to formulas of its own':

> Thus there is much that is all too recognisable. We have already witnessed, more than once, the dingy family background, the parental misunderstanding and youthful resentment, the stark, irreverent language, the general air of cynical defeatism – and even certain specific sequences, such as those showing us a smoke-belching industrial city as seen by the young lovers on a 'romantic' outing to a neighbouring hill-top.

'We have', in short, 'been there before; and the impact is no longer what it was.'[22]

That same day, the weeklies offered a reappraisal and an obituary. 'I see Kingsley gets a bit of a ragging in the *N.S.* today by this John Gross character,' Philip Larkin reported with some distinct pleasure to Monica Jones. 'Good division of his characters into heroes who can do nothing wrong and stooges who can do nothing right.' It was now eight years since *Lucky Jim* had overnight made its author's name, and Gross's *New Statesman* review of Amis's new collection of stories, *My Enemy's Enemy*, included the reader's reaction to him by this stage of his career: 'We begin by assenting, "Ah, that's what life is really like"; in the end we find ourselves muttering, "Well, there's more to life than *that*".' The obituary was of the New Left, at whose recent summer school, held in Burley-in-Wharfedale, Sandy Hobbs had chaired a debate between Perry Anderson and the historian E. P. Thompson. 'I made a vain, and probably naive, attempt to stress the common ground between the two, but conversations with them suggested to me they were on quite different intellectual trajectories,' recalled Hobbs in

2006. 'Thompson could see that the journal [the *New Left Review*] he had helped to found was changing its character radically. He asked me my views, as a psychologist, of the recent article by R. D. Laing. He was pleased that I shared his scepticism of its worth, but of course its publication was only an early sign of Anderson's taste for grandiose theory-mongering ...'

Now, in the *Spectator*, a young journalist, Stephen Fay, wrote a lengthy piece headed 'The Late New Left', declaring at the outset that 'the New Left is exhausted', that indeed, some six years after it had begun in the wake of Suez and the Soviet invasion of Hungary, 'it barely exists in capital letters any longer'. At the heart of Fay's analysis was what he saw as the New Left's wishful thinking in relationship to the working class:

> Their revolution had to be working-class. They were the intellectuals who would lead it. But they were confronted by an apathetic working class, unaware, they thought, of political and social realities ...
>
> They never really rejected the idea of the manipulated masses, unwittingly seduced by commercial television. They continued to think of the working class in romantic or literary terms, guided by Richard Hoggart's *The Uses of Literacy*. 'It is the mythology of prosperity which induces apathy,' Stuart Hall said. Obviously Macmillan's 'you've never had it so good' enraged and encouraged them. But they were never able to show many workers in, say, the engineering industries that it was untrue. Even the working class in less prosperous areas, in Scotland and the North-East, could not be convinced. They were relatively much better off than they were in the thirties, and although the New Left said this does not matter, it does to the working class.

'In the end,' reckoned Fay, 'their appeal for the revolutionary overthrow of capitalism too often degenerated into an appeal for moral revulsion.' And he went on to itemise other failings, including the lack of close economic analysis, the inability to understand let alone influence the trade unions, the fact that 'they rarely asked themselves how the content of some of the plays, films and novels they admired was to be communicated to the people whose interest was marginal, or whose minds needed changing', and above all their unwillingness to accept the need for firm leadership within the movement. 'But for all that,' Fay conceded, 'the New Left was an important symptom of British life in the fifties. After years of full employment, economics seemed less important (which they are not), culture and society much more important. For many people this was their first introduction to politics, and it will possibly influence many of them for the rest of their political lives. Theirs was a revolt against age, and against a static society.' Yet ultimately, he concluded, 'it will take more than the New Left to change the system'.[23]

Among the many young writers and creative figures loosely affiliated to the New Left was Dennis Potter. ' "Culture" ', he declared on Saturday the 22nd in his *Daily Herald* TV column, 'has become too suspect for too many people.' His particular object of wrath was what he saw as the BBC's overly highbrow arts programme, *Monitor*, and he added: 'TV can help, must help, break down these false barriers.' That day, the Tyne Tees edition of *TV Times* included a letter (from K. Irving of Hexham) complaining that the beer served in *Coronation Street*'s Rover's Return was invariably flat ('I have never seen a pint with even a bubble of froth on it'); guests on *Juke Box Jury* included Mike Sarne, whose single 'Come Outside' (featuring an eventually obliging Wendy Richard) had been so integral to the summer's soundscape; and next day the struggling left-wing Sunday paper *Reynolds News* reinvented itself as the *Sunday Citizen* ('still the same old drearily plebeian "paper without a peer" ', observed Heap). Early afternoon on Monday the 24th had Henry St John at Shepherd's Bush market. 'I asked if I could look through a box of pin-up magazines which were still out of reach, as they had been twice on Saturday,' noted this most dogged and least empathetic of diarists. 'I bought 3 back numbers of "Connoisseurs Choice" but not vol. 3 no. 1 which continued to elude me.' Elsewhere that day, 18-year-old Ray Davies was taking his first classes at Hornsey College of Art, and in Birmingham's evening paper Peter Griffiths was asserting that 'the socialists are attempting to obtain the coloured vote because they think it will hold Smethwick for them'. Tuesday the 25th belonged, unhappily enough, to Trevor Howard, up before Middlesex Sessions for driving a car under the influence of drink. 'The public', declared the chairman (the Hon. Ewen Montagu, QC), 'need protection from you, because even after that warning [a previous conviction for drink driving] you are a man who drinks vast quantities every night – according to your own evidence equivalent to six double whiskies.' The upshot was a £50 fine and disqualification from driving for eight years – punishment perhaps increased as a result of Howard's insouciant remark to the jury that he had never before had the experience of being in a police station for 'this sort of thing'.[24]

'I wish that the whole planning business would stop for a week so that everybody – developers, designers and administrators – could read this book. Really read it, not come armoured against it with preconceptions and statistics.' So, in next day's *Daily Telegraph*, declared Ian Nairn at the outset of his review of Jane Jacobs's book on what had been happening to American cities and what should now be happening. A great architectural writer reviewing a great writer on urban life: a signal moment, but just a shame that it was in a paper relatively seldom read by Britain's post-war generation of progressive and well-meaning 'activators', a generation still very influential in their self-appointed task of creating a New Jerusalem – a task that in Nairn's eyes had gone badly wrong. After crisply summarising the Jacobs thesis as 'city vitality depends on the vitality of streets, definite places with a definite shape, and a street's vitality depends on the mixture of uses in it', he went on:

> Yet the staples of our urban rebuilding at the moment [in Britain] are *first* sorting out of uses into residential, commercial and industrial. *Second*, 'comprehensive redevelopment', so that whole areas termed outworn – and in fact forced to be outworn because they have been so designated – are replaced wholesale, instead of being renewed slowly and organically. *Third*, except in shopping centres, where the absurdity is too evident, disintegration of the street into a collection of buildings in landscape, decorously spaced out and fragmented.
>
> All this, applauded by everyone, is in the name of good design and good planning. The sufferers are inarticulate and carry no political weight – imagine the fuss if someone proposed to redevelop Chelsea in the way that the LCC [London County Council] are now disembowelling the East End.

Who cares about a little business in Camberwell, compulsorily purchased with nowhere else to go to? Or the little back streets of Stepney, humble enough but with all the magnificent spark of urban life that planners applaud and sigh for abroad? They are being demolished wholesale, to be replaced by a collection of isolated blocks with the old street continuity gone, the old corner shops and small businesses gone, the pub standing gaunt on the corner because it was too much trouble to acquire ...

Nairn then brilliantly compared town planning in 1960s Britain to bloodletting in the early nineteenth century – 'clearance and redevelopment is prescribed just as comprehensively and complacently for parts of cities which are as complex as the human body' – before continuing:

With kindness and understanding, a large part of the slums could clear themselves, pulling themselves up by their own bootstraps, with public aid only for the irrecoverable corners. But this demands a complete reversal of architectural and town planning theory, and a complete change of attitude of the planners to the planned. We have killed more of Cockney London with kindness after the war than the bombs ever did.

Not one post-war scheme, to my knowledge, has been prepared to accept a few old terraces, an existing corner shop or two, a small, inoffensive industry that does not want to move. To do so would be 'anathema, chaos, the negation of planning, untidiness ...'. In fact, to do so is the only hope of keeping the city alive as an organism. It must renew itself as naturally as the body does. If that obscures someone's tidy vision of how people live, then *tant pis*.

'Our city life has been almost destroyed, doubtless with the best of intentions,' concluded this passionate, troubled, humane man. 'To the shame of the profession, it has taken a 46-year-old American journalist to say so and to say why. What she did was to look and feel and analyse – which is what our planners and architects should have done 25 years ago.'

This Wednesday daytime, the Light Programme went on, as ever, its own sweet, untroubled way. At 10 o'clock, *At Your Request*, with Sandy MacPherson at the BBC theatre organ and Joe McBride on tenor; at 10.31, *Music While You Work*, with the Metropolitan Police Band; at 11.00, *Morning Story* ('The Cherry Wood Chair'); at 11.15, *The Dales*; at 11.31, the BBC Midland Light Orchestra, conducted by Gilbert Vinter; at 12.00, 'Derek Roy with his Twelve O'Clock Spin introducing a cavalcade of star entertainers on record'; at 12.31, *Parade of the Pops*, introduced by Denny Piercy and featuring half a dozen regulars (Bob Miller and the Millermen, Lynn Collins, Dougie Arthur, Gordon Somers, The Milltones, Vince Hill) as well as a trio of guests (Kathie Kay, Johnny De Little, Eden Kane); at 13.36, *Downbeat*, with Charles Melville; at 13.45, *Listen with Mother* (today's story 'Jenny Goes Out to Tea'). Among those listening was D. W. Ramm, probably male, probably young, definitely from Lincoln. 'Illness kept me in bed for a day,' began his far from gruntled letter to *Melody Maker*:

> I tuned to the BBC.
>
> After three minutes, I turned off Sandy MacPherson. The Metropolitan Police Band sounded like the British police. Left with 'The Dales', Scottish dance music and the BBC Midland Light Orchestra, I picked up my book again.
>
> Derek Roy's '12 o'clock Spin' was a breath of fresh air. 'Parade of the pops' was awful.
>
> But what was this? Nine minutes of 'Downbeat' with Charles Melville.
>
> First word, 'Basie' – marvellous! Second, the Four Freshmen. Interrupted by a shipping forecast which lasted just long enough for us to hear 'Downbeat was introduced by Charles Melville ...'
>
> Let's have another channel which broadcasts the best in everything.

'Meanwhile,' he asked, 'is there any wonder why I am emigrating to Australia?'

That evening, Bangor City played their away leg in Naples and went down 3–1. No away-goals-counting-double rule then, so a decider on neutral ground was arranged for Highbury in mid-October. All of which, or any other of life's small transitory pleasures and amusements, mattered not a jot to Andrée Bokitko, whose daughter was born next day, Thursday the 27th:

It was the summer of 1962 [she recalled many years later for an anthology compiled for the National Childbirth Trust], and the papers were full of stories about the thalidomide babies. I was expecting my first baby, so naturally I was very interested in it all. I remember discussing it with a friend one day, who was also pregnant. She said if she knew she was having an affected baby she'd have an abortion, but I said no, I couldn't do that.

Simone was a breech birth, so I was taken into hospital and induced. I had gas and air during the delivery, so I was a bit woozy. But I remember there were lots of medical people in the room, and I just had this feeling something was wrong after she was born. They kept trying to put the mask over my face so I couldn't ask anything or see what was going on. And then a doctor came quite close to me and asked had I taken any drugs during my pregnancy? And then I knew, I just knew, that I'd had one of *those* babies.

They showed Simone to me very briefly in the delivery room, but I only saw her face as she was wrapped in a shawl. And I remember thinking, well, she's a pretty little thing, whatever else might be wrong with her.

I was really tired after the delivery, and back on the ward I slept. When I woke up it was night, and everyone else was asleep. I called the nurse, and told her I wanted to see my baby. She said it wasn't possible, but I insisted. I thought maybe I'd dreamt it, that there wasn't anything wrong, but I had to know, one way or the other. Eventually she agreed to get Simone, and we unwrapped her shawl together. I saw everything then – Simone has elbow-length arms, with three fingers on each, and part of her femur missing on both legs. I just cried and cried and cried. But I prayed too: I said to God, if she's going to suffer, take her now. Because I wanted her, but not if she was going to have an awful life.

My husband was in a terrible state when he discovered what was wrong. They called him in to the hospital, but they didn't give him any idea on the phone what it was about – he thought something had happened to me. When he arrived they took him into a sluice room to show Simone to him – they said they didn't want to frighten other people. He was horrified, he said if she's like that on the outside, what's going to be wrong with her inside? But I persuaded him that Simone would be okay, that she was our baby, and that things would work out alright.

A few days later the consultant came to see me and said he'd heard I'd been putting it about that I'd taken thalidomide during my pregnancy. He warned me not to talk about it any more, which annoyed me enormously. In the end I got the drugs I'd taken during my pregnancy analysed, and sure enough the one I'd taken for anxiety had contained thalidomide.

'Simone', she added, 'was one of the last thalidomide babies born. In some ways that helped, in that there were lots of parents with affected two- and three-year-olds to give support and advice. In other ways it was awful – why hadn't they publicised the ban on the drug I was taking, to alert me to the dangers of keeping on taking it once I was pregnant?' It is a heartbreaking (as well as revealing) account; but at least, irrespective of subsequent matters of blame and compensation over the whole dreadful thalidomide scandal, the last two sentences offer some comfort: 'I didn't feel I had anything to apologise for. She was my baby, and I loved her exactly as I would if she hadn't had anything wrong.'[25]

Merciful normality reigned in Chingford, where on Friday morning at 10.30, after shopping, Judy Haines went to the hairdresser. Nevertheless, like many suburban housewives as the relative certainties of the 1950s began to give way to the relative uncertainties of the 1960s, she was not at the age of fifty-three at an entirely happy stage of her life. 'Met Mrs Saunders on way home, who is more resigned to her changed husband since his illness (cancer),' continued her entry:

He is back at work but most disagreeable. She says she makes her 'life' during the day. It struck me I always do this. John never goes out with me in the week, and very little is said in the evening. I have got used to it and quite like it. Felt very lonely after first retiring from office life. Wouldn't mind having another bash if the right job turned up.

Nothing suburban about the Liverpool photoshoot that day for the Beatles, as Brian Epstein geared up publicity a week ahead of 'Love Me Do' hitting the world. One black-and-white image in particular would prove iconic. Four young men coolly (but with just a hint of a smile from John and George) looking out at the world, the location a strip of wasteland between Saltney Street and Dublin Street up by Clarence Graving Dock, behind them a huge, prison-like, brick-stone warehouse – altogether, at a time when (in Mark Lewisohn's apt words) 'pretty much every pop publicity photo was formulaic and studio-bound', it did the business.

The first review (praising the record's 'refreshing do-it-yourself approach') appeared next day, the 29th, in the *Liverpool Echo*; 'Telstar', acme of yearning modernity, entered the Top Ten; not regretting East Suffolk noisiness ('daylong shots as the farmers tried to scare the crows from the crops, the roar of tractors and harvesters'), the New Zealand novelist Janet Frame left her cottage near Eye after living there since May; the 72-year-old Gladys Langford made a rare foray from north London to see Noël Coward's *Sail Away* at the Savoy Theatre but regretted it ('Yankee accents of players, near-nude characters, such silly songs & even sillier dialogue made me sigh for 12/6 spent on seat'); and on the small screen, the first of a new series of *Thank Your Lucky Stars* included Petula Clark, Mark Wynter and Chubby Checker, the near-pioneer consumer programme *On the Braden Beat* made its debut, and Honor Blackman appeared for the first time in *The Avengers* as the black-leather-clad Cathy Gale. For E. P. Thompson in Halifax, it was time for the grand remonstrance to Lawrence Daly after the latter's rationale for disbanding the Fife Socialist League. 'In order to make the commonplace Labourist points, you use emotionally loaded phrases – such as the spectre of vote-splitting, "when millions of people ... sick of Tory rule" would condemn us etc,' he wrote reproachfully to the Scottish miner. 'I have heard these arguments from Labour and C.P. [Communist Party] ideologues, but I didn't expect to get them from Lawrence Daly.' And Thompson declared that he remained 'convinced that the Labour Party, certainly in England, is both sick and essentially reactionary' – that, indeed, 'it can only be changed by a shake-up on a scale which will involve breakaways and fights outside the Party, and cannot be confined to inner-Party pressure'.

But for Scotland's widely read the *People's Journal* the issue this Saturday was (as in one corner of Chingford) quite different. 'WITH SO MANY MEN IDLE IN SCOTLAND, SHOULD MARRIED WOMEN WORK?' it asked, before providing some of the answers that a survey on this question had elicited:

> I think most married women fill jobs which men couldn't and wouldn't take. However, if a married woman and an unemployed man applied for the same job, the job should go to the man. After all, a man is the breadwinner in any household. *(Bill Mackenzie, Clachnaharry, Inverness)*

> They should give all work to unemployed men. A woman's place is in the home looking after her family. *(Archie Brown, retired coal miner, Musselburgh)*

> I have no objection to married women working. Taking their jobs is not the answer to the unemployment problem in Scotland. What we want is more work for the men. I say it will be a good thing if more firms provided nurseries so that more women with families could go out and work. Of course, the complete answer is to see that every man earns sufficient so that his wife doesn't have to go out and work to get extras. *(William Stabler, redundant miner, Glenrothes)*

> It's not up to the women of Scotland to provide jobs for unemployed men. The responsibility lies solely with the Government. Anyhow I doubt if men, especially skilled tradesmen, would want the majority of jobs married women have. If married women were forced to give up their jobs it would cause even more discontent. *(Mrs Margaret Wood, Edinburgh)*

> If a woman has a young family, and her husband is working, she should be at home looking after her children and cooking her husband's meals. That is a wife's job. In our parents' day a man would have been ashamed to admit that he couldn't keep his wife and family. Now it just doesn't mean a thing. No woman can be expected to do two jobs – working all day and doing the housework at night – and be a success at them both. If a woman

does a good job at home she should not be asked to do more. *(Ken Grant, Edinburgh)*

Don't be daft! I'm a waitress, and I don't know any man who would wait at table if I gave my job up. *(Mrs Sadie Jamieson, Glasgow)*[26]

––––––

Saturday, 29 September, more than a quarter of the way through the decade, was also the date for the second pilot of the TV programme which more than any other, and despite its relatively short life-span, would define the 1960s. Millicent Martin singing the opening song, a gag about Gaitskell and the new Liberal defector (Lieutenant-Colonel Patrick Lort-Phillips) to Labour, a sketch about James Meredith trying to get into the all-white University of Mississippi, an item on the Common Market, a confrontation between Bernard Levin and a group of lawyers, a sketch about Henry Brooke (the new Home Secretary), a parody of the TV advertising magazine *Jim's Inn*, a calypso by Lance Percival – such, as recalled by David Frost, were among the treats of take two of *That Was The Week That Was*, a final iteration before somewhat reluctantly being given permission to go live for real later in the autumn. What was *TW3*'s world-view? Almost by definition, no precise answer is possible, yet perhaps a cluster of negatives gets somewhere close. Essentially, it was anti-establishment, anti-Tory (whatever its professions of political neutrality), anti-authoritarian, anti-discrimination, anti-snobbery, anti-moralising. And who in September 1962 were the *type* of public figures whom Frost and co. instinctively felt less than warm towards? A much longer list would be entirely possible, but here are ten plausible examples, all but one of them obituarised between 1991 and 2003 (a golden age of obituary writing).

Julian Amery (aged 43), Minister for Aviation and son-in-law of Macmillan, 'possessed courage, dash and abundant self-belief' as well a 'deep and plummy voice', an 'old-fashioned manner' and a penchant for double-breasted suits. His father Leo, Colonial Secretary in the 1920s, had been a passionate imperialist, and so was Julian, 'convinced that God was an Englishman' and dismayed by Britain's rapid dismantling of its Empire. In truth he was a more subtle operator (opposing capital punishment, upholding the welfare state, believing that Britain belonged firmly in Europe), but this pro-Franco member of the Carlton Club, of White's, of the Beefsteak, seldom there without glass in hand and cigar in mouth, did not always give that impression.

Hardy Amies (53), the Queen's dressmaker, was courtier almost as much as couturier. From a relatively modest suburban background, he had made a 'close scrutiny of upper-class life' and 'moulded himself into an MGM depiction of an urbane and educated English gent'. 'A splendidly partisan snob', albeit arguably redeemed by 'a splendidly mocking sense of humour', he 'dearly loved to consort with duchesses, and felt that a duke spoke with only less authority than God himself, especially in matters of taste and breeding'. As for his legacy: 'From his elegant Georgian premises in Savile Row, the home of Richard Brinsley Sheridan, he distilled and crafted the quintessential English gentlewoman's look: tweeds by day and jewel-framing silks by night. It was a virtually immutable style that he honed over six working decades and which became a shibboleth of British upper-class dressing.'

Lord (Rowley) Cromer (44) was a member of the long-established merchant-banking Baring family, a grandson of the great proconsul of the British Empire (Sir Evelyn Baring, first Earl of Cromer), son-in-law of the *Daily Mail*'s chairman, a member of Brooks's and the Beefsteak, and for the past fifteen months Governor of the Bank of England. Seeing himself as 'guardian of the old values of low inflation and a sound currency', he was wholly out of sympathy with 1960s-style growthmanship – not least as starting to be exemplified by the new, mildly irreverent Chancellor, Reginald Maudling. 'Lord C. has a nose,' reflected Macmillan after his appointment, and undeniably in a financial sense that was true. Yet inside the Bank he seemed to many not only self-important, but also, in an unwelcome patrician way, lacking in sympathy for life's toilers in the ranks. It had, in other words, been a choice by Macmillan that had far from aligned the Old Lady with an incipient social quasi-revolution in the country at large.

Lord (Alfred, or 'Tom') Denning (63), son of the village draper in Whitchurch in rural Hampshire, was the new Master of the Rolls. Viewed as a radical within the legal system because of his strong belief that it was the function of the courts to change, and not just to interpret, the law, what he cared most 'deeply and passionately' about were 'fundamental and traditional values – religion, the Christian orthodox morality, the rule of law, an ordered society, and fair play'. He was in favour of the death penalty; he maintained more generally that retribution had an essential place in the penal system; and in 1957, in a distinctive contribution to the House of Lords debate on the Wolfenden Report which had recommended the decriminalisation of homosexual acts between consenting adults, he declared that unnatural vice was even worse than natural sin, lamented that 'Hell fire and damnation hold no terrors nowadays' and advocated that the law should continue to punish homosexual conduct. A famously moral man in an age of changing morality: the rest, soon enough, would be history.

John Junor (43) was a quarter of the way through his thirty-two-year editorship of the *Sunday Express*, which in 1962 still had a circulation of well over 4 million. 'Middle-brow, deliberately sober, quaint, relentlessly right-wing': such, in Roy Greenslade's words, were its key qualities. 'There was plenty of castigation but no investigation. Though it relied on the war as its main source of content, it was redolent of the pre-war era. Its stock-in-trade were series about acts of valour by unknown seamen, soldiers and pilots who had undergone private ordeals in wartime, illustrated by heavily inked drawings. The leader page was so Tory it was a wonder it wasn't printed in blue.' Junor himself had not yet started writing his own column, but undoubtedly the paper reflected how he saw things: a belief in homely Scottish values (he had grown up in working-class Glasgow); an instinctive dislike of social workers, of homosexuals, of intellectuals; an intense respectability. 'Prejudiced and absolutely certain of his own righteousness,' noted an obituary, 'he was just the sort of editor many male (though very few female) journalists like working for.'

Betty Kenward (56) was a different kind of journalist, not that she ever called herself that. The creator at the end of the war of 'Jennifer's Diary', first in the *Tatler* and by this time in *Queen*, she faithfully if blandly (at least to the untrained eye) chronicled the social gatherings – weddings, balls, royal occasions, cocktail parties, race meetings – of the English upper classes. 'Remorselessly, she stuck to an all but vanished view of the social order,' noted the *Daily Telegraph*'s perhaps surprisingly unfriendly obituary. 'Arrivistes – journalists, politicians (except Sir Ian Gilmour, Bt), writers (except

John Julius Norwich), advertisers and publishers – had no place in her column.' Instead, 'the shires were Jennifer's spiritual heartland', and it was from 'county families that Jennifer drew most of her "dear friends", that privileged few granted the special dignity of remaining nameless in her column'. The snobbishness was undeniable, including at times a 'telephone manner brusque towards anyone she judged her social inferior'; yet out of difficult personal circumstances she forged a writing career, with erratic punctuation but a very distinctive identity, which celebrated people – albeit people from an almost absurdly narrow social range – coming together rather than staying apart.

John Morrison (55), the future Lord Margadale, had been chairman of the 1922 Committee since 1955 and was the most powerful Tory backbencher of the day. Immense inherited wealth, including a large estate in Wiltshire and a huge one on the Isle of Islay, fortified his independence of ministers; his natural authority was 'enhanced by his imposing physical presence – he had a countryman's ruddy glow and was heavily built'; though 'not an elegant shot as he rounded his shoulders and crouched over his gun', he was 'an exceptional one', with a record bag of 128 snipe in one day; and 'his personality was, by turns, charming and brutal'. MP for Salisbury since 1942, he followed one rule in his political life: namely, that 'the only way of serving the interests of the nation was to sustain a Conservative government'. Or to characterise in a different way this effective and formidable man of instinct rather than intellect, 'his simple conviction, in politics, was that what he felt was right'.

E. W. ('Jim') Swanton (55) was cricket's grand panjandrum. He wrote about the game for the *Daily Telegraph* with unrivalled authority if seldom a graceful or memorable sentence; delivered on radio and television solemn and seemingly omniscient judgements; believed fervently in cricket's continuing two-class system of amateurs and professionals; exhibited (unlike his great rival, John Arlott) little or no interest in the welfare of the paid fraternity; and was, at his worst, the snob's snob, perhaps because he had been to neither a major public school nor Oxbridge. Over the years the stories about him would proliferate – so snobbish that, the joke went, he would not even travel with his chauffeur – yet he not only prioritised the game being played in the right way over any narrow partisanship, but was a critic of South African apartheid at a time when the great majority of his readers saw no problem there. 'The Archbishop of Lord's', he was sometimes called; and the great tragedy was that his pomposity, his crustiness and his apparently reactionary views alienated so many, especially the young, from the religion he devoted his life to.

Roy Thomson (68) was the smiling, unpretentious, unfalteringly commercial and wholly self-made Canadian newspaper owner who had taken Britain by storm since arriving in 1953: first the acquisition of the *Scotsman*; then becoming the majority owner in Scottish Television (the proverbial 'licence to print money', though in fact he called it a 'permit', not a 'licence'); and from 1959 the ownership of the *Sunday Times*. The politics of this man who 'devoured balance sheets as other men do crossword puzzles' were straightforward enough, combining a belief in Conservatism with a hatred of nationalisation – within which broad parameters, understood rather than spelled out, his editors were free to work unhindered by interference. As folksy media moguls go ('You make a dollar for me, I'll make a dollar for you,' would be his invariable greeting to new recruits), or even non-folksy, there have been plenty worse.

Hugh Trevor-Roper (48), 'thin and donnish in appearance', was Regius Professor of Modern History at Oxford, a post he had acquired in 1957 – thanks to prime ministerial patronage – against keen competition from the stormy petrel of British historians, A. J. P. Taylor. Three years later he had repaid the favour by organising at the Oxford end the campaign for Macmillan to become the university's new Chancellor. Like Swanton, the cartoon version (implacable enemy of the left; hostile to new forms of social history starting to bubble up from below; a stuffiness exemplified by insisting that undergraduates wear gowns to his lectures) did significantly less than justice to a man with a mischievous, subversive streak and, in his best, most wide-ranging essays, capable of turning the writing of history into an art form.[27] Yet, also as with Swanton, it was the cartoon which most people knew: unhelpful to the man himself, even more unhelpful to history's appeal in the dawning age of sociology and other alluring new attractions.

But if those ten were in some sense 'establishment' figures, and easy prey for the satirists, what about the alternative establishment, generally more left-liberal in inclination, that was by now taking shape and would on the whole become increasingly comfortable with itself over the next two decades? Obituarised between 1989 and 2019, here are ten of *their* representatives, using the word in the loosest possible sense.

Noël Annan (45), Provost of King's College, Cambridge and a vigorous public intellectual, actually had the headline 'Pillar of the liberal Establishment' above his *Times* obituary. In time his best-known book would be a remarkable collective biography, *Our Age: Portrait of a Generation* (1990), where he sought to delineate 'the commonest *mentalités*' of his particular generation of (often Oxbridge-educated) intellectuals, activators and others:

> Our belief in giving the greatest possible freedom to people in their private lives, and in the way they expressed that life through the arts, conflicted with our belief in the duty of the state intervening to prohibit factories being built in the heart of the countryside or to compel parents to send their children to school. The fact that this conflict existed confirmed us in our belief that men of good will must sit down together and work out sensible solutions to their problems. The brave new world was to be a pluralist world. People should acknowledge that there was no single model of belief and behaviour, such of that of the gentleman in bygone days. Freedom and tolerance demanded that each must find his own level and ideals. Tolerate rebels because they were quite likely to be the innovators of the next decade. Tolerate irreverence. It was a positive virtue to tweak the Establishment and keep it on the hop. In this way, so we hoped, the next generation would not fall into self-hatred as the young communists of the thirties had done.
>
> We wanted all classes in society to enjoy what formerly had been the privileges of the rich. We rejoiced in the fifties as travel became cheaper and the package tour to Spain became a recognized mass holiday. We liked seeing clothes become less formal. We saw in the clothes the Teds wore in the fifties a sign of working-class independence. Something of the contempt of the modernist movement for the routine of office and factory lingered on. Men and women were owed parties, leisure, enjoyment by virtue of having to work; and one objective in one's work was to mix as much pleasure as possible with the job

through the expense account or the discovery of an obligation to travel. And similarly there was a disinclination to take too severe a view of skiving and scrounging among the workforce, overmanning and moonlighting: what were they but the analogue of directors' lunches and perks? But our generation was not composed solely of vulgar hedonists. They believed in spreading Arnold's sweetness and light. They thought that if the authorities supported the arts, people would realize what intense joy the greatest works of man could bring to their lives.

'The cardinal virtue', added Annan in heartfelt conclusion, 'was no longer to love one's country.' Instead: 'It was to feel compassion for one's fellow men and women.'

A. J. Ayer (51), Wykeham Professor of Logic at Oxford, lived mainly in Camden Town (just starting to become a favoured place for the counter-establishment) and was married to the journalist Dee Wells. A quarter of a century earlier he had made his name with *Language, Truth and Logic*, whose resolutely anti-metaphysical stance would be such a turn-off for those immersed in 1960s' 'alternative' culture; but by this time he was best known for his media appearances (especially TV's *Brains' Trust*), his seemingly relaxed approach to personal morality, his unwavering support of liberal causes and his equally staunch devotion to Tottenham Hotspur. Some years later, after listing the main things he regularly protested against (war + maltreatment of political prisoners + censorship + capital/corporal punishment + persecution of homosexuals + racial discrimination), he conceded that 'it would be more romantic to be marching forward shoulder to shoulder under some bright new banner towards a brave new world'. 'Perhaps,' he added, 'it is the effect of age': 'I do not really feel the need for anything to replace this mainly utilitarian, mainly tolerant, undramatic type of radicalism. For me the problem is not to devise a new set of political principles, but rather to find a more effective means of putting into operation the principles that most of us already profess to have.'

Asa Briggs (41) was a human dynamo: Yorkshire in background and outlook; pre-eminent Victorian historian; a pioneer in broadening history out from high political to urban, labour and business as well as more broadly social and cultural; fingers in many pies, including the presidency of the Workers' Educational Association (WEA); the first volume recently published of what would be a five-volume history of British broadcasting; and now, at the newly established University of Sussex, Professor of History, Dean of Social Studies and Pro-Vice-Chancellor. There, in the defining 'plate-glass' university of the era, he 'set about "re-drawing the map of learning", as he put it. Students would major in the "core subject" of their choice while also studying a series of "contextual" subjects. Buzz words in this academic *terra nova* were "interdisciplinary" and "cross-cultural".' All very trendy (the word is impossible to avoid), but how would 'Sussex' values mesh with Briggs's own? A deep-dyed social democrat hostile to Marxism; an unswerving admirer of Clement Attlee and the '1945' settlement; a liberal, but a pragmatic liberal. Two worlds were poised to collide, and Briggs would find himself, not always easily, somewhere in the middle.

Ian Gilmour (36) was impeccably well connected (Eton, Balliol, Grenadier Guards, heir to a baronetcy, married to a daughter of the Duke of Buccleuch), owned the *Spectator*, had recently stepped down after five years as editor, and was about to become Conservative MP for Norfolk Central. His editorship had seen the magazine closely mirror his own views, as – to the dismay of some of its traditional readers – it opposed the death penalty, campaigned against censorship of books and theatre, supported Britain going into Europe and backed the legalisation of homosexuality. Now, given also his considerable intellectual gifts as well as personal charm when he chose to use it, a shining political future seemed assured. But potentially there were three problems: his adoption of 'the languorous manner of a dilettante'; the suspicion that, like Lord Rosebery in the 1890s, he wanted the palm without the dust; and the awkward fact that that patrician tradition in Conservatism whereby 'the elite of society sets civilised, liberal standards' for the rest of society was in terminal decline. One way and another, the future of liberal, one-nation Conservatism was not necessarily safe in the hands of someone who, as the saying went, could box but could not punch.

Peter Hall (31) was the force-of-nature theatre director who two years earlier had founded the Royal Shakespeare Company (RSC), putting on productions (including of new plays) in London as well as at Stratford. He was the classic post-war meritocrat: brought up at

Barnham in rural Suffolk, where his father rose from railway clerk to stationmaster; a Cambridge education (first as a scholarship boy at a direct-grant school, the Perse, then at the university); and aged twenty-four, the first English director of *Waiting for Godot*. An 'undoctrinaire socialist' (his own words) who once contemplated going into politics, an increasingly unwavering believer in the state's responsibility to the arts, a larger-than-life figure who combined metropolitan hedonism with workaholic East Anglian puritanism, he seems increasingly in retrospect one of the titans of the age – a leader rather than a follower of public taste and fashion.

Lord (George) Harewood (39), son of the Princess Royal and sixteenth in line to the throne, was the royal with a difference. 'It's very odd about George and music,' reflected the Duke of Windsor. 'You know, his parents were quite normal – liked horses and dogs and the country!' Or in a variant on the story, the Queen was reputedly once heard to say, 'Funny thing about George. You know, in most respects he's perfectly normal.' At this point in the early 1960s he was director of both the Edinburgh Festival and the Leeds Festival (as well as the actively involved president of Leeds United FC); he 'genuinely valued British music and knew a great deal about it'; and over the years his 'overriding concern' would be 'to help transform British people's attitude to opera'. Tom Sutcliffe in his 2011 obituary neatly summed him up: 'George – as colleagues called him – was unconventional, though not quite as unclass-conscious as he was sometimes assumed to be. Opera in English, and opera in Britain, benefited from his far-sighted leadership. He was the right royal, in the right place, at the right time. Indeed the only thing that was not right about him was his politics, which were liberal and democratic.'

Roy Jenkins (41) was a Labour MP, a friend of the Gilmours and in his penchant for high society had long left behind his South Wales roots. Politically, his main achievement to date was having piloted through the Commons in 1959 what became the Obscene Publications Act, reforming in a liberal direction the law of censorship. By the early 1960s, a senior Labour colleague, Douglas Jay, seriously doubted whether Jenkins (in the middle of writing a sympathetic, full-scale biography of Asquith) belonged any longer in the Labour Party, given his assimilation into 'the Liberal way of life' (including a close connection to the Bonham Carter family) and strongly pro-European views. 'Belief in the Common Market had a natural attraction for Liberals,' recalled Jay. 'First it could be represented as "progressive" and "new"; secondly it kept one away from sordid, backstairs subjects like housing, food prices and old-age pensions. It was a seductively drawing-room form of radicalism.' 'I was at first', he added, 'surprised that Jenkins, with his South Wales mining background, should have been susceptible to these influences when Gaitskell [to whom Jenkins was very close] was completely immune to them.' Great and honourable liberal reforms lay ahead; for better or worse, Jenkins would be a central figure in Britain's stop–start European journey; but of housing, of food prices, of old-age pensions, of how most people lived their necessarily mundane day-to-day lives, not so much.

Lady (Bridget) Plowden (52), chairman of the Working Ladies Guild and of the Professional Classes Aid Council, was best known at this stage for being married to Lord (Edwin) Plowden, the former Whitehall mandarin whose 1961 report on Treasury control of public expenditure was a classic case, thought *The Times*, of 'treading with such extreme delicacy that its footsteps are scarcely audible'. 'Her commitment to public service was as strong as his,' noted Robert Armstrong in his 2001 obituary of him, 'but they ploughed different furrows and did not overlap. She was energetic, busy and brisk, where he was reflective and deliberate; but they complemented each other ideally. It was almost as if neither could be happy unless each was as fully engaged as the other in public service of some kind.' And soon, after she happened at an official dinner to sit next to the Education Minister (Sir Edward Boyle, another liberal-minded member of the counter-establishment), her great progressive moment would come.

Stephen Spender (53) was, thought the critic and poet G. S. Fraser, the nearest to a continental intellectual that Britain could muster; their fellow poet Peter Porter would remember Spender not only as 'the proof that the fresh qualities of idealism and innocence which we assume, however mistakenly, to be the hallmark of the poet can survive all the long littlenesses of life, including modulations of fashion and the wit of competitors', but also as 'a brilliant journalist, a gatherer and virtuoso presenter of ideas, and a shrewd judge of people and art'. Having made his reputation in the 1930s, as part of that mythical composite poet later known as 'MacSpaunday' (MacNeice,

Auden and Day Lewis as well as Spender), he was now co-editor of *Encounter* (where the other co-editor, Melvin Lasky, was the fervent Cold Warrior, not Spender); a regular on the burgeoning international lecture-and-conference circuit; and 'an unstinting and dependable supporter of good causes, both private and public'. Equally reliable, once he had put behind him a flirtation in the 1930s with Communism, were his politics and general outlook: left-liberal, with an emphasis on the second 'l'. And unlike many intellectuals who had turned their backs on Communism – even, like Spender, contributing to Richard Crossman's 1949 anthology *The God That Failed* – 'his own disenchantment', as Porter notes, 'never turned him into a right-wing fanatic or professional apologist for capitalism'. Years later, in the Thatcherite 1980s, he would be identified by the Cambridge neo-Conservative don Maurice Cowling as (along with Ayer, Berlin and three others) one of 'the unbearably self-satisfied authors of the fifties and sixties'; but in the tall and handsome Spender, an egotist but not a self-justifier, he had got the wrong man.

George Weidenfeld (43), the son of middle-class Viennese Jews, was one of several leading post-war publishers who had come to Britain as refugees from Nazism. His politics were broadly centre-left, but he was as happy to publish Vladimir Nabokov (well to the right) as he was to publish Eric Hobsbawm (well to the left). A legendary party-giver, a legendary lover, a man with a gift for sniffing out whatever seemed new and interesting (especially if it had an exotic tinge), he was above all as a publisher an internationalist, relaxed – even at significant commercial cost – about introducing relatively obscure French or German authors to English-language readers. 'Polyglot and cosmopolitan' was the verdict on him of his fellow publisher John Calder in his 2016 obituary; and by that fateful year, when Thomas Dibdin's two immortal lines from 1797 had a particular resonance ('Oh! it's a snug little island! / A right little, tight little island!'), Weidenfeld had done his best for not far short of three-quarters of a century to turn the tide the other way.[28]

So, in early autumn 1962, ten members of the male-dominated establishment, ten rather younger members of the emerging alternative establishment, equally male-dominated. Logically, and not just because of age, the unfolding 1960s should have seen the collective influence of the former group wane, the collective influence of the latter group increase. In practice, given the country's deeply embedded social conservatism, it would be a bit more complicated than that. Or put another way, the birth of liberal England – if indeed it ever happened – would be long as well as strange.

6

Deceptively Simple Beater

'This year, the first child born to free secondary education for all is university age,' noted Ruth Adam in the *Observer* on Sunday, 30 September. 'He has grown up to take the effects of the 1944 Act – streaming, and 11-plus selection, and the rush for university education – as the normal, ordained steps up the school ladder.' He and his peers, even including the odd female peer, were the children of Rab Butler's celebrated wartime Education Act, opening up grammar schools to the working class (though not always to the extent assumed); and now, eighteen years on, a full-scale grammar-school elite was poised to emerge, in time threatening the traditional dominance of the privately educated elite.

Adam then sought to capture the values and ambitions of a particularly high-performing heir to the 1944 Act:

Seven years in grammar school cut him off from his working-class way of life. He speaks and thinks differently from his parents. He is not hampered by their prejudices. But he has lost their loyalties as well.

His father's interest in the class war seems to him as out-dated as horse-drawn traffic. The social system, as it stands, is providing him with his passport to the meritocracy, and he has no burning memories of poverty and unemployment to smoulder in him. His father thinks of him as a prospective white-collar worker, but he thinks of himself as a white-coated one, classless. When he admits that one of the things he is looking forward to most at the university is 'meeting really interesting people', he is thinking more of African students than of boys (or girls) from upper-class schools.

Unlike those privileged 18-year-olds, arriving at university 'stamped with the pattern of their public school' and over the years ahead 'keeping the old-school-tie manufacturers in business', her grammar-school leaver was 'impossible to imagine' as 'being drawn back there [his old school] by wistful nostalgia':

> He has never regarded it as his alma mater, perhaps because the original one was always on the premises where he lived, solid and mundane, during the years when he needed her most. He is on friendly, respectful terms with his schoolmasters, and unemotionally grateful for what they have done for him. But he has never had a romantic relationship with a member of his own sex. There were always girls available, from the first moment when he began to look round for them. Sexually, he is more sophisticated than any undergraduate before him.
>
> But, while avoiding the tangled sentimentalities of his predecessors, he has also missed the ideals which made them tick. He has no underlying obligation of service and leadership. And (unless his grammar-school head was very exceptional indeed) he has not been provided with any foundation of dogma on which to build a personal religion. He thinks of the churches as the kind of societies which odd people join, like CND.

'Unsentimental, uncommitted, tolerant, he is innocent of racial and national prejudice, and almost entirely free from small snobberies and vanities,' concluded Adam, 'the one exception' being 'his belief in the superior status of the graduate'. And 'Classless, agnostic, politically uninvolved, his only guiding light, for years, has been this passionate aim to get a university education. To him, university is the only certain good. He is not so certain just what it is that he is to be educated for.'

Also this Sunday, on the eve of Labour's annual conference (this year at Brighton), the party's national executive issued a statement urging the government not only to pass a law making incitement to racial hatred an offence, but also to outlaw racial discrimination in public places. 'The Labour Party', declared the statement, 'deplores the recent growth of Fascist and other racialist propaganda, which, it believes, is deeply repugnant to the overwhelming majority of British people.' That evening, ABC Television's *Armchair Theatre*, directed by Philip Saville and produced by Sydney Newman, was Robert Muller's bitter satire *Afternoon of a Nymph*, starring Janet Munro and Ian Hendry. Half a century later, Saville filled in some of the background, starting with how he had first got to meet Muller:

I asked how I would recognise him [at the assigned Mayfair club]. 'Well,' said Muller, 'I'm a short, balding, unprepossessing sort of guy with glasses.' I replied, 'I'm a tall, prepossessing guy with lots of brown curly hair, so we shouldn't have any trouble.' When I remember that now, I cringe at what an insufferable prick I must have sounded. But that's how we all were in the sixties. It was part of the shameless new narcissism we operated within: a sort of insensitivity and barbarism was flaring up in media and fashion.

Robert's play was about a day in the life of a young girl on the fringes of show business. In a matter of days, we were like two peas in a pod. This drama fitted my current personal obsession: themes about the individual in society and their constant struggle to resist group pressures from those who wanted to force them into a pattern that's not strictly their own. This was the nub of the drama about 'Elaine', a young starlet being dictated to about how she should behave on the road to success.

'Who am I...? What am I?' she cries ...[1]

The new narcissism, the new individualism: there would of course be much else to the 1960s, but – in certain worlds anyway – that strain was never far from the surface.

'No message: no commercial value: no claim to art,' insisted David Bailey in the new issue of *Vogue*, explaining a double-page spread by him of photographs of London parks. 'I'm tired of photo-journalism which just goes on and on, more boring each time, especially if there is no war to report. These six are pictures to look at, creating a moment rather than capturing one, photographed just for kicks.' Just north of Hyde Park, at Lancaster Gate, the Football Association decided that Monday, 1 October, on Alf Ramsey as England's favoured new manager; in Devon, an abandoned Sylvia Plath wrote the first of her almost shockingly intense *Ariel* poems ('The Detective'); and at Cheltenham the town's annual literary festival – directed this year by Elizabeth Jane Howard – got under way with a panel of young writers, including Edna O'Brien and Lynne Reid Banks. But no invitation for J. G. (Jim) Farrell, living in a basement in Redcliffe Square, Earl's Court, teaching English as a foreign language and trying to write. 'I am eating well,' he reassured a German friend. 'This evening I cooked myself two eggs and some radishes (uncooked!) and some bread and cheese. I bought a new frying-pan for which one does not need fat or grease. You must have them in Germany too. It is wonderful and much easier.' A bed-sit in Earl's Court was classic Tony Hancock territory, but this evening the two programmes attracting most attention were *Coronation Street* (where baby Christopher went missing, having been left by his mother in a pram outside Gamma Garments) and *Panorama*, back from its summer break. Two days ahead of a threatened one-day rail strike in protest against the proposed closure of railway workshops, the Transport Minister Ernest Marples and the leader of the National Union of Railwaymen, Sid Greene, had a combative head-to-head. 'Although a small group considered this "public" meeting to be in bad taste or of doubtful value,' noted audience research, 'their discussion was widely praised as lively, informative and thoroughly enjoyable television, "a real scoop for the BBC".' Significantly less enthusiasm, though, for another returning warhorse, *What's My Line?*, with Eamonn Andrews still in the chair, Isobel Barnett, Barbara Kelly and David Nixon still the three regular panellists, and this week Sid James the guest panellist. 'Why have you dragged out this corpse?' asked a surveyor. 'Same carefully assumed personalities, the same ponderous jokes; the show just creaks along. Even the great big plug for the celebrity's current play and film.'[2]

It was surprising the surveyor had time to watch, for every day there seemed to be a new story reflecting the relentless, ever-quickening pace of urban redevelopment. That Monday evening, Eccles Borough Council debated whether it should support Lancashire County Council's plan to build a South Lancashire motorway linking Manchester with Liverpool. The motorway would pass through the centre of Eccles, some 300 shops and houses would be demolished, and

2,000 local people had signed a petition protesting against the route; but the decisive argument (14 votes to 11 in favour of going ahead) came from Councillor G. Nolan, highways committee chairman, who said that upon the approval of the motorway scheme depended a new shopping precinct planned for the town centre of Eccles. Or, from the October issue of the magazine *Official Architecture and Planning*, take 'Scottish Notes': in Paisley, the town council deciding to proceed with a £2 million plan to build a new civic centre, including a banqueting hall and councillors' dining rooms; in Edinburgh, the city's planning committee considering an £8 million scheme (including an eighteen-storey office block and a sixteen-storey hotel) for the redevelopment of the St James's Square and Leith Street area, 'said to be the biggest project in the city for 200 years'; in Glasgow, preparatory work under way on the hugely ambitious Red Road multi-storey development (seven tower blocks, aiming to be Europe's highest); and also in Glasgow, likewise aimed at providing mass public housing, details of a planned 'interesting comprehensive development [eight tower blocks] at Hillpark'. This last development was intended to be 'on a 40-acre site just inside the city boundary' – but it would also, the report tactfully failed to mention, be in a sedate, middle-class district full of bungalows, whose residents might not necessarily welcome being surrounded and overlooked by former inner-city slum-dwellers.[3]

Neither bungalows nor high-rise at Balmoral, where the Privy Council was due to meet on Tuesday. 'London airport by 8 a.m.,' recorded Bill Deedes:

> Quintin Hailsham in bowler hat, blue suit and boots. [Geoffrey] Rippon in brown tweeds. Very smart pilot officer. Comfortable Heron with four seats and a steward. Substantial elevenses. Arrive Aberdeen 11 a.m. Two cars. Fifty-three miles to Balmoral. Straight fast road. Not very Highland. Dee in full water. Met by private secretary and aides. Welcome visit to the loo. With half an hour before 12.30, walk across some very springy turf to kitchen gardens, greenhouse, then John Brown's statue. A fine statue with a couplet of appalling banality. Back to Balmoral. Wait in the drawing room. Quintin summoned to the library. Corgi sniffs at the door. We follow. Corgi in with us. Quintin reads Orders as we stand on his right. HM calls 'approved'. Clerk of

the Privy Council, Geoffrey Agnew, handles the paper. All over in three minutes. Back to the drawing room. One bar electric. Fires not lit. Sherry in the drawing room.

The drawing room has some splendid Landseers. Queen Victoria on a pony. Also some excellent heads by Landseer of Balmoral gillies. Plain rooms with natural wood doors, shiny chintzes. Tray of drinks. Lunch at 1 p.m. HM with Margaret and Anne plus two staff, three women, ourselves and three girls. Roast potatoes with poached egg. Chicken *à la king*. Very rich. Wine or beer. Profiteroles. Cheese board. More than enough. Princess Anne on the Loch Ness monster. Then an hour's slightly difficult conversation. Discuss public buildings. New Hilton Hotel in London overlooks Buckingham Palace. 'No privacy,' says the Queen. Rippon [Minister of Public Building and Works] looks suitably contrite. Queen sits on a footstool. Princess Anne looks as if she would like to be elsewhere. Disappears.

It was all over at 3 p.m., by which time day two at Cheltenham was moving into gear. 'The meetings are held in the town hall,' noted Andrew Sinclair. 'The audience is largely female, with its age and class and centre of gravity dead middle.' Theme of the day was autobiography, with a panel comprising Laurie Lee, Alec Waugh, Elspeth Huxley and the Spurs footballer Danny Blanchflower – the last, according to Sinclair, putting 'to literary shame the other writers of autobiography' by accepting the need for a much greater degree of candour. Elsewhere on the literary front, while Plath wrote 'The Courage of Shutting-Up', John Fowles gave in private his mixed verdict on Keith Waterhouse's *Billy Liar* ('I liked this. Its briskness and harshness and shortness ... But as with all these Northcountry horror-stories, there is no depth – a staggeringly good surface-skin of contemporary reality, of hard post-war language. But beneath that something, nothing') and Muriel Spark's first play, *Doctors of Philosophy*, premiered at the New Arts Theatre Club, with a mainly female cast including Fenella Fielding. The critics generally sharpened their pens – like 'a late Eliot play extensively rewritten by an adolescent Iris Murdoch', thought Kenneth Tynan – but subsequent reassessments justifiably suggest that the proto-Stoppardian playfulness was at the time too out of kilter with the still continuing fashion since the late

1950s for more masculine, realist drama. By contrast, a Reaction
Index of 75 for the return of *This Is Your Life*, with this week Rupert
Davies (TV's Maigret) the subject. 'I would not like to see anyone else
in Eamonn Andrews' shoes,' commented a lorry driver's wife. 'When
Brian Johnston came on I had a horrible feeling he was to take over.
I'm sure I would not have enjoyed it so much.'4

Next morning at the Labour Party conference, after a sleepless night,
Gaitskell spoke for an hour and twenty minutes in the overheated hall
of the Brighton ice rink. The issue was Europe. And among those in
the audience for one of the great political setpieces of the era was the
Guardian's John Cole:

> The speech revealed the depths of Mr Gaitskell's contempt for the
> way in which the public debate has been conducted. A passage
> on the desire of 'top people' to arrogate to themselves the right
> to judge this issue, instead of educating the public in its rights
> and wrongs, was as furiously angry as anything Mr Gaitskell has
> ever said about the Communists and fellow travellers.
>
> Mr Gaitskell's superb control of this conference has always
> depended on his painstaking preparation, and this was revealed
> today in his heavily documented argument as to why he regards
> the economic terms for or against entry as equally balanced. But
> he regarded the political factors as more important.
>
> Federation would mean 'the end of Britain as an independent
> nation state', which might be either a good or a bad thing, but
> was certainly a fundamental issue. 'The end of a thousand years
> of history,' he quoted from his broadcast [of 21 September], and
> added in a self-mocking understatement: 'It needs a little care
> and attention.' It meant the end of the Commonwealth ...

'Mr Gaitskell, looking pale and tired when he finished,' added Cole,
'received a long standing ovation in which some of his parliamentary
colleagues – and some of his oldest political friends – ostentatiously
abstained.' It was indeed a remarkable spectacle: a sustained standing
ovation from Gaitskell's erstwhile enemies on the left, prompting his
wife Dora to remark in a worried voice that 'all the wrong people are
cheering'; while, among his closest and indeed personal intimates, Roy
Jenkins stood but did not applaud and Bill Rodgers ('I was outraged,

particularly the chauvinism of "a thousand years of history"') sat firmly with arms folded. For Jenkins, wholly committed emotionally to Britain being part of Europe, the sense of betrayal was acute. And not long after the speech, in which his leader had looked back to the First World War and declared that 'we at least do not intend to forget [the sacrifices of] Vimy Ridge and Gallipoli', he was heard to remark sourly that if Gaitskell lost the next election he could always become chairman of the Commonwealth War Graves Commission.[5]

No green lights on the railways that Wednesday, as the one-day strike went ahead, but yet more green lights for redevelopment: in Banbury, with the ancient market place now 'threatened'; in Bury, with the town council making a compulsory purchase order to enable a £3 million rebuilding ('new roads, car parks, a modern market, a shopping precinct in Italian style') of the town centre; and in Liverpool, as the city council formally approved, without debate, Graeme Shankland's proposals for the development of forty-two acres of the city centre. All the more piquant, then, that that very day, in his presidential address to the Royal Institute of British Architects (RIBA), Sir Robert Matthew was contending that too many redevelopment schemes had already created 'arid wastes in place of teeming vitality, and failed to create the character, the community life, the diversity of people and uses, the compactness and visual interest that characterise so many older so-called unplanned and blighted areas'. It sounded as if he had been reading Jacobs, or anyway Nairn on Jacobs, and he went on to ask: 'Are we satisfied that the limitations imposed by use zoning, density controls, sight lines, widths between buildings, are in fact essential and desirable?' At Cheltenham, while the historian Cecil Woodham-Smith spoke in the Town Hall, the building labourer and playwright Henry Chapman, a Wesker protégé, was speaking in the trades union club on behalf of Centre 42. 'He said', reported Sinclair, 'that class art and class censorship now existed. He wanted a new art to rise from the working people, so that art could be known immediately by its quality "as a plasterer knows a good piece of plastering by a look".' Nothing proletarian about Rowley Cromer, who in a speech at the Mansion House that evening – while distraught viewers in 8.4 million homes watched an unavailing search for baby Christopher – in effect called for the abolition of exchange controls, a cornerstone since 1939 of the controlled management of the British economy. 'The time has now come', he declared, 'when the City once again might well provide an international capital market where the foreigner can not only borrow long-term capital but where, equally important, he will once again wish to place his long-term investment capital.' An undeniably bold vision, of London as the world's centre of 'entrepot business in capital', but not yet an economic runner, let alone a political one.[6]

If Cromer wanted a less *dirigiste* economy, that was certainly not the case with Labour, whose shadow Chancellor, James Callaghan, spoke next day at Brighton, stressing above all the need for planning in order to ensure continuous economic expansion, as opposed to the stop–go economy that had characterised Tory governments since 1951. But as to what 'planning' actually meant in practice, he was somewhat light on detail, apart from offering the aspiration that 'we want to assemble the facts to shape the future'; as for incomes policy specifically, always the likeliest Achilles heel for a planned economy under a Labour government, he gained loud applause by declaring that 'it will be an incomes policy for all', including 'rents, dividends, capital gains, and gifts', and he talked reassuringly of 'a gigantic essay in persuasion and co-operation' – but beyond that he felt (or was) unable to go.

Elsewhere in conference-world that Thursday, a two-day conference on factory production of housing, organised by the Cement and Concrete Association, began in London, albeit 'plagued by considerably more than its fair share of technical hitches with slides, films, lights and microphone'. Opening speaker was the Housing Minister, Sir Keith Joseph, who demanded that 'we must bypass shortages by doing over 12 months in the dry factory what at the moment too often has to be done in seasonal conditions on the site'; and from later speakers there ensued a flow of dazzling productivity claims about factory-made housing, such as a new house ready for occupation in three days, a block of flats in barely two months. Even so, as one observer reflected at the end of the first day, there was a regrettable missing dimension to the whole occasion:

> Valuable though the conference is proving to be, the questions of human scale, comfort, and the satisfactory and economical use of land for the new factory-built housing, will not be discussed,

and many delegates showed their disappointment in the agenda. Here, they felt, was an opportunity to form a core of moral, political, economical and architectural codes which could prevent the new industry from creating precedents the public might learn to regret.

Prefabrication, in housing, is still not widely accepted. Mechanised building is prefabrication, and to be accepted by the majority as the only means of producing the much-needed cheap housing, emphasis must be placed upon emotional requirements, as well as the commercial gain.

The day's other conference was at Southport: a meeting of the National Health Service Executive Councils' Association, which was told by a dental surgeon (Mr A. D. Page of Huddersfield) that the UK had the worst incidence of dental decay in the Western world, with one in five people wearing false teeth by the age of twenty. Accordingly, he backed a resolution calling for the national fluoridation of water supplies – a resolution which, after one of the executive (Dr W. Marshall of Soke of Peterborough) had insisted that fluoride was not 'an unproven thalidomide' but had been 'exhaustively tested', was passed unanimously.[7]

This Thursday the 4th also saw the launch of *New Society* – the weekly magazine which over the next two decades not only had its finger on the pulse of British society, taken as a whole, more than any other publication, but also in its own right played a major part in the seemingly irresistible rise of social sciences. It was, moreover, an influencer. 'Every Thursday,' a future long-serving editor, Paul Barker, would recall, 'copies flowed into the in-trays of senior civil servants especially at the home policy departments (education, environment, administration of justice, health, social security). To television documentary producers, it was meat and drink.' Tagging itself on its cover as 'The Social Science Weekly', the first issue included articles on 'Our redundancy problem', 'Science applied to society', 'What makes a horse sell whisky?', 'Meeting of sociological minds' and, given pride of place in the billing, 'The full report on teenage marriage'. Many notable writers would contribute over the years, from right as well as left, but not Kingsley Amis, who might instead this day have glanced at a very different weekly, *Country Life*, for its review by Geoffrey Grigson of his new collection of stories. Two bits stood out: a reference to Amis's 'wary, 1960-ish ethos'; and, about his fiction in general, how he 'always seems to be saying, incidentally and between the lines, "Can't catch me."' Can't catch me indeed: indisputably that day, Amis travelled to Cheltenham, where he was due to appear in the evening on a panel comprising Romain Gary, Joseph Heller and Carson McCullers as well as himself. Their topic was 'Sex in Literature'; and the panel had been assembled by Elizabeth Jane Howard, albeit with Amis foisted upon her, against her wishes, at the behest of the event's sponsor, the *Sunday Telegraph*, which also provided a rather dud chairman in the person of the paper's editor, Donald McLachlan. The festival's official climax turned out to be something of a flop, to judge by Sinclair's report. The four 'were meant to make good copy', but instead 'made little except jokes'; and, in the only memorable quote, Amis said he despised 'an affectation of hairy-chestedness', pointing out that (in Sinclair's paraphrasing words) 'many of the best sexual descriptions in literature never passed beyond the bedroom door'. That night, after the post-event dinner, Amis and Howard stayed up talking until 4 a.m. 'When he kissed me,' she wrote forty years later, 'I felt as though I could fly.'[8]

As Friday – a momentous Friday – dawned soon afterwards, Amis's old mucker had a poem, 'Essential Beauty', in the *Spectator* ('a long skid towards the end', Larkin would reflect soon afterwards to Monica Jones); Richard Hoggart in the *Guardian* gave a modified welcome ('the nostalgia for working-class life and the sensuous pleasure in expense-account living sometimes have an expected quality') to John Braine's *Life at the Top*, successor to *Room at the Top*; Robert Taubman in the *New Statesman* did not go overboard ('I would rather have something more natural in the circumstances than tight-lipped restraint and good dialogue') for Penelope Mortimer's future Penguin Modern Classic, *The Pumpkin Eater*, about a woman's breakdown; and in the same magazine the philosopher Richard Wollheim offered the crispest of summaries of Bryan Magee's *The New Radicalism*, a political manifesto that the author himself (described that week by Raymond Williams as part of 'the generation of political driftwood') would come to see, not unjustifiably, as the earliest intellectual godfather of New Labour: 'He is against Clause Four; fellow-travellers; nostalgia for the bad old days; Michael Foot; haters of affluence; CND; cultural paternalism; and Socialists who prefer purity of doctrine to political power.' As ever, diarists that day faithfully recorded the quotidian. For Georgiana Tench, staying in an old people's home in south-west London while her daughter was away, a day of 'rather low spirits' until 'an attendant stopped in her evening bed-doing & had nice long chat with me & was interested in my photos, etc'; for Veronica Lee at her girls' grammar school in Devon, frustration that 'French lessons are so boring and we have so many of them', while feeling 'depressed and useless' after a teacher had told her that it would be 'too difficult' for her to get into London University; and for Dennis Dee, smallholder in East Yorkshire, the usual taciturn take-away from the daily round: 'Fine again today. Mr Blacker called to check the pigs. Did some concreting in the cattle shed.'[9]

Almost certainly none of them was reading the latest *Melody Maker*, dated the 6th but out this Friday the 5th. 'Telstar', its sales already north of 250,000, was ensconced at No. 1, followed by Elvis Presley's 'She's Not You', Cliff Richard's 'It'll Be Me', Tommy Roe's 'Sheila' and Little Eva's 'Loco-Motion'; at No. 20 and on the way down was Pat Boone's 'Speedy Gonzales'; at equal No. 40 and going up was Mark Wynter's 'Venus in Blue Jeans'; in the Top Twenty, there were only seven British representatives; and anything 'beat' was conspicuous by its absence. Best-selling LP of the week was the soundtrack of *West Side Story*, followed by *The Golden Age of Donegan*; top of the EPs was Elvis's 'Follow that Dream'. The briefest of news items – just sixteen words followed by three pregnant dots – noted that 'Liverpool's top beat group The Beatles make disc debut today (Friday) with "Love me do" (Parlophone) ...'; another news item noted that Brian Matthew was set to compere that evening the Twist and Trad Show at Blackpool Winter Gardens; while, to judge by the ads near the back, the main musical action that Friday was going to be in London: at Ronnie Scott's Club, the Tubby Hayes Quintet; at the Flamingo in Wardour Street, the Don Rendell Quintet with Graham Bond, plus Kathy Stobart and the Brian Auger trio, followed from midnight by All-Nighter Club, starring Georgie Fame with the Blue Flames; and far from Soho, in unglamorous outer suburbia at the Woodstock Hotel in North Cheam, not so far from Railway Cuttings, 'Rhythm 'n Blues, with the Rolling Stones'.[10]

On the cusp: a moment to savour, in retrospect anyway, for a cast of thousands, largely unaware on 5 October 1962 that cultural tectonic plates were about to shift and that they would be part of the story. To take just some. Leo Abse (45, future decriminaliser of homosexual activity between consenting adults) was sitting on the Labour back benches as MP for Pontypool; Fiona Adams (27, future photographer of the Beatles in bombed-out Somers Town) was working for the weekly teen magazine *Boyfriend*; Tariq Ali (18, future Grosvenor Square star) was at Punjab University organising demonstrations against Pakistan's military dictatorship; Joan Bakewell (29, future presenter of freewheeling *Late Night Line-Up*) was doing audition after audition in search of television work; Reginald Ball (21, future Reg Presley of the Troglodytes-turned-Troggs) was laying bricks in Andover; Mary Barnes (39, future resident of R. D. Laing's Kingsley Hall) was working in a hospital; George Best (16, future pioneer footballing superstar) was being quietly nurtured by Manchester United's Matt Busby; John Bindon (19, future upwardly mobile machismo actor) was laying asphalt; Brian Cant (29, future legendary presenter of *Play School*) was making do with bit parts in *Dixon of Dock Green*; Chas Chandler (23, future discoverer of Jimi Hendrix) was playing bass in the Tyneside-based Alan Price Trio; Brian Clough (27, future outspoken football manager) was playing centre-forward for second-division Sunderland; Joe Cocker (18, future opening act at Woodstock) was working as a fitter for the East Midlands Gas Board; Sandy Denny (15, future folk immortal) was at school in New Malden; Basil D'Oliveira (31 or so, future England cricketer and *cause célèbre*) had just had a disappointing third season with Middleton in the Central Lancashire League; Michael Duane (47, another future *cause célèbre*) was in his third year as headmaster of Risinghill School, London's showpiece mixed comprehensive; Brian Duffy (29, future key photographer of the 'Swinging Sixties') was working for *Vogue* and thinking about going freelance; Tony Elliott (15, future founder of initially radical *Time Out*) was at school at Stowe; Kenny Everett (17, future maverick disc jockey) was working as a copy boy in a Liverpool advertising agency; Marianne Faithfull (15, future voice of innocence and experience) was at convent school in Reading; Mick Farren (19, future Deviant and provocateur) was at art college in Worthing; Julie Felix (24, future 'Britain's first lady of folk') was hitching her way round Europe; Paul Foot (24, future scourge of Peter Griffiths, Harold Wilson and Enoch Powell) was working for the *Daily Record* and learning his socialism from Glasgow's shipyard firebrands; Margaret Forster (24, future author of zeitgeist-laden *Georgy Girl*) was teaching at Barnsbury Girls' School in Islington; Sandra Goodrich (15, future Sandie Shaw) had just left school and was working at the huge Ford's plant in Dagenham; Peter Green (15, future equal-greatest British blues guitarist) was a butcher's boy in London's East End; Bob Guccione (31, future creator of men's magazine *Penthouse*) was running a mail-order business in London; David Hemmings (20, future star of Antonioni's era-defining *Blow-Up*) was a former boy soprano now hoping for the big adult break; Adrian Henri (31, future one-third of *The Mersey Sound*) was teaching art at Manchester and Liverpool Colleges of Art; Cyril Nicholas Henty-Dodd (27, future all-purpose disc jockey and TV chatshow host Simon Dee) was earning £25 a week plus commission as an estate agent; Lesley Hornby (13, future Twiggy) was having a happy childhood at 93 St Raphael's Way, Neasden, and starting as an embryonic mod to make her own clothes; Glenda Jackson (26, future star of Ken Russell's *Women in Love* and so much else), still had it almost all to do, albeit complimented this very day by the *Watford Observer* as 'pale and edgy' in a play of two marriages, *Double Yolk*, at the local Palace Theatre; Terry Jones (20, future Python) was reading English at Oxford and about to meet Michael Palin; Samantha Juste (18, future applier of needle-to-record on *Top of the Pops*) was a teenage model, real-name Sandra Slater, based in Rochdale; Lindsay Kemp (24, future legendary-but-unloved-by-the-critics mime artist, dancer and choreographer) was in the process of forming his own company and the start of an underground reputation; Bruce Kenrick (42, future founder of Shelter) was a clergyman who had just moved to Notting Hill and was seeing the problem of homelessness first-hand; Anne Lantree (19, future Honeycombs' drummer Honey Lantree) was a trainee hairdresser in Hackney; Kenneth Leech (23, future founder of the Centrepoint charity) was training for the priesthood; Donovan Leitch (16, future British Dylan, or not) was living at 230 Bishops Rise in Hatfield New Town; Ken Loach (26, future director of *Up the Junction*, of *Cathy Come Home*, of *Kes*) was trying to start a theatre company; Cathy McGowan (19, future presenter of *Ready, Steady, Go!*) was working in the fashion department of *Woman's Own* and was on her marks; Tom McGrath (21, future founding editor of *International Times,* Britain's first counter-cultural newspaper) was running a late-night jazz club in Glasgow; Barry MacSweeney (14, future teenage candidate for the poetry chair at Oxford) was at grammar school in Newcastle upon Tyne; David McWilliams (17, future singer-songwriter of the much hyped 'The Days of Pearly Spencer') was playing truant from Ballymena Technical School; Howard Marks (17, future cannabis-smuggling, not necessarily so Mr Nice) was at the Welsh-speaking grammar school in Pontycymer; Phil May (17, future Pretty Thing and godlike figure to the young David Jones/Bowie) was at Sidcup Art College; Barry Miles (19, future second-most-celebrated counter-cultural Miles) was at art college in Cheltenham; Dougie Millings (49, future supplier of round-collared suits to the Beatles) was operating out of a poky first-floor workshop in Old Compton Street, Soho; Adrian Mitchell (29, future star of the first Poetry Internationale at the Albert Hall) was working on the *Evening Standard*'s Londoner's Diary; Alex Moulton (42, about to launch at the Earl's Court Cycle Show a lightweight bicycle for the age of lightness) had recently had his design turned down by Raleigh; Gordon Murray (41, future creator of *Camberwick Green, Chigley* and *Trumpton*) was working for the BBC, still wedded to string-operated puppets; Richard Neville (20, future creator of *Oz* magazine) was living with his parents in suburban Sydney; Andy (Thunderclap) Newman (19, future piano soloist on anthemic 'Something in the Air') was a trainee telephone engineer for the General Post Office; John Noakes (28, future semi-leftfield *Blue Peter* presenter) was working in rep; Tommy Nutter (19, future dresser of all except George walking across Abbey Road) was an apprentice with Donaldson, Williams & Ward, traditional Savile Row tailors; Ivan Owen (35, future creator of Basil Brush) was working as a floor manager for the BBC; Nyree Dawn Porter (22, future unhappy, trapped wife of Soames Forsyte) had left New Zealand two years earlier, never having seen a television set; John Ravenscroft (23, future musical arbiter as John Peel) was selling crop-hail insurance to farmers in Texas; Diana Rigg (24, future Emma Peel) was playing middle-ranking roles at the RSC; Lynn Ripley (14, future Twinkle) was at school in South Kensington with Camilla Shand; Jim

Slater (33, future ruthless asset-stripper shaking up the old, paternalistic corporate order) was deputy sales director at British Leyland; Millie Small (14, future lover of her boy Lollipop) was living in Jamaica and already a music veteran; Allan Smethurst (34, future Singing Postman) was a Norfolk postman who sang on his rounds; Dusty Springfield (23, future own woman, gay icon and unsurpassable female pop singer of the decade) was still part of the Springfields (half-folk, half-pop, time to leave); George Steiner (33, future cutting-edge European, anti-American polymath) was a founding fellow at Churchill College and already an object of Cambridge suspicion for the sin of intellectual exhibitionism; Roy Strong (27, future youthful extrovert director of the National Portrait Gallery) was an assistant keeper there and still living wholly in the past; Penny Valentine (19, future 'first woman to write about pop music as though it really mattered') was *Boyfriend*'s agony aunt; Carol White (18, future homeless, pram-pushing Cathy) was married to the oldest of the singing King Brothers and being a homemaker; Mary Whitehouse (52, future guardian of British morals) was senior mistress at Madeley Secondary Modern School in Shropshire; Marcia Williams (30, future 'imperious, impulsive and unpredictable' insider's insider at No. 10) was the daughter of a Northamptonshire brickworks manager and now working in Harold Wilson's private office; and Harold Wilson (46, future PM) was shadow Foreign Secretary, a chapel-formed Yorkshireman watchful and waiting ...[11]

'For John, Paul, George and Ringo, it was a satisfyingly *single* moment,' relates their collective biographer, Mark Lewisohn. 'Here, from Friday 5 October, was a disc seven inches in diameter that said and played Beatles: black plastic, red labels, silver lettering and Parlophone's seemingly patriotic £ trademark. They stared at it so long they memorised the catalogue number, R4949.' Both numbers, 'Love Me Do' on the A-side and 'PS I Love You' on the B-side, were essentially Paul's songs – but, probably through an error at EMI's label-printing department at the Hayes factory, they were attributed not to McCartney–Lennon (as Brian Epstein had intended) but instead to Lennon–McCartney, a songwriting combination henceforth set in stone. In the two national reviews now out, *Disc* called 'Love Me Do' a 'deceptively simple beater which could grow on you' but gave it only two stars; while *Record Retailer* saw it as 'the strongest outsider of the week' and noted that this 'new group from the Liverpool area' already had 'a strong following', that is, locally. Put another way, amid national indifference as a whole, sales in the north-west, especially in Liverpool itself, would be substantial from the start. And remarkably enough, that Friday evening while the Beatles played a gig at the Co-op Ballroom in Nuneaton, the other great future icon of the 1960s also hit the world, as the first James Bond film, *Dr No*, was premiered at the London Pavilion. 'Absolutely awful – fatuous & tedious, not even erotic,' reckoned Evelyn Waugh (a friend of Ian Fleming's wife, Ann); but he was a grumpy outlier about what one critic called a 'crisp and well-tailored' adaptation in which 'all the characters are suitable for the guided-missile age' as they 'move along predestined courses steered by no consideration of right or wrong, love or hate'. In short, amoral fantasy ('impenetrably steely motivation, dollops of gratuitous violence, a strong line in sex') for a new age of eroding norms.

And the Stones this Friday evening? How were they getting on in North Cheam? Reputedly, only two people paid to see them perform in a back room of the Woodstock pub, while four people stood outside listening for free.[12] The 'real' 1960s were off to a patchy start.

Notes

Abbreviations

Abrams	Mark Abrams Papers (Churchill Archives Centre, Churchill College, Cambridge)
AJ	*Architects' Journal*
AR	*Architectural Review*
BBC WAC	BBC Written Archives Centre (Caversham)
CL	*Country Life*
Daly	Lawrence Daly Papers (Modern Records Centre, University of Warwick)
Darlington	Diary of Roger Darlington (private collection of Roger Darlington)
Dee	Diary of Dennis Dee (East Riding of Yorkshire Archives, Beverley)
DM	*Daily Mail*
DT	*Daily Telegraph*
Fowles	Charles Drazin (ed), John Fowles, *The Journals: Volume 1* (2003)
Fowles	John Fowles Papers (Special Collections, University of Exeter)
FT	*Financial Times*
GDP	Great Diary Project (Bishopsgate Institute, London)
Hague	Frances and Gladys Hague Papers (Keighley Library)
Haines	Diary of Alice (Judy) Haines (Mass-Observation Archive, University of Sussex, The Keep, Brighton)
Halle	Diary of William Halle (Wandsworth Heritage Service)
Heap	Diary of Anthony Heap (London Metropolitan Collections)
Hill	Diary of Jennie Hill (Hampshire Record Office, Winchester)

Hodgson	Diary of Vere Hodgson (Kensington Central Library)
Jackson	Brian Jackson Papers (Special Collections, University of Essex)
Langford	Diary of Gladys Langford (Islington Local History Centre)
Larkin	Anthony Thwaite (ed), Philip Larkin, *Letters to Monica* (2010)
Larkin	Unpublished letters of Philip Larkin to Monica Jones (Bodleian Library, Oxford)
Last	Diary of Nella Last (Mass-Observation Archive, University of Sussex, The Keep, Brighton)
Lee	Diary of Veronica Lee (later Porter) (private collection of Veronica Porter)
LPA	Labour Party Archives (People's History Museum, Manchester)
Macmillan	Harold Macmillan, *At the End of the Day* (1973)
Martin	Diary of Madge Martin (Oxfordshire History Centre, Oxford)
NS	*New Statesman*
NY	*New Yorker*
Raynham	Diary of Marian Raynham (Mass-Observation Archive, University of Sussex, The Keep, Brighton)
St John	Diary of Henry St John (Ealing Local History Centre)
ST	*Sunday Times*
Tench	Diary of Georgiana Tench (Modern Records Centre, University of Warwick)
TLS	*Times Literary Supplement*
Willmott	Diary of Phyllis Willmott (Churchill Archives Centre, Churchill College, Cambridge)

All books are published in London unless otherwise stated.

I NOTHING TO OFFEND

1. Lee, 10 Jun 1962; *Accrington Observer*, 12 Jun 1962; *The Times*, 9 Jun 1962, 11 Jun 1962; BBC WAC, R9/7/58–VR/62/331, 10 Jun 1962; (Brighton) *Evening Argus*, 11–12 Jun 1962.
2. GDP/7/1960–64, 11 Jun 1962; *Guardian*, 12 Jun 1962; Last, SxMOA1/4/275, 11 Jun 1962; https://coronationstreet.fandom.com/wiki/Episode_156.

3. Haines, SxMOA99/34/8/15, 12 Jun 1962; Last, SxMOA1/4/275, 12 Jun 1962; GDP/458/June–July 1962; *DM*, 13 Jun 1962; Gyles Brandreth, *Something Sensational to Read in the Train* (2009), p 31.

4. *Scotsman*, 13 Jun 1962; Russell Davies (ed), *The Kenneth Williams Diaries* (1993), p 192; *Country Life*, 14 Jun 1962; BBC WAC, R9/7/58 – VR/62/337, 14 Jun 1962.

5. *Guardian*, 14–16 Jun 1962.

6. Christopher Harvie, *Scotland and Nationalism* (third edn, 1978), p 175; *Scotsman*, 6 Jun 1962; *Guardian*, 13 Jun 1962; Harvie, p 175; *Scotsman*, 16 Jun 1962; *Guardian*, 14 Jun 1962.

7. *Shrewsbury Chronicle*, 15 Jun 1962; *TLS*, 15 Jun 1962; *NS*, 15 Jun 1962; Mark Lewisohn, *All These Years, Volume 1* (2013), p 676; www.tvpopdiaries.co.uk/needle.

8. www.tvpopdiaries.co.uk/1962; *Macmillan*, p 86; Kevin Cann, *Any Day Now* (2010), pp 23–4.

9. Based mainly on Dunn in *NS*, 22 Jun 1962, this paragraph is also derived from *Guardian*, 16 Jun 1962 ('Labour at play'), *Observer*, 17 Jun 1962 ('Tickled pink'), *Guardian*, 18 Jun 1962 ('Labour to Win' and 'London Letter').

10. This account of Mandela in London comes from: Mary Benson, *A Far Cry* (1989), p 144; Anthony Sampson, *Mandela* (1999), pp 167–9; Emily Buchanan, 'Nelson Mandela's death', *BBC News*, 7 Dec 2013; Nelson Mandela Foundation, 'Foundation receives 1962 photos' (2020).

2 OUR FRIEND TELSTAR

1. *ST*, 8 Jul 1973; *Guardian*, 21 Jun 1962; *AJ*, 20 Jun 1962; *South London Press*, 22 Jun 1962; *Manchester Evening News*, 18 Jun 1962; *Guardian*, 20 Jun 1962.

2. Roy Bullock, *Salford 1940–1965* (Salford, 1996), p 56; Heap, Acc 2243/36/1, 18 Jun 1962; *Guardian*, 19 Jun 1962; *NS*, 22 Jun 1962; *Observer*, 24 Jun 1962; Heap, Acc 2243/36/1, 21 Jun 1962; *Observer*, 24 Jun 1962.

3. *Listener*, 28 Jun 1962; BBC WAC, R9/7/58 – VR/62/351, 22 Jun 1962; *Sunday Express*, 24 Jun 1962; Hill, vol 30, 18–19 Jun 1962; BBC WAC, R9/7/58 – VR/62/349, 21 Jun 1962; Ray Galton & Alan Simpson, *Steptoe and Son* (2002), pp 45–6; BBC WAC, R9/7/58 – VR/62/357, 26 Jun 1962.

4. Martin, P5/2J/37, 25 Jun 1962; *Fife News*, 30 Jun 1962; *Bath and Wilts Evening Chronicle*, 26 Jun 1962; Hodgson, 26 Jun 1962.

5. John Goldsmith (ed), Stephen Spender, *Journals, 1939–1983* (1985), p 242; *Guardian*, 29 Jun 1962, 28 Jun 1962.

6. *FT*, 28 Nov 1962.

7. R. Wilkinson, 'A Statistical Analysis of Attitudes to Moving', *Urban Studies*, May 1965, pp 1–14.

8. Wilkinson, p 5; Fred Inglis, *Richard Hoggart* (2014), pp 143–4; Michael Tracey, *A Variety of Lives* (1983), pp 189, 197; William Glock, *Notes in Advance* (Oxford, 1991), p 115.

9. *Guardian*, 28 Jun 1962; *Observer*, 1 Jul 1962; Inglis, *Hoggart*, pp 145–6; Jeffrey Milland, 'Courting Malvolio', *Contemporary British History*, Summer 2004, p 95.

10. Charles Stuart (ed), *The Reith Diaries* (1975), p 503; Denis Forman, *Persona Granada* (1997), p 265; *NS*, 6 Jul 1962 (Williams); *NY*, 14 Jul 1962; Richard Hoggart, *An Imagined Life* (1992), pp 59–60; *NY*, 14 Jul 1962; Christopher Mayhew, *Time to Explain* (1987), pp 131–2; Lawrence Black, *The Political Culture of the Left in Affluent Britain, 1951–64* (Basingstoke, 2003), p 101.

11. Milland, p 96; Forman, p 265; Joe Moran, 'Mundane millionaires', *Guardian*, 22 Feb 2011; Krishan Kumar, 'Holding the Middle Ground', *Sociology*, Jan 1975, pp 67–88; Heap, Acc 2243/36/1, 29 Jun 1962; Willmott, WLMT 1/24, 1 Jul 1962.

12. *DM*, 30 Jun 1962; *Guardian*, 30 Jun 1962; Artemis Cooper, *Writing at the Kitchen Table* (1999), p 218; *Littlehampton Gazette*, 6 Jul 1962; *Wikipedia*, 'Jimi Hendrix'; Eric James, *A Life of Bishop John A. T. Robinson* (1987), pp 112–13; *Guardian*, 2 Jul 1962; *British Medical Journal*, 3 Oct 1964; *Dundee Courier*, 2 Jul 1962; *Observer*, 4 Nov 2012 (Dalya Alberge); Bevis Hillier, *Betjeman: The Bonus of Laughter* (2004), p 178; Halle, D 121/2, 2 Jul 1962.

13. *Fowles*, pp 511–12; *Observer*, 24 Jun 1962; *CL*, 28 Jun 1962; *ST*, 24 Jun 1962; *Spectator*, 8 Jun 1962; *Guardian*, 8 Jun 1962; *Observer*, 10 Jun 1962; *Fowles*, pp 512–13.

14. *Guardian*, 7 Jul 1962; *NS*, 6 Jul 1962; Daly, 302/3/19, 7–8 Jul 1962; Fred Inglis, *Radical Earnestness* (Oxford, 1982), pp 178–80.

15. *Surrey Comet*, 7 Jul 1962; *Bexhill-on-Sea Observer*, 7 Jul 1962; Russell Thompson, *Basildon* (Salisbury, 2002), p 32; *AR*, Nov 1962, p 333 (Kenneth Browne); Michael Crick, *Jeffrey Archer* (1995), p 73; BBC WAC, R9/7/59 – VR/62/378; *The Morecambe and Wise Show*, ITV, 7 Jul 1962; Richard Davenport-Hines, *The Pursuit of Oblivion* (2001), p 249; Hill, vol 30, 7 Jul 1962; Haines, SxMOA99/34/8/15, 7–8 Jul 1962.

16. *DT*, 9 Sep 2006 (Yehuda Koren and Eilat Negev). For a discussion of the uncertainties surrounding that day's events, see *NS*, 16 Oct 2020 (Anna Leszkiewicz, reviewing Heather Clark's biography of Plath).

17. Joe Moran, *Armchair Nation* (2013), pp 143–4; *The Strange Story of Joe Meek*, BBC Two, 8 Feb 1991; *Birkenhead News and Advertiser*, 14 Jul 1962; Raynham, SxMOA99/60/1/9, 12 Jul 1962; Colin Harper, *Dazzling Stranger* (2000), pp 137–8; *DT*, 9 Sep 2006 (Koren and Negev).

18. *Guardian*, 11 Jul 1962; *AJ*, 11 Jul 1962, 18 Jul 1962; *AR*, Jul 1962, p 47.

19. David Kynaston, *The City of London, Volume 4* (2001), p 276; *Guardian*, 12 Jul 1962.

20. Rebecca Stott, *In the Days of Rain* (2017), pp 17, 184–7, 386; *Hampstead & Highgate Express*, 20 Jul 1962; Galton & Simpson, pp 50–3.

21. *Observer*, 8 Jul 1962; Peter Catterall (ed), *The Macmillan Diaries, Volume II* (2011), p 481; Ferdinand Mount, *Cold Cream* (2008), pp 248–9; *DM*, 10 Jul 1962; D. R. Thorpe, *Supermac* (2010), p 521; *Guardian*, 12 Jul 1962; *DM*, 12 Jul 1962; Thorpe, p 521; *Guardian*, 13 Jul 1962.

22. Christopher Sandford, *Mick Jagger* (Cooper Square Press edn, 1999), pp 49–50; Keith Richards, *Life* (2010), p 97.

23. *Listener*, 5 Jul 1962.

24. Anthony Sampson, *Anatomy of Britain* (1962), pp xi, 350–1, 637–8.

25. *Spectator*, 13 Jul 1962; *TLS*, 13 Jul 1962; David Hughes, 'Simon Raven', *Independent*, 16 May 2001; *Guardian*, 20 Jul 1962; *Punch*, 11 Jul 1962.

26. *The Times*, 17–28 Jul 1962.

27. *Observer*, 29 Jul 1962 (Mark Arnold-Foster); Marjorie Morgan, 'Carmen Bryan and the Commonwealth Immigrants Act 1962', *blackpresence*, 12 Jan 2013.

28. *Macmillan Diaries*, p 484. In general, see: Keith Alderman, 'Harold Macmillan's "Night of the Long Knives"', *Contemporary Record*, Autumn 1992, pp 243–65.

29. David Profumo, *Bringing the House Down* (2006), p 169; Ian Gilmour, *Whatever Happened to the Tories?* (1997), p 173; W. F. Deedes, *Dear Bill* (1997), p 148; *Listener*, 19 Jul 1962 (Peter Green); *The Times*, 14 Jul 1962, 16 Jul 1962; *NS*, 20 Jul 1962 (Francis Williams).

30. *FT*, 17 Jul 1962; *Sunday Telegraph*, 15 Jul 1962; Heap, Acc 2243/36/1, 16 Jul 1962; *NY*, 4 Aug 1962; Mount, p 263.

31. Russell Davies (ed), *The Kenneth Williams Diaries* (1993), p 194; Andrew Barrow, *Gossip* (Pan edn, 1980), p 226; www.tvpopdiaries.co.uk/1962; Haines, SxMOA99/34/8/15, 14 Jul 1962; St John, 68/47, 15 Jul 1962; *Observer*, 15 Jul 1962.

32. Miles Jebb (ed), *The Diaries of Cynthia Gladwyn* (1995), p 271; David Frost, *An Autobiography* (1993), pp 43–6.

33. John Campbell, *Margaret Thatcher, Volume One* (2000), pp 149–50; *Guardian*, 17 Jul 1962; https://coronationstreet.fandom.com/Episode_166; BBC WAC, R9/7/59 – VR/62/399, 16 Jul 1962; *Listener*, 26 Jul 1962 (Derek Hill).

34. *Macmillan*, p 100; *The Times*, 18 Jul 1962; *Observer*, 22 Jul 1962 ('Sayings of the Week'); *Guardian*, 18 Jul 1962; *Wikipedia*, 'Ian Horobin'; Mark Lewisohn, *Radio Times Guide to TV Comedy* (2003 edn), pp 398–9; *Listener*, 26 Jul 1962; BBC WAC, R9/7/59 – VR/62/401, 17 Jul 1962.

35. Elizabeth Longford, *Elizabeth R* (1983), p 210; *Guardian*, 19 Jul 1962; *Wiltshire Gazette & Herald*, 26 Jul 1962; John Osborne, *Almost a Gentleman* (1991), p 242; *Manchester Evening News*, 18 Jul 1962; *Guardian*, 19 Jul 1962; *Manchester Evening News*, 18 Jul 1962.

36. Stephen Fay and David Kynaston, *Arlott, Swanton and the Soul of English Cricket* (2018), pp 125–6; Charles Williams, *Gentlemen & Players* (2012), pp 174–5; *Wisden Cricketers' Almanack, 1963* (1963), p 357.

3 THINGS THEY DO CHANGE

1. *Wiltshire Gazette & Herald*, 12 Jul 1962; *East Anglian Daily Times*, 19 Jul 1962; *Shrewsbury Chronicle*, 20 Jul 1962; *Lincolnshire Echo*, 20 Jul 1962; *East Anglian Daily Times*, 19 Jul 1962; diary of Sidney Jackson (West Yorkshire Archives Service, Bradford), 18 Jul 1962.

2. Howard Newby, *Country Life* (1987), pp 184–5; H. E. Bracey, *People and the Countryside* (1970), p 37; John Martin, *The Development of Modern Agriculture* (Basingstoke, 2000), p 114; Bracey, *People*, pp 36, 44; Graham Harvey, *The Killing of the Countryside* (1997), p 114; Newby, *Country Life*, p 187; LPA, 'A suggested policy for British Agriculture' (Jan 1963), Sub-Committee on Agriculture, Nov 1962–May 1963; E. J. Hobsbawm, *Industry and Empire* (Harmondsworth, 1969), p 205; William Smethurst, *The Archers* (1996), pp 12, 126–7.

3. Martin, pp 98, 102; Alun Howkins, *The Death of Rural England* (2003), pp 151–2; Martin, pp 106–7; *Guardian*, 3 Sep 1963 (Stanley Baker); Howkins, pp 155–6.

4. Martin, pp 108, 110.

5. Martin, p 126; Dan Cherrington (ed), John Cherrington, *Candidly Yours* … (Ipswich, 1989), p 55; Frances Donaldson, *A Twentieth-Century Life* (Bloomsbury Reader edn, 2013), p 263; C. David Edgar, 'Sir John Eastwood', *Independent*, 4 Oct 1995; Gerald Frost, *Antony Fisher* (2002), pp 45–51; Cherrington, p 55.

6. Martin, pp 111–12, 118; Howkins, pp 151, 155; *Guardian*, 9 Nov 1962.

7. Harvey, p 19; Howard Newby, *Green and Pleasant Land?* (1979), p 214; John Young, *Farming in East Anglia* (1967), p 81; Howkins, p 196; Oliver Rackham, *The History of the Countryside* (Phoenix Press edn, 2000), pp 206, 302, 340, 96; C. Henry Warren, *Content with What I Have* (1967), pp 68–9.

8. Jeremy Burchardt, *Paradise Lost* (2002), p 169; Newby, *Country Life*, pp 227–8.

9. *Wikipedia*, 'Jack Hargreaves'; Trevor Rowley, *The English Landscape in the Twentieth Century* (2006), p xiv, quoting Hoskins; Victor Bonham-Carter, *The Survival of the English Countryside* (1971), p 189.

10. *Listener*, 19 Mar 1964; Lionel Brett, *Landscape in Distress* (1965), pp 50, 52, 54, 68, 70, 159.

11. *ST*, 17 Feb 1963; *Guardian*, 26 Jan 1963, 14 Feb 1963; *CL*, 8 Aug 1963. On Lincolnshire birds: *Observer*, 17 Feb 1963 (John Davy).

12. Hetty Saunders, *My House of Sky* (Toller Fratrum, 2017), pp 100–5; J. A. Baker, *The Peregrine* (William Collins edn, 2017), pp 32, 121.

13. Leeds & District Bird Watchers' Club, Annual Report, 1962 (Local and Family History, Leeds Central Library); Charles Sinker (ed), *Hilda Murrell's Nature Diaries* (1987), p 104.

14. Notes by Steve Roud for: The Copper Family of Rottingdean, *Come Write Me Down* (Topic Records CD, 2001).

15. *CL*, 14 Nov 1963 ('Farming Notes'); Newby, *Country Life*, pp 199–200; LPA, 'A suggested policy'; *Guardian*, 22 Aug 1962; LPA, 'A suggested policy'.

16. Howard Newby, 'Agricultural Workers in the Class Structure', *Sociological Review*, Aug 1972, pp 421–2; *The Times*, 2 Dec 1963; Newby, *Country Life*, p 207; Howard Newby, *The Deferential Worker* (1977), p 297.

17. Newby, 'Agricultural Workers', p 426; Newby, *Deferential Worker*, pp 301–2; *The Countryman*, Winter 1964, p 311; Ronald Blythe, *Akenfield* (Penguin edn, Harmondsworth, 1972), p 92; Colin Bell and Howard Newby, 'The Sources of Variation in Agricultural Workers' Images of Society', *Sociological Review*, May 1973, pp 244–5.

18. Burchardt, pp 154–5; Blythe, p 101; Newby, *Deferential Worker*, pp 284–9; Burchardt, pp 155–6; Martin, pp 129–30.

19. W. M. Williams, *A West Country Village* (1963), pp 100–5; John S. Nalson, 'Quiet Revolution in Traditional Society', in Ronald Frankenberg (ed), *Custom and Conflict in British Society* (Manchester, 1982), pp 84–6; Warren, pp 165–70.

20. Miss Read, *Winter in Thrush Green* (Orion Books pbk edn, 2007), pp 6–7; Automobile Association, *Illustrated Road Book of England and Wales* (1963), pp 228–33; Mike Pitcher, *Of Bales and Banking* (Portsmouth, 2013), pp 15, 30, 32, 75, 78, 113, 117–18.

21. Burchardt, p 157; David Phillips and Allan Williams, *Rural Britain* (Oxford, 1984), pp 177, 186; Howkins, p 184; Newby, 'Agricultural Workers', pp 430–1; Ruth M. Crichton, *Commuters' Village* (Dawlish, 1964), p 47.

22. Howard Newby, 'Urbanization and the rural class structure', *British Journal of Sociology*, Dec 1979, p 478; Burchardt, p 152; H. E. Bracey, *English Rural Life* (1959), p 41; Phillips and Williams, pp 77, 80; E. W. Martin, *The Shearers and the Shorn* (1965), pp 191, 195; Howkins, p 200; Bracey, *English*, pp 33–4.

23. Phillips and Williams, p 110; Bruce Wood and Jackie Carter, 'Towns, Urban Change and Local Government', in A. H. Halsey (ed), *Twentieth-Century British Social Trends* (2000 edn, Basingstoke), pp 423–4; Burchardt, p 188; Howkins, p 177, quoting J. K. Bowers and Paul Cheshire, *Agriculture, the Countryside and Land Use* (1983), p 47; Newby, 'Urbanization', p 482.

24. John Connell, *The End of Tradition* (Henley-on-Thames, 1978), p 54; Bracey, *English*, pp 50–1; Newby, *Green*, p 194; Bracey, *English*, pp 44, 48; Crichton, p 46; Bracey, *English*, p 236; Newby, *Deferential Worker*, pp 329–35; Crichton, pp 80–92.

25. Jean Robin, *Elmdon* (Cambridge, 1980), chap 11; Burchardt, pp 195–6; Marilyn Strathern, *Kinship at the Core* (Cambridge, 1981), p xxii.

26. Geoffrey Moorhouse, *Britain in the Sixties: The Other England* (Harmondsworth, 1964), pp 63–7; Crichton, chap 6.

27. Tony Aldous, *Goodbye, Britain?* (1975), chap 4; Moorhouse, pp 72, 184–5, 61–2.

28. Ronald Frankenberg, *Communities in Britain* (Harmondsworth, 1966), summarising and quoting Margaret Stacey's *Tradition and Change*; Martin, pp 147–8, 153; nostalgiacentral.com, 'Swizzlewick'; *The Times*, 24 Aug 1964; *Illustrated Road Book*, p 471; Warren, pp 58–60; *Betjeman Revisited* (Green Umbrella video, 1995).

4 NO JAM ROLL? GIVE OVER!

1. Andrew Bradstock, *David Sheppard* (2019), p 129; *The Times*, 20 Jul 1962; Rob Chapman, *Syd Barrett* (2010), p 39; *Guardian*, 20 Jul 1962; Heap, Acc 2243/36/1, 19 Jul 1962; *Guardian*, 20 Jul 1962 (Fay); *NS*, 27 Jul 1962 (Gellert); *ST*, 22 Jul 1962 (Hobson); Andrew Barrow, *Gossip* (Pan edn, 1980), pp 226–7.

2. *FT*, 20 Jul 1962; *Guardian*, 20–21 Jul 1962; *The Times*, 21 Jul 1962.

3. Haines, SxMOA99/34/8/15, 21 Jul 1962; Chris Waters, *Fred Trueman* (2011), pp 25–7, cf www.tvpopdiaries.co.uk, 20 Jul 1962; *Guardian*, 23 Jul 1962; *Record Collector*, Feb 2007 (Rob Bradford); *Observer*, 22 Jul 1962; David Kynaston, *Till Time's Last Sand* (2017), p 453; *Guardian*, 24 Jul 1962; Darlington, 23 Jul 1962; *Guardian*, 24 Jul 1962; Humphrey Carpenter, *Dennis Potter* (1998), p 127; Stephen Fay and David Kynaston, *Arlott, Swanton and the Soul of English Cricket* (2018), p 185; BBC WAC, R9/7/59 – VR/62/419, 25 Jul 1962; *Guardian*, 27 Jul 1962; John Biffen, *Semi-Detached* (2013), p 211; Mark Lewisohn, *All These Years, Volume 1* (2013), p 688; BBC WAC, R9/7/59 – VR/62/421, 26 Jul 1962; *The Times*, 27 Jul 1962; *Listener*, 2 Aug 1962 (Peter Green); *Observer*, 29 Jul 1962; D. R. Thorpe, *Supermac* (2010), p 525.

4. David Selbourne (ed), *A Doctor's Life* (1989), pp 167–8; *Guardian*, 30 Jul 1962, 1–2 Aug 1962; *South London Press*, 10 Aug 1962, 14 Aug 1962; *Guardian*, 12 Sep 1962.

5. *Guardian*, 20 Jul 1962; *The Times*, 1 Aug 1962; *Guardian*, 1 Aug 1962; *The Times*, 3 Aug 1962; *Observer*, 5 Aug 1962 (Roy Perrott); Automobile Association, *Illustrated Road Book of England and Wales* (1963), p 455; Paul Foot, *Immigration and Race in British Politics* (Harmondsworth, 1966), pp 41–2, 25.

6. *Radio Times*, 26 Jul 1962; https://coronationstreet.fandom.com/ Episode_171; *The Times*, 6 Aug 1962, 3 Aug 1962; (Northampton) *Mercury and Herald*, 3 Aug 1962; *Guardian*, 24 Jul 2014 (Simon Hattenstone); Michael Willmott (ed), Rev Oliver Willmott, *The Parish Notes of Loders, Dottery and Askerswell: Volume 1* (Shrewsbury, 1996), Aug–Sep 1962.

7. *Observer*, 5 Aug 1962; Last, SxMOA1/4/277, 5 Aug 1962; *Bexhill-on-Sea Observer*, 4 Aug 1962, 11 Aug 1962; Selbourne, p 169; Last, SxMOA1/4/277, 6 Aug 1962.

8. *Ipswich Evening Star*, 7 Aug 1962; Anthony Thwaite (ed), *Selected Letters of Philip Larkin* (1992), p 343; *Guardian*, 8 Aug 1962; Last,

SxMOA1/4/277, 7 Aug 1962; Barrow, p 228; Dominic Shellard, *British Theatre since the War* (1999), p 101.

9. *NS*, 10 Aug 1962; *Listener*, 9 Aug 1962.

10. Heap, Acc 2243/36/1, 11 Aug 1962; *Sunday Express*, 12 Aug 1962; Selbourne, p 171; *Blackpool Gazette and Herald*, 7 Jul 1962; *West Lancashire Evening Gazette*, 9 Aug 1962; Nicholas Parsons, *The Straight Man* (1994), p 163; Hague, Jul 1962; *NS*, 24 Aug 1962; *Guardian*, 25 Aug 2012 (Robert Booth); Robert Colls, 'English journeys', *Prospect*, Jul 2007, pp 46–50.

11. Barrow, p 228; *Observer*, 12 Aug 1962; Bevis Hillier, *Betjeman: The Bonus of Laughter* (2004), p 179; Foot, p 25; Larkin, Ms. Eng. c. 7425, fo 42, 13 Aug 1962; *Guardian*, 14 Aug 1962; *Fife News*, 18 Aug 1962; *The Times*, 15 Aug 1962; *Wikipedia*, 'BMC ADO16'; Roy Greenslade, *Press Gang* (Pan edn, 2004), p 177.

12. Geoffrey Moorhouse, *Britain in the Sixties: The Other England* (Harmondsworth, 1964), pp 14–15; *Guardian*, 15 Aug 1962; Moorhouse, p 13; *Guardian*, 28 Jul 1962 ('Stopping drift of population'); Peter Shapely, 'Civic pride and redevelopment in the post-war British city', *Urban History*, 2012 (39/2), p 325; *Liverpool Daily Post*, 22 Sep 1962; Shapely, p 325. In general, for a stimulating and insightful long-run narrative, see: Tom Hazeldine, *The Northern Question* (2020).

13. Haines, SxMOA99/34/8/15, 16 Aug 1962; Lewisohn, pp 701–2; *Scarborough Evening News*, 17 Aug 1962; Carpenter, p 127; BBC WAC, R9/7/59 – VR/62/461, 16 Aug 1962.

14. *Bideford and North Devon Gazette*, 17 Aug 1962; *Guardian*, 18 Aug 1962 ('London Letter'); Bill Morgan (ed), *Rub Out the Words: The Letters of William S. Burroughs, 1959–1974* (2012), p 110; Darlington, 17 Aug 1962; *Guardian*, 18 Aug 1962; Selbourne, p 172; BFI, *Screenonline*, 'Plater, Alan'; BBC WAC, R9/7/59 – VR/62/463, 17 Aug 1962.

15. *Charles Buchan's Soccer Gift Book, 1962–1963* (1962), p 93; *Littlehampton Gazette*, 24 Aug 1962; *Mojo*, Nov 1995, p 29; Mark Amory (ed), *The Letters of Evelyn Waugh* (1980), p 592; *Listener*, 30 Aug 1962 (Burns Singer); *Observer*, 19 Aug 1962.

16. Haines, SxMOA99/34/8/15, 21 Aug 1962; Barrow, p 228; *AJ*, 22 Aug 1962; GDP/7/1960–64, 22 Aug 1962; Haines, SxMOA99/34/8/15, 22 Aug 1962; Lewisohn, pp 711–12; Spencer Leigh, 'Johnny Keating', *Independent*, 9 Jun 2015; Heap, Acc 2243/36/1, 22 Aug 1962.

17. *Guardian*, 23 Aug 1962; *Wikipedia*, 'Paraquat'; *NS*, 24 Aug 1962; Last, SxMOA1/4/277, 24 Aug 1962.

18. The main source for this account is Angela Bartie and Eleanor Bell, '1962 International Writers Conference, Edinburgh: An edited history', www.

edinburghworldwritersconference.org/background, but material also from: Margaret Drabble, *Angus Wilson* (1995), pp 308–11; *Guardian*, 11 Aug 2012 (Stuart Kelly); Barry Miles, *William S Burroughs* (2014), p 404; *NS*, 31 Aug 1962 (Muggeridge).

19. *Observer*, 2 Sep 1962 ('Comment'); *Guardian*, 27 Aug 1962; Martin, P5/2J/37, 27 Aug 1962; Local and Family History, Leeds Central Library, LP HUN 796.

20. BBC WAC, R9/7/59 – VR/62/487, 30 Aug 1962; Foot, p 58; *Guardian*, 28 Aug 1962, 31 Aug 1962; W. Stephen Gilbert, *Fight and Kick and Bite* (1995), p 100; Carpenter, p 127.

21. *DT*, 31 Aug 2002 (Mick Brown); *The Times*, 4 Sep 2020 (Will Hodgkinson); *Birkenhead News and Advertiser*, 1 Sep 1962; *Guardian*, 3 Sep 1962; *FT*, 3 Sep 1962; Elizabeth Wilson, *Jacqueline du Pré* (1998), p 93; *Wikipedia*, 'Anita West'.

22. *Listener*, 13 Sep 1962; Jackson, Working-Class Community papers, File (Box) C1, 3 Sep 1962.

23. Robert Jeffrey and Ian Watson, *Clydeside* (Edinburgh, 2000), p 75; Lewisohn, pp 724–8; *Guardian*, 6 Sep 1962; Joe Moran, 'Crossing the Road in Britain, 1931–1976', *Historical Journal*, Jun 2006, p 489; *Observer*, 2 Sep 1962 (Ben Wright); *Guardian*, 6 Sep 1962.

24. Welsh Football Data Archive, 'Welsh Cup 1877 – to date'; *Illustrated Road Book*, pp 263, 371; Hywel Francis and David Smith, *The Fed* (1980), pp 427–8; Michael P. Jackson, *The Price of Coal* (1974), p 108; Francis and Smith, p 428; Martin Johnes, *Wales since 1939* (Manchester, 2012), p 70; Francis and Smith, pp 453–4; Johnes, p 91.

25. Johnes, pp 149–51, 81; *Guardian*, 26 Sep 1962; R. S. Thomas, 'The Welsh Hill Country', in A. Alvarez (ed), *The New Poetry* (Harmondsworth, 1962), pp 77–8. The following Thomas poem in Alvarez's anthology (published in spring 1962) is 'Welsh Landscape', pp 78–9, the last ten lines of which offer an utterly bleak prediction of the future facing Wales, especially rural Wales.

26. Isabel Emmett, *A North Wales Village* (1964), pp 120, 9–13, 23, 28–9; George Thomas, *Mr Speaker* (1985), p 96; Johnes, chap 7; Dai Smith, 'Alun Richards', *Guardian*, 19 Jun 2004.

27. Johnes, p 89; Mervyn Jones, *Michael Foot* (1994), p 251; Johnes, p 269.

28. Kenneth O. Morgan, *Callaghan* (Oxford, 1997), p 678; Johnes, pp 216, 221–2; *Wikipedia*, 'Welsh Language Society'; Johnes, p 220; Meic Stephens, 'Gwynfor Evans', *Independent*, 22 Apr 2005; John Beavan, 'Viscount Tonypandy', *Independent*, 23 Sep 1997; *Observer*, 19 Aug 1962; D. Ben Rees, 'Eddie Thomas', *Guardian*, 4 Jun 1997; *Observer*, 19 Aug 1962.

5 BROTHERS AND FRIENDS

1. *Fowles*, p 527; Anthony Sampson, *Anatomy of Britain* (1962), p 11; *Guardian*, 7 Sep 1962; Graham McCann, *Frankie Howerd* (2004), pp 190–5; *NS*, 14 Sep 1962 (Roger Gellert).

2. *Wisden Cricketers' Almanack, 1963* (1963), p 741; BBC WAC, R9/7/60 – VR/62/505, 8 Sep 1962; British Railways, *Passenger Services: London (Paddington), Bristol & West of England, etc* (1962), p 289 (Table 163); *Radio Times*, 6 Sep 1962; www.tvpopdiaries.co.uk/needle; *Wisden*, p 741; *Wikipedia*, 'Robert Soblen'; Robert Pearce (ed), Patrick Gordon Walker, *Political Diaries, 1932–1971* (1991), pp 273–4.

3. 'John Vassall', *The Times*, 6 Dec 1996; *Guardian*, 13 Sep 1962; *The Times*, 13 Sep 1962; *Guardian*, 13 Sep 1962; Daly, 302/3/18, 12 Sep 1962.

4. Lawrence Black, *Redefining British Politics* (Basingstoke, 2010), p 152; *Guardian*, 8 Sep 1962; *Observer*, 16 Sep 1962; Black, *Redefining*, p 158; *ST*, 16 Sep 1962; Black, *Redefining*, p 152.

5. Willmott, WLMT 1/24, 13 Sep 1962; Tam Dalyell, 'Sir Timothy Raison', *Independent*, 11 Nov 2011; Haines, SxMOA99/34/8/15, 13 Sep 1962; *Independent*, 27 Sep 1996 (Bayan Northcott); Colin Harper, *Dazzling Stranger* (2000), pp 105–7; John Lahr, *Prick Up Your Ears* (Bloomsbury pbk edn, 2002), pp 87–9; *Guardian*, 11 Sep 1962; BBC WAC, R9/7/60 – VR/62/517, 15 Sep 1962.

6. *Guardian*, 17 Sep 1962; *ST*, 16 Sep 1962; *Listener*, 27 Sep 1962; Ben Watt, *Romany and Tom* (2014), pp 339–40; Walter Hooper (ed), C. S. Lewis, *Collected Letters: Volume III* (2006), pp 1,371–2; Simon Gunn and Rachel Bell, *Middle Classes* (2002), p 137; *Listener*, 27 Sep 1962 (Peter Green); Abrams, ABMS 2/4/11, file 'L.P. Study of Public Opinion (Political), Aug 1962–May 1965'; *Where?*, Summer 1962, p 3, Autumn 1962, pp 4–5; Asa Briggs, *Michael Young* (2001), pp 196–8. For a different interpretation of public attitudes to secondary education, and in particular of the surveys done for Labour by Mark Abrams, see: Peter Mandler, *The Crisis of the Meritocracy* (Oxford, 2020), chap 4.

7. David Kynaston, *The Financial Times* (1988), pp 292–3; *The Times*, 20–21 Sep 1962; Local and Family History, Leeds Central Library, *Roundhay High School Magazine*, Dec 1963, p 24; Stuart Laing, 'Banging in Some Reality', in John Corner (ed), *Popular Television in Britain* (1991), p 135; Harry Thompson, *Peter Cook* (1997), p 134; Sheila Hancock, *The Two of Us* (2004), p 123; Larkin, Ms. Eng. c. 7425, fo 53, 20 Sep 1962; *Banbury Guardian*, 20 Sep 1962.

8. *Guardian*, 21 Sep 1962; Sheila Patterson, *Immigration and Race Relations in Britain, 1960–1967* (1969), pp 3, 16.

9. Matthew Press, 'Tassaduq Ahmed', *Guardian*, 8 Jul 2002; Chris Boothman, 'Rudy Narayan', *Independent*, 6 Jul 1998; Margaret Busby, 'Frank Crichlow', *Guardian*, 27 Sep 2010; 'Errol Brown', *DT*, 7 May 2015; Colin Grant, *Homecoming* (2019), pp 147, 270 (Campbell); Mike Phillips and Trevor Phillips, *Windrush* (1998), pp 128, 149–50 (Weekes, Jones); Grant, pp 116–17, 281 (Trotman); Max Eilenberg, 'HS Bhabra', *Independent*, 27 Jun 2000; David Matthews, *Voices of the Windrush Generation* (2018), pp 46, 66 (Charlie Phillips); *Wikipedia*, 'Anwar Pervez'; Atika Rehman, 'Sir Anwar Pervez', www.dawn.com/news, 5 Oct 2019; Robert Verkaik, 'DS Roberts calls it a day', *Independent*, 25 Mar 1997; Phillips, pp 123, 329–31 (Phoenix); Grant, pp 156, 272 (France); Phillips, p 143 (Ouseley); *Guardian*, 25 Oct 2016 (Frances Perraudin on Cole); *Guardian*, 11 Nov 2020 (Dave Simpson on Armatrading); *Wikipedia*, 'Joan Armatrading'; 'Lord Bagri', *The Times*, 20 Jul 2017; *Independent*, 1 Feb 1997 (John Walsh on Caryl Phillips); Chris Mullard, 'Dame Jocelyn Barrow', *Guardian*, 27 May 2020; *Guardian*, 3 Sep 2020 (Joseph Harker on Pascall); *NS*, 11 Oct 2013 (Sophie McBain on Rabbatts); *Wikipedia*, 'Eddy Grant'; Fenella Brown et al (eds), *Acland Burghley* (2002); 'Laurel Aitken', *The Times*, 26 Jul 2005; 'Leonard Woodley, QC', *The Times*, 7 Mar 2020; *Big Issue*, 30 May 2016 (Rushdie); *Wikipedia*, 'Wilfred Wood (bishop)'; Robin Bunce and Paul Field, *Darcus Howe* (2014), pp 23–4; 'Mustapha Matura', *The Times*, 4 Nov 2019.

10. Dilip Hiro, *Black British, White British* (1971), p 18; Clair Wills, *Lovers and Strangers* (2017), p 196, quoting from Peter Wright, *The Coloured Worker in British Industry* (1968); Matthews, pp 206–7.

11. Wills, pp 196–7; Patterson, *Immigration*, p 174; Phillips, p 226; Helen McCarthy, *Double Lives* (2020), p 305; Grant, p 115; Marcus Collins, 'Pride and Prejudice', *Journal of British Studies*, Jul 2001, p 402.

12. Sheila Patterson, *Immigrants in Industry* (1968), chap 9.

13. Wills, p 233; *Independent*, 20 Jul 1998 (Peter Popham); Wills, pp 230–3; Robert Winder, *Bloody Foreigners* (2004), p 357; Campaign against Racism and Fascism/Southall Rights, *Southall: The Birth of a Black Community* (1981), pp 11–14; Piotr Stolarski, *Ealing in the 1960s* (2013), p 237; Hiro, p 151.

14. Patterson, *Immigration*, chap 6, especially pp 195–6, 221.

15. Wills, pp 247–54; Phillips, pp 191–2 (Weekes); Grant, p 99 (DeAbreu); Phillips, pp 132–4 (Huntley); Alison Shaw, *A Pakistani Community in Britain* (Oxford, 1988), pp 35–6.

16. McCarthy, pp 307–8; Wills, p 201; Winder, p 372; Collins, 'Pride', pp 402–5, 408; Shaw, p 43.

17. Grant, pp 214, 219–20; Hiro, pp 30–1; Grant, pp 237, 233 (Letts); *Guardian*, 12 Jan 2017 (Bee Wilson); Wills, pp 325–6.

18. Michael Dawswell, 'The Pigmentocracy of Citizenship', in Lawrence Black et al, *Consensus or Coercion?* (Cheltenham, 2001), p 75; Chris Waters, '"Dark Strangers" in Our Midst', *Journal of British Studies*, Apr 1997, p 232, quoting from Michael Banton, *White and Coloured* (1959).

19. Phillips, pp 138–40 (Dennison, Mark, Bousquet); Winston James, 'Migration, Racism and Identity Formation', in Winston James and Clive Harris (eds), *Inside Babylon* (1993), p 249, quoting from Donald Hinds, *Journey to an Illusion* (1966).

20. D. R. Thorpe, *Supermac* (2010), p 514; *NY*, 29 Sep 1962; Michael Cockerell, *Live from Number 10* (1988), pp 83–4; Giles Radice, *Friends & Rivals* (2002), p 119; Philip M. Williams, *Hugh Gaitskell* (1979), pp 724, 729; Michael McManus, *Jo Grimond* (Edinburgh, 2001), p 184.

21. Heap, Acc 2243/36/1, 27 Sep 1962; *NY*, 29 Sep 1962; *Macmillan*, p 137; Brian Brivati, *Hugh Gaitskell* (1996), p 407; Radice, p 120, quoting from Anthony Crosland, *The Conservative Enemy* (1962); Henry Hardy and Mark Pottle (eds), Isaiah Berlin, *Building: Letters, 1960–1975* (2013), pp 105–6.

22. Williams, p 729; *Guardian*, 22 Sep 1962; *Wikipedia*, 'University Challenge'; *New Musical Express*, 21 Sep 1962; David Burgess-Wise, *Ford at Dagenham* (2001), p 157; *DT*, 21 Sep 2002 (Graham Robson); *Barking & Dagenham Recorder*, 21 Feb 2002; *Independent*, 5 Oct 1988; *Guardian*, 25 Sep 1962.

23. Larkin, Ms. Eng. c. 7425, fo 53, 21 Sep 1962; *NS*, 21 Sep 1962; *TLS*, 4 Aug 2006; *Spectator*, 21 Sep 1962.

24. Humphrey Carpenter, *Dennis Potter* (1998), p 128; *TV Times*, 22 Sep 1962; www.tvpopdiaries.co.uk/1962; Heap, Acc 2243/36/1, 23 Sep 1962; St John, 68/47, 24 Sep 1962; Doug Hinman, *The Kinks* (San Francisco, 2004), p 10; Paul Foot, *Immigration and Race in British Politics* (Harmondsworth, 1965), p 25; *Western Morning News*, 26 Sep 1962.

25. *DT*, 26 Sep 1962; *Radio Times*, 20 Sep 1962; *Melody Maker*, 6 Oct 1962; Joanna Moorhead, *New Generations* (Cambridge, 1996), pp 44–5.

26. Haines, SxMOA99/34/8/15, 28 Sep 1962; Mark Lewisohn, *All These Years, Volume 1* (2013), pp 739–40, 750; Janet Frame, *The Complete Autobiography* (1990), p 409; Langford, 29 Sep 1962; www.tvpopdiaries. co.uk/1962; televisionheaven.co.uk/reviews/bradens-beat-on-the-braden-beat; Ronald Bergan, 'Honor Blackman', *Guardian*, 7 Apr 2020; Daly, Ms 302/3/18, 29 Sep 1962; *People's Journal*, 29 Sep 1962.

27. David Frost, *An Autobiography* (1993), pp 48–50; 'Lord Amery of Lustleigh', *The Times*, 4 Sep 1996, *DT*, 4 Sep 1996; Patrick Cosgrave,

'Lord Amery of Lustleigh', *Independent*, 5 Sep 1996; 'Sir Hardy Amies', *The Times*, 6 Mar 2003; Jane Mulvagh, 'Sir Hardy Amies', *Independent*, 6 Mar 2003; Keith Middlemas and John Orbell, 'The Earl of Cromer', *Independent*, 19 Mar 1991; David Kynaston, *Till Time's Last Sand* (2017), p 449; 'Lord Denning', *The Times*, 6 Mar 1999; Roy Greenslade, *Press Gang* (2003), pp 120–1; 'Sir John Junor', *The Times*, 5 May 1997; Julian Critchley, 'Sir John Junor', *Independent*, 5 May 1997; 'Betty Kenward', *DT*, 26 Jan 2001, *The Times*, 26 Jan 2001; 'Lord Margadale', *DT*, 29 May 1996; Patrick Cosgrave, 'Lord Margadale', *Independent*, 30 May 1996; Stephen Fay and David Kynaston, *Arlott, Swanton and the Soul of English Cricket* (2018); *Wikipedia*, 'Roy Thomson, 1st Baron Thomson of Fleet'; *Guardian*, 5 Aug 1976 (David Leitch); 'Lord Thomson, newspaper owner', *Guardian*, 5 Aug 1976; Sampson, p 118; Philip Mansel, 'Lord Dacre of Glanton', *Independent*, 27 Jan 2003.

28. 'Lord Annan', *The Times*, 23 Feb 2000; Noel Annan, *Our Age* (1990), pp 18–19; 'A. J. Ayer', *The Times*, 29 Jun 1989; Ben Rogers, *A. J. Ayer* (1999), p 269; 'Lord Briggs', *The Times*, 17 Mar 2016, *DT*, 17 Mar 2016; Edward Pearce and Julian Critchley, 'Lord Gilmour of Craigmillar', *Guardian*, 24 Sep 2007; 'Lord Gilmour of Craigmillar', *The Times*, 24 Sep 2007; David Kynaston, 'Lord Gilmour', *FT*, 24 Sep 2007; 'Sir Peter Hall', *The Times*, 13 Sep 2017; Michael Billington, 'Sir Peter Hall', *Guardian*, 13 Sep 2017; Elizabeth Longford, *Elizabeth R* (1983), p 185; Tom Sutcliffe, 'The Earl of Harewood', *Guardian*, 12 Jul 2011; 'Lord Jenkins of Hillhead', *The Times*, 6 Jan 2003; Douglas Jay, *Change and Fortune* (1980), pp 283–4; Leonard Marsh, 'Lady Plowden', *Independent*, 6 Oct 2000; Sampson, p 284; Robert Armstrong, 'Lord Plowden', *Independent*, 19 Feb 2001; Peter Porter, 'Sir Stephen Spender', *Independent*, 18 Jul 1995; 'Sir Stephen Spender', *The Times*, 18 Jul 1995; Annan, p 597; John Calder, 'Lord Weidenfeld', *Independent*, 21 Jan 2016; J. M. and M. J. Cohen (eds), *The Penguin Dictionary of Quotations* (Harmondsworth, 1960), p 133. On Amery, Hall and Jenkins respectively, see also: David Faber, *Speaking for England* (2005); Stephen Fay, *Power Play* (1995); John Campbell, *Roy Jenkins* (2014).

6 DECEPTIVELY SIMPLE BEATER

1. *Observer*, 30 Sep 1962; *Guardian*, 1 Oct 1962; Philip Saville, *They Shoot Directors, Don't They?* (Birmingham, 2019), pp 72–3. See also on *Afternoon of a Nymph*: John Russell Taylor, *Anatomy of a Television Play* (1962).

2. *Vogue*, 1 Oct 1962; Leo McKinstry, *Sir Alf* (2006), p 197; Heather Clark, *Red Comet* (2020), pp 765–6; *Listener*, 11 Oct 1962 (Andrew Sinclair); Lavinia Greacen (ed), *J. G. Farrell in his Own Words* (Cork, 2009), p 49; https://coronationstreet.fandom.com/wiki/Episode_188; *Listener*, 11 Oct 1962 (Peter Green); BBC WAC, R9/74/3, Nov 1962 (no 273), 1 Oct 1962, R9/7/60 – VR/62/548, 1 Oct 1962.

3. *Guardian*, 2 Oct 1962; *Official Architecture and Planning*, Oct 1962, p 632; Miles Glendinning and Stefan Muthesius, *Tower Block* (1994), p 243.

4. W. F. Deedes, *Dear Bill* (1997), pp 152–3; *Listener*, 11 Oct 1962; Clark, p 766; Fowles, EUL Ms 102/1/12, fo 17, 2 Oct 1962; *Guardian*, 9 Aug 2018 (Charlotte Higgins); BBC WAC, R9/7/60 – VR/62/550, 2 Oct 1962.

5. Brian Brivati, *Hugh Gaitskell* (1996), p 413; *Guardian*, 4 Oct 1962; Roy Jenkins, *A Life at the Centre* (1991), p 146; Bill Rodgers, *Fourth Among Equals* (2000), p 70; Giles Radice, *Friends & Rivals* (2002), p 121; John Campbell, *Roy Jenkins* (2014), p 225.

6. *Banbury Guardian*, 4 Oct 1962; *Guardian*, 4 Oct 1962; *AJ*, 10 Oct 1962; *Listener*, 11 Oct 1962; https://coronationstreet.fandom.com/wiki/Episode_189; *FT*, 4 Oct 1962.

7. *Guardian*, 5 Oct 1962; *AJ*, 17 Oct 1962; *Guardian*, 5 Oct 1962.

8. Paul Barker, 'Painting the Portrait of "The Other Britain"', *Contemporary Record*, Summer 1991, pp 47–9; *New Society*, 4 Oct 1962; *CL*, 4 Oct 1962; *Listener*, 11 Oct 1962; Elizabeth Jane Howard, *Slipstream* (2002), pp 334–8.

9. *Spectator*, 5 Oct 1962; *Larkin*, p 306; *Guardian*, 5 Oct 1962; *NS*, 5 Oct 1962; *Listener*, 4 Oct 1962 (Williams); *NS*, 5 Oct 1962; Tench, Ms 255/13, 5 Oct 1962; Lee, 5 Oct 1962; Dee, DDX 829/2, 5 Oct 1962.

10. *Melody Maker*, 6 Oct 1962.

11. 'Leo Abse', *The Times*, 21 Aug 2008; 'Fiona Adams', *The Times*, 18 Jul 2020; *Wikipedia*, 'Tariq Ali'; Joan Bakewell, *The Centre of the Bed* (2003), p 159; 'Reg Presley', *The Times*, 6 Feb 2013; Morton Schatzman, 'Mary Barnes', *Independent*, 11 July 2001; Duncan Hamilton, *Immortal* (2013), chaps 1–3; 'John Bindon', *DT*, 15 Oct 1993; 'Brian Cant', *The Times*, 21 Jun 2017; Chris Welch, 'Chas Chandler', *Independent*, 18 Jul 1996; Brian Glanville, 'Brian Clough', *Guardian*, 21 Sep 2004; Adam Sweeting, 'Joe Cocker', *Guardian*, 24 Dec 2014; Clinton Heylin, *No More Sad Refrains* (Omnibus Press edn, 2011), p 19; Peter Oborne, *Basil D'Oliveira* (2004), p 82; Graham Wade, 'Michael Duane', *Guardian*, 27 Jan 1997; Eamonn McCabe, 'Brian Duffy', *Guardian*, 7 Jun 2010; Nigel Fountain and John Fordham, 'Tony Elliott', *Guardian*, 22 Jul 2020; David Lister, *In the Best Possible Taste* (1996), p 22; Marianne Faithfull, *Faithfull* (1994), pp 11–12; Richard Williams, 'Mick Farren', *Guardian*, 30 Jul 2013; 'Julie Felix', *The Times*, 4 Apr 2020; Richard Stott, 'Paul Foot', *Guardian*, 20 Jul 2004;

Chris Maume, 'Margaret Forster', *Independent*, 9 Feb 2016; *Wikipedia*, 'Sandie Shaw'; 'Peter Green', *The Times*, 27 Jul 2020; Rupert Cornwell, 'Bob Guccione', *Independent*, 22 Oct 2010; Tom Vallance, 'David Hemmings', *Independent*, 5 Dec 2003; 'Adrian Henri', *The Times*, 22 Dec 2000; Spencer Leigh, 'Simon Dee', *Independent*, 2 Sep 2009; Twiggy Lawson, *Twiggy in Black and White* (1997), chaps 2–3; Chris Bryant, *Glenda Jackson* (1999), p 43; Stuart Jeffries, 'Terry Jones', *Guardian*, 23 Jan 2020; 'Samantha Juste', *DT*, 11 Feb 2014; Michael Coveney, 'Lindsay Kemp', *Guardian*, 29 Aug 2018; Michael White, 'The Rev Bruce Kenrick', *Guardian*, 19 Jan 2007; Spencer Leigh, 'Honey Lantree', *Guardian*, 10 Jan 2019; Paul Oestreicher, 'The Rev Ken Leech', *Guardian*, 25 Sep 2015; *Welwyn Hatfield Times*, 29 Apr 2019; Anthony Hayward, *Which Side Are You On?* (2004), p 27; *Wikipedia*, 'Cathy McGowan'; Michael Horowitz, 'Tom McGrath', *Independent*, 27 Jul 2009; Nicholas Johnson, 'Barry MacSweeney', *Independent*, 13 May 2000; Pierre Perrone, 'David McWilliams', *Independent*, 16 Mar 2002; 'Howard Marks', *The Times*, 12 Apr 2016; 'Phil May', *The Times*, 22 May 2020; www.barrymiles.co.uk (Biography); 'Dougie Millings', *The Times*, 3 Oct 2001; Michael Kustow, 'Adrian Mitchell', *Guardian*, 22 Dec 2008; Marcus Williamson, 'Alex Moulton', *Independent*, 12 Dec 2012; Stuart Jeffries, 'Gordon Murray', *Guardian*, 1 Jul 2016; Marsha Rowe, 'Richard Neville', *Guardian*, 5 Sep 2016; Adam Sweeting, 'Andy "Thunderclap" Newman', *Guardian*, 4 Apr 2016; Stuart Jeffries, 'John Noakes', *Guardian*, 30 May 2017; Meredith Etherington-Smith, 'Tommy Nutter', *Independent*, 18 Aug 1992; Anthony Hayward, 'Ivan Owen', *Independent*, 20 Oct 2000; Dennis Barker, 'Nyree Dawn Porter', *Guardian*, 12 Apr 2001; Spencer Leigh and D. J. Taylor, 'John Peel', *Independent*, 27 Oct 2004; 'Diana Rigg', *The Times*, 11 Sep 2020; Dave Laing, 'Twinkle', *Guardian*, 27 May 2015; Chris Maume, 'Jim Slater', *Independent*, 21 Nov 2015; Chris Salewicz, 'Millie Small', *Guardian*, 7 May 2020; Spencer Leigh, 'Allan Smethurst', *Independent*, 26 Dec 2000; Lucy O'Brien, *Dusty* (1989), p 27; Eric Homberger, 'George Steiner', *Guardian*, 8 Feb 2020; Roy Strong, *The Roy Strong Diaries, 1967–1987* (1997), pp 3–6; Richard Williams, 'Penny Valentine', *Guardian*, 13 Jan 2003; 'Carol White', *The Times*, 20 Sep 1991; David Winter, 'Mary Whitehouse', *Independent*, 24 Nov 2001; Julia Langdon, 'Lady Falkender', *Guardian*, 18 Feb 2019; 'Lord Wilson of Rievaulx', *The Times*, 25 May 1995.

12. Mark Lewisohn, *All These Years, Volume 1* (2013), pp 745–51; Charlotte Mosley (ed), *The Letters of Nancy Mitford and Evelyn Waugh* (1996), p 463; *Guardian*, 8 Oct 1962; Lewisohn, p 752; Ian M. Rusten, *The Rolling Stones in Concert, 1962–1982* (Jefferson, North Carolina, 2018), p 9.

Image Credits

All reasonable efforts have been made by the author and publishers to trace the copyright owners of the material quoted in this book and of any images reproduced in this book. In the event that the author or publishers are notified of any mistakes or omissions by copyright owners after publication, the author and publishers will endeavour to rectify the position accordingly for any subsequent printing.

Acknowledgements

The following kindly gave permission to reproduce copyright material: Dominic Abrams (Mark Abrams); BBC Written Archives Centre (BBC copyright content reproduced courtesy of the British Broadcasting Corporation. All rights reserved.); Roger Darlington; Pamela Hendicott and Ione Lee (Judy Haines); Islington Local History Centre (Gladys Langford); Sue Lowndes (Vere Hodgson); Veronica Porter; Marian Ray and Robin Raynham (Marian Raynham); Wandsworth Libraries and Heritage Service (William Halle); Lewis and Michael Willmott (Phyllis Willmott); The Trustees of the Mass Observation Records (The unpublished diaries of Nella Last, reproduced with permission of Curtis Brown Group Ltd, London on behalf of The Trustees of the Mass Observation Archive © The Trustees of the Mass Observation Archive); Orion Publishing Group (RS Thomas, 'The Welsh Hill Country' © RS Thomas); Proper Music Group (The Copper Family, 'The Seasons Round', lyrics courtesy of The Copper Family, as sung by Bob and Ron Copper); Pan Macmillan (*Dear Bill*, WF Deedes, © WF Deedes); HarperCollins Publishers (*The Peregrine* © 2017, JA Baker); estate of Geoffrey Moorhouse (*Britain in the Sixties: The Other England*, Geoffrey Moorhouse © 1964, Geoffrey Moorhouse); the estate of John Fowles (© John Fowles).

I would like to thank the following archivists for their help: Emma Anthony; Mark Aston; Sophie Bridges; Nigel Cochrane; Stefan Dickers; Helen Ford; Louise North; Polly North; Jonathan Oates; Andrew Riley; Jessica Scantlebury; Alison Smith.

Various friends made time to read all or part of this book at draft stage and offer helpful suggestions: Mike Burns; Patric Dickinson; Prudence Fay; Veronica Porter; Harry Ricketts; David Warren.

Many thanks also to Amanda Howard (Superscript Editorial Services) for transcribing my audio tapes; to Peter James for his copy edit; to David Atkinson for compiling the index; to Catherine Best for reading the proofs; to my agent Georgia Garrett and her assistant Honor Spreckley; and, at Bloomsbury, to my editor Michael Fishwick and his colleagues Lauren Whybrow, Lilidh Kendrick and Amanda Waters.

My greatest debt is to my wife Lucy, who not only did some of the research, checked the transcriptions and read a draft, but also gave me much else besides.

December 2020

Index

A Note on the Author

David Kynaston was born in Aldershot in 1951 and has been a professional historian since 1973. His four-volume history of the City of London was published between 1994 and 2001, and more recently he has written *Till Time's Last Sand*, a history of the Bank of England. His continuing history of post-war Britain, 'Tales of a New Jerusalem', has so far comprised *Austerity Britain*, *Family Britain* and *Modernity Britain*. His most recent three books have been *Arlott, Swanton and the Soul of English Cricket* (with Stephen Fay); *Engines of Privilege: Britain's Private School Problem* (with Francis Green); and *Shots in the Dark: A Diary of Saturday Dreams and Strange Times*.

A Note on the Type

The text of this book is set in Linotype Stempel Garamond, a version of Garamond adapted and first used by the Stempel foundry in 1924. It is one of several versions of Garamond based on the designs of Claude Garamond. It is thought that Garamond based his font on Bembo, cut in 1495 by Francesco Griffo in collaboration with the Italian printer Aldus Manutius. Garamond types were first used in books printed in Paris around 1532. Many of the present-day versions of this type are based on the *Typi Academiae* of Jean Jannon cut in Sedan in 1615.

Claude Garamond was born in Paris in 1480. He learned how to cut type from his father and by the age of fifteen he was able to fashion steel punches the size of a pica with great precision. At the age of sixty he was commissioned by King Francis I to design a Greek alphabet, and for this he was given the honourable title of royal type founder. He died in 1561.